AND

THE TWO
SHALL   BECOME
ONE

AND
THE TWO
SHALL BECOME
ONE

THE
Frank J. Atwood
& Rachel L. Atwood
STORY

HOLY ROYAL AND STAVROPEGIC
Monastery of Machairas
———— CYPRUS ————

Typesetting, pagination and overall design by:
The Holy Royal and Stavropegic Monastery of Machairas, Cyprus

Proof-reading and Editing by:
Eleftheria Kaimakliotis, Cyprus

Copyright © by:
Frank & Rachel Atwood, AZ, USA
&
The Holy Royal and Stavropegic Monastery of Machairas, Cyprus

ISBN-13: 978-1985391055
ISBN-10: 1985391058

This book has also been published in the Greek language.

To order additional copies or the Greek edition, please contact:

The Holy Royal and Stavropegic Monastery of Machairas
P. O. Box 25272
1308 Nicosia
Cyprus

Tel.: +357-22359334
Fax: +357-22359318
Email: bibliopoleio@maherasmonastery.org.cy

Dedicated to:

Metropolitan of Limassol, Cyprus
Athanasios

Bishop of Ledra
and Abbot of the Holy Royal and Stavropegic
Monastery of Machairas, Cyprus
Epiphanios

Abbot of Saint Anthony's Holy Monastery
Florence, AZ, USA
Archimandrite Paisios

*faithful monks and obedient servants of God,
who humbly shepherd souls toward hope of eternal life.
May God grant you Paradise.*

TABLE OF CONTENTS

PROLOGUE

It is with much joy that I greet this publication, which is the autobiography of Anthony and Sarah. More than twenty years have gone by since I came across a letter from the United States, while going through my mail one day. As my knowledge of English was not very good, I put the letter aside in order to go over it later on, when I could, with quietude, better devote myself to it. Yet, I could not dismiss the strong impulse that drew my heart to that letter. So, I picked it back up, read it, and immediately wrote and sent my response.

Many years later, when God granted the blessing that I visit the United States, He guided my footsteps to meeting with the sender of that letter in person. That sender was none other than Anthony, the author and protagonist of this book. His adventurous life and God's wondrous providence for him – and through him, for every single person – fascinate the reader who, amazed and surprised, will not hesitate to exclaim, "Great are You, O Lord, and wonderful are your works, and no word is adequate to sing the praise of your wonders!"

Accordingly, we thank God "in all and for all", "for all things we know and do not know, for blessings manifest and hidden that have been bestowed upon us". For, as we know, the Lord assured us that "God wants all people to be saved and to come to the knowledge of the truth."

We therefore entrust this autobiography to the readers, with the goal of benefitting every person, so that he will not despair, no matter how difficult and complicated his life may become. Rather, with hope and strong conviction, he should hasten to our captain and helmsman, God, our Lord Jesus Christ, asking Him to safely guide his life to the harbor of salvation.

With this in mind, we wish the devout readers of this book salvation and sanctification in Christ.

Metropolitan of Limassol

Athanasios

1 April 2018

A FEW WORDS
BY THE AUTHORS

HOW do we reconcile the death sentence – specifically, a sentence of death that was pronounced on the 8th of May in 1987 – with our marriage, and more importantly, with eternal life? In order to answer this question, we need not only to look back, but especially, to look forward.

Before we were joined in marriage, we were two people from two extremely divergent backgrounds. Frank, the only child born to affluent parents, had a childhood of privilege; Rachel, the only daughter of a couple who later divorced, had a childhood racked with difficulties. In spite of the difficulties, Rachel became "one of us" – a hard-working American with a kind and gentle heart and a rock-solid belief in God. Despite the privileges and the affluence, Frank's "choices" – some that he made and some that had been foisted upon him – led him down the dark trail that ended, eventually, on Death Row in an Arizona prison.

The stories of our lives are the stories of the two very different people, who, several years after the death sentence had been pronounced, were married on December 17, 1991. They are the stories of how Rachel become "one of us" and of how Frank's "choices" led him so far astray. They are the stories of how we met and married; but they go further, for they are the stories that explain how each of us discovered Orthodoxy and came to be Eastern Orthodox Christians, and especially, of how the trajectory of our lives has so completely changed. Merely being Orthodox Christians can never be enough; we have learned to lead lives of prayer, repentance, and most of all, hope. With our hope firmly grounded in our risen Lord and Savior, Jesus Christ, we look forward to life in Him, because only in Him are all things possible.

We must emphasize that we did not "become one" upon our marriage, but years later. Through our individual life experiences and through our shared experiences, we have learned, at last, what is meant by "And The Two Shall Become One". At the request of clergy near and dear to us, we offer these, first, our individual and then, our shared experiences to the scrutiny and prayers of all who read them. And we pray, always for the salvation of all.

Chapter One

Frank: the Early Years

I was born, an only child, on a beautiful Sunday afternoon in January of 1956 at the Queen of Angels Hospital, considered then to be a prestigious facility, in Los Angeles, California. My parents, John and Alice Atwood were both products of the upper middle class; however, their backgrounds were literally worlds apart.

Frank as a newborn.

Frankie J. with his dad in 1956.

Like his father before him (my grandfather had been a colonel in the United States Army), my father, who was born in February of 1920 in San Diego, California, also embarked upon a military career. After entering the United States Military Academy at West Point in New York (Class of 1942), he fought in World War II, in Japan and the Philippines. His expertise in communications (he served in the Signal Core) found him engaging

Frank 1, with boxer, Rusty.

in excursions behind enemy lines to establish the means for critical intelligence sharing. Dad was a highly decorated army officer, rising quickly up the ranks from lieutenant, to captain, and then a major, prior to his return stateside as a colonel.

My mother, who was born in Vienna, Austria, in March of 1916 to influential parents, later studied fashion design in Paris. Soon after her matriculation at university, unrest due to Hitler's invasions of European countries led to my mother's migration to America, where she eventually met my father.

Frank at 3 years old, sitting and smiling.

My mother and father met and fell in love while water skiing at Lake Arrowhead (a mountain resort northeast of Los Angeles in the San Gabriel Mountains), and were married in 1950. Initially they resided at Fort Monmouth, in New Jersey, while my dad completed his tour of active duty. Eventually they settled in the upscale Los Angeles neighborhood of Brentwood. My father, although on retired reserve military status, continued attending regular meetings at a local military installation and serving on active duty several weeks a year. Simultaneously, he pursued a civilian career in the communications industry as an executive with the Hughes Aircraft Company.

It was into this advantageous setting that I was born.

Frank, 6.

Having no brothers and sisters, I was the sole focus of my loving parents and enjoyed their undivided attention. Educational endeavors began around 1960, when I was enrolled at Bonner School, a private establishment that functioned as an advanced learning institution for the children of the well-to-do. Even at that early age I felt a sense of privilege as I entered the gates of that prestigious facility each weekday. I got along well with the other students and my teachers. Aside from one terrifying memory of having gashed my chin open on a jungle gym and requiring stitches, most of my memories of my experiences at the Bonner School are quite pleasant. I excelled scholastically and made many friends who enhanced my feelings of inclusion by attending my birthday parties and inviting me to theirs.

That bountiful period of happiness and success followed me as I was enrolled at Brentwood Elementary School. This learning center was also inundated with the offspring of many affluent families. For the most part I enjoyed the classes and was a good student; however, it is my extra-curricular activities that I recall with the most fondness and the greatest clarity.

My participation in organized athletics began when I joined the ice hockey team on which my dad was a coach. It was an experience that was a bit daunting and intimidating at first since, at seven years old, I was the youngest member of the squad. We were playing a game on enemy ice, when, for the very first time, I got onto the ice myself. I felt disoriented.

Playing ice hockey (1964).

Several minutes later, I found myself back on the bench. That experience in humility actually encouraged me toward what eventually became a cornerstone in subsequent sporting endeavors, as I spent weeks and months hard at work in my backyard, tirelessly practicing stick handling skills. While I never did excel on that ice hockey team, mostly due to

Frank (second from left) with his ice hockey team.

Frank practising baseball in his back yard.

Frank 8, a boy scout.

All-star baseball player (c. 1968).

being small in stature and so young in age, I still developed a sense of significant accomplishment once the pride my parents took in my painstaking efforts became manifest. It was that determined drive to excel that was rewarded with success in my later forays into both baseball and football.

At around age eight or nine I joined a local Little League baseball conference. The ice hockey experience provided a leg up on other participants, as did the indefatigable labor by myself and a few neighborhood kids. We managed our own baseball practice, using every spare moment to work on some aspect of our skills – fielding grounders, catching pop-ups and fly balls, becoming accurate in both infield and outfield throwing, pitching, batting and running the bases. Sometimes we were able to recruit my mom to take us to the batting cages in a nearby town or to a local park, where there was more room to practice, but usually we would hone our abilities in my backyard, the street, or on an empty parking lot. I even practiced alone by tipping a garbage can on its side so I could practice throwing or by drawing a square on the garage door with chalk in order to work on my pitching. At the height of my short-lived career in baseball, my friend, Peter and I both became perennial all-stars and were awarded co-most valuable player trophies.

As the summers faded to autumns I felt a renewed sense

of energy and excitement; football season was beginning! Many of the same companions who had labored so vigorously with me during baseball season also enthusiastically engaged in daily football activities. How fondly do I recall some of the pick-up games in front of my house, tackle football games... on concrete. I also recall how much time my dear father spent practicing with me, and how intently he coached me. Dad had always been, and will forever be, my coach.

Frank 11,
in his football uniform.

I never did enjoy as much prowess in football as I did in baseball. Still, I became second-string linebacker and starting quarterback, a position I cherished and for which I was honored by a write-up in a local newspaper and a couple of appearances in bowl games, including the Pioneer Bowl, which was played in the snow in Salt Lake City, Utah.

In addition to having been involved in sports with my dad, my mother also encouraged my athletic endeavors. After undergoing a rigorous screening process, including interviews, our family obtained membership at the exclusive Riviera Country Club, complete with the entry of our names into its "Blue Book"[1]. Mom immediately enrolled me in tennis classes, where I trained under a famous Romanian tennis pro. Additionally, during

Frank 13, at Lake Arrowhead
water skiing (c. 1967).

1   The "Blue Book" contains a list of socially influential people. Entry in it carries societal influence.

At Lake Arrowhead, water-skiing.

family vacations at Lake Arrowhead my mom introduced me to water skiing. At first it was an awkward venture, and I remember how warily I stepped off of the pier and into the water, making sure that the tow rope was between my skis and that the ski tips were out of the water. Then the instructor would yell "hit it" and the boat, with my mom on board, would take off. In the beginning the instructor grabbed my upper arm and held me up ("like a sack of potatoes" my mother would say), but soon I was able to go it alone. I still relish the excitement and glee of rushing across the water's surface. In fact, it was this exhilarating sensation that soon led to one of the loves of my life, body surfing.

The summers on the beach with my mother, and usually my best friend Chad, were paradise. Early in the morning my mom would pack a picnic lunch and we would drive the few miles to Will Rogers Beach and spend the day in the sun and surf, returning in the late afternoon. My mom would lie in the sun (an activity that she absolutely loved but which in later years proved to have inflicted severe skin damage), while Chad and I would body surf for hours. Every once in a while my mom would make us exit the water and, water-logged, shriveled like prunes and nearly blue, we would bask in the glorious southern California sun until my mom acceded to our pleas to reenter the ocean for more body surfing. Those were truly endless summers.

In the winter we would often vacation at a ski resort – Big Bear (next to Lake Arrowhead), northern California's Heavenly Valley, or Mt. Mammoth, and northern Arizona's Snow Bowl were amongst our favorite destinations. It was during those expeditions that my mother introduced me to snow skiing; being from Austria, she was a master skier. This was another initially awkward venture, as I found myself dangling above cliffs while sitting in a fragile ski chair suspended in

Frankie J. and Mom skiing at Heavenly Valley (1967).

mid-air. Still, I caught on rapidly and soon was zipping down mountainsides like an expert. With my parents consistently facilitating my endeavors, sports were a huge part of my early years.

While participation in athletics was a dominant feature during those years, there also was frequent attendance at sporting events. My parents took me to Dodger Stadium to watch Sandy Koufax pitch, or to the Los Angeles Memorial Coliseum to see O. J. Simpson run for the USC Trojans, or to observe the "Fearsome Foursome" (Rosey Greer, Deacon Jones, Merlin Olson, and Lamar Lundy) play for the Los Angeles Rams. We also attended UCLA Bruin basketball games at Pauley Pavilion and watched the masterful John Wooden coach players like Lew Alcindor (later known as Kareem Abdul Jabar) and win an astonishing ten out of twelve national championships.

I recall family vacations that found us journeying by car one summer from Los Angeles to visit relatives in Winnipeg, Manitoba (southern Canada), or flying to lavish resorts in Aspen, Sun Valley and Honolulu. Sometimes we would vacation in California and drive to Yosemite National Park in northern California or summer at the Hotel Del Coronado resort near San Diego. Even my dad's periods of active duty were an occasion for a family event. Once, we drove over to Fort Huachuca, in southern Arizona, where there was a riding stable and I fell in love with a horse named "Chubby". Being a city slicker, I was not at all comfortable on horseback, but Chubby seemed to sense my absence of proficiency. He made our ride together such a pleasant experience, unlike other horses which, sensing discomfort, would use the opportunity to be most troublesome. In all, there were many wonderful family journeys.

Of course, family events were not limited to sporting endeavors and vacations. We were season ticket holders for the Hollywood Bowl, a mainstay of classical music performances, where we enjoyed Zubin Mehta conducting the Los Angeles Philharmonic Orchestra. Many times, we visited the downtown Los Angeles Music Center or Dorothy Chandler Pavilion to listen to the unparalleled pianist, Arthur Rubenstein in concert. Undoubtedly, my childhood was filled with an environment of love and privilege, a time in which I felt included and adored.

Other significant childhood activities included attendance at St. Alban's Church, where I was an acolyte and exuberantly participated with regularity in Sunday services and in Sunday school, sang in the choir, and engaged in special events like: church plays, holiday caroling, fund raisers and so on. Christmas caroling was especially fun. As dusk approached, we would gather in the church parking lot with our assigned groups of carolers and then walk through nearby neighborhoods. Going from house to house, we would momentarily pause in front of each and sing the classics: Joy to the World, Silent Night Holy Night, O Come All Ye Faithful, Onward Christian Soldiers, and other favorites. Sometimes we would be lucky enough to get assigned to one of the hayrides. This encompassed a flatbed truck with railings, with the back filled with hay. We would climb on board and be driven to outlying areas, gleefully singing Christmas carols. I also took great pleasure in the weekly lessons given at both

Frankie J. in the Church Choir as an Acolyte.

Sunday services and Sunday school. I studiously practiced those devotionals throughout the week. They provided a sense of belonging and a firm foundation in Episcopalian doctrine, and they promoted a strong faith in God.

It is with a sense of joy that I recall my childhood nightly prayer routine, initially performed with my mother's guidance. At her prompting, I would retrieve my carefully folded prayer cloth from the closet, kneel at the side of my bed with my mother, and recite my prayers. Nightly supplications included liturgical prayers, such as the Lord's Prayer and the Nicene Creed, as well as private devotionals. One of my favorites that I still continue to frequently recite prior to retiring for the evening is: "Now I lay me down to sleep, I pray the Lord my soul to keep, and if I die before I wake, I pray the Lord my soul to take. God bless my mommy and daddy. Amen."

Frank giving a cello recital at age 13.

Near the conclusion of my studies at Brentwood Elementary School, my fondness for classical music found me studying several instruments. Initially I took trumpet lessons, but as it turned out to be quite an "inconvenience" to neighbors, I began studying cello. Ultimately I settled on the piano, with the advantage of studying under an accomplished master. Although quite nerve-racking, the several recitals in which I took part produced a real sense of achievement.

The close circle of friends I had at elementary school were all athletically gifted, so we dominated schoolyard contests. A game that we called "Socko", similar to dodge ball, was one favorite, but we also enjoyed kickball and sockball competitions (similar to baseball but played with a rubber ball, the size of a basketball, that was socked or kicked). We were a close knit group who attended each other's birthday parties. My own birthday parties commonly included a trip to the Los Angeles Sports Arena to watch the Harlem Globetrotters or to see the Ice Capades; those trips were great fun for all. Childhood, including school, was a good experience, a wonderful and productive time, intertwined as it was with the outpouring of my parents' love and the joy of friendship.

The one emotionally traumatic occasion of my childhood occurred when I was eight and my mother was pregnant. The excitement of a little brother or sister turned to despair when Mom miscarried. I cried and cried. A year later, one of our neighbors and my dad wondered why I was still so upset. (Psychiatrists have since concluded that the emotional strain I had undergone contributed to a weakened mental condition and functioned to exacerbate my much-later diagnosed post-traumatic stress disorder [PTSD]).

In 1968, at the age of twelve, I entered Paul Revere Junior High School, an educational center where the rich kid lifestyle was the norm. For me, the change from courses in a single classroom (under the same teacher's instruction) to each subject being taught by a different educator in separate classrooms was a difficult transition. I think that one reason for this was the alteration in class constituency. In elementary school the entire day was spent with the same students which allowed for the forging of strong friendships. Under the system employed in junior high schools, relations were extremely casual and superficial. To get to know anyone became quite difficult for me and extremely disconcerting... it created a disturbing sense of unease. After toughing it out for that initial school year, I sat down with my parents in the summer of 1969 to discuss the disquietude that had accompanied my attendance at Paul Revere. Soon thereafter my parents suggested the more formal and rigorous format of the Brentwood Military Academy. I eagerly concurred with the idea of attending military school, as I had always been very proud of my family's line of army officers. Consequently, in the fall of 1969, at the age of thirteen, I very proudly embarked upon the road to fulfilling my dream of following in my father's footsteps as I entered the halls of Brentwood's exclusive military academy.

I felt an incredible sense of honor and enthusiasm; I was actually pursuing my dreams. At the outset I was a model cadet. The plebes (first year cadets) were taught how to march – forward march, where our every step was in accord with the platoon's cadence, left or right march, and about face, where we would pivot 180° to then march in the opposite direction. There were also the commands to halt, which meant coming to a complete stop, and to stand at attention. In addition to marching drills, we also learned the variant rifle positions: right shoulder arms and left shoulder arms (the rifle resting on the right or left shoulder), present arms (holding the rifle in front of us), and attention (the rifle at one's side with the rifle butt on the ground). There was also the twenty-one-point manual of arms, a routine during which the rifle would be smoothly transitioned between different positions. We were taught how to dismantle, clean, and reassemble our M1 rifles. I practiced the marching drills and manual of arms daily in my backyard. Of course, we wore uniforms so I routinely polished my brass (belt buckle and shirt lapel insignia) and shined my shoes.

That first semester I was a good student and an aspiring cadet. My father, who had been promoted to brigadier general in 1967, was so very proud of me.

Chapter Two

Rachel: the Early Years

I was born on the evening of August 5, 1962, the second child to Robert and Earlene Tenny. While both of my parents were raised in diverse segments of the country, they did initially enjoy the innocence of small town America.

Rachel, a cute baby.

My father was born in the eastern reaches of Washington State in April of 1930, but lost both of his parents while still in his infancy. Although this tragedy resulted in my dad having been ushered into foster care, it eventually led to his adoption by two wonderful and kind people, Clyde Tenny and his adorable wife, Edna. Edna, whom we all called Gammy, was a grand woman who would become a most important role model in my life. The Tennys were also from eastern Washington, but shortly after having adopted my dad, the family relocated to the cozy little town of Port Angeles on Puget Sound. There, Clyde earned a good living as the owner of a soda fountain, selling, in fact, as much as five hundred gallons of ice cream on some days.

After about ten years or so, the Tennys left the evergreen

wilds of Washington and settled in the desert of Arizona, where soon thereafter, my father graduated from Tucson High School (Class of 1948). In Tucson, my grandfather purchased a property known as the El Corona, a sprawling guest ranch. Gammy, my grandmother, did all of the cooking and indoor work, while Grandpa and my father performed the many laborious chores that the operation of a guest ranch required. The proprietorship of the El Corona ensured Grandpa's stature in the community, as he was well-liked and admired by all, and especially well-known for the grilling and delectable barbecuing that were guest favorites. Sadly, my paternal grandfather died of a heart attack on June 2, 1956. This dour development found Gammy and my dad, then in his early twenties running the dude ranch on their own. My father toiled tirelessly and the El Corona became quite a success. In fact, my dad became a big presence in Tucson's horse community and went on to build the original Sabino Vista Stables.

My mother, Earlene Blackmore, entered the world together with her fraternal twin, Mary in April of 1935. They were the beloved daughters of Earl Blackmore, a prominent cattle rancher, and his wife, Rachel, whom her grandchildren later called Gigi. The family dwelt in the small town of Canadian that is nestled in

Rachel and her brother, Rob.

the Panhandle of the Lone Star state. Earlene and Mary were preceded by a brother, Loren, who was born five years earlier. My mother and her sister were known in town as the "Blackmore twins," and their upbringing was typical for small town prairie life. Both my mom and her twin attended university at Texas Tech, in Lubbock, Texas.

It was my Aunt Mary who first emigrated from Texas and journeyed west, after having graduated from Texas Tech, to Tucson, Arizona, where a promising teaching opportunity beckoned. Initially my mother remained behind in Texas with her mom – my grandparents had divorced while their twin daughters were still attending Texas Tech. Eventually my mother and Gigi joined Aunt Mary in Tucson in the mid-1950s.

Not too long after having arrived in Arizona, Gigi and my mother accompanied Mary on a visit to the El Corona Ranch, where my mom met and fell in love with my dad. After a short courtship my mother, Earlene and my father, Robert were married in May of 1958. Soon afterward my mother's twin, Mary wed a military man, Jim Embry in 1959.

Life on the ranch did not at all agree with my mom. She did not fully appreciate all of the requisite hard work involved in operating such an enterprise. My mother preferred to entertain, a penchant that may have served her well on the guest ranch... had she not favored the lifestyle of a socialite over that of a blue collar existence. Unfortunately, my mom gave Gammy little assistance in the kitchen. Nevertheless, married life was not too rocky, at least not at first, and in February of 1959 my brother was born. For a while he was the center of my parents' focus and helped them to forge a closer bond. However, the tension arising from their separate aspirations – my father had a career as a rancher, but my mother had aristocratic desires – eventually erupted. It was also around this time that it became somewhat obvious that my mother had a drinking problem. My mother wanted to dissolve the marriage.

It was also during this time, in 1962, when my mom learned that she was pregnant with me. On a hot summer evening in Tucson, while my father was grilling steaks for ranch guests, my mother went into labor. At first my dad's service to his guests inclined him toward completing the barbecue; however, I could not wait, so my dad rushed my mom off to St. Joseph's Hospital. This was well before the days when an expectant father could accompany his wife into the delivery room. So, since my dear brother's delivery had spanned some eighteen hours, my dad settled down in the waiting room to watch some television. No sooner had he inserted the coins into a pay slot than a nurse appeared to inform him that he had a baby girl. I had burst upon the world in near record time! It has always been a family joke that my brother, who took such a long time to be delivered, does everything so slowly, whereas I, who was born so quickly, tend to do everything speedily.

At any rate, my dad called his mother, to tell her the wonderful news. Of course, the occasion having unfolded so quickly initially incited an aura of disbelief, but doubt soon turned into joy and I was named Rachel Lee, after my maternal grandmother, Gigi.

The first year of my life was spent on the El Corona Ranch, where I, although I don't recall having done so, adopted the habit of bucking in my crib. My family is always quick to remind me that whenever I was placed in my crib I would begin to butt against the crib's siding with enough force to move the crib. There were times that I actually propelled the crib to the door, as on more than one occasion my poor dad had to enter my room via the window, since my bucking had effectively blocked the door. I guess that I really took to ranch life... as a budding bucking bronco!

Rachel about one and a half, already strong enough to... propel her crib.

Unfortunately, my mom persisted in her aversion to life at El Corona and constantly urged my dad to sell it. When I was a year old, my beloved dad relented and sold the El Corona... a decision he has regretted to this very day. It broke his heart to leave the ranch and the life he so loved, but he stoutly moved the family to a house just a few miles away from the El Corona. As the profits from the sale of the ranch had gone to his mother, my father then entered a career in retail in order to provide for his family. At about this time it became apparent that, in addition to an increase in alcohol consumption, my mom had also begun to misuse prescription drugs. As for me, I did not abandon my impish ways, and on one occasion, was found by my dad, outside, clad in only his cowboy boots... that I had filled with water!

In 1966 we moved again and took up residence where we still dwell, on the east side of Tucson. At around this time my dad began work at Skagg's drugstore and my mother's substance abuse became far more noticeable. Although the area was rather sparsely populated, there was a family across the street with two girls, one a little older than me and one a bit younger. I soon became good friends with the family and when I was particularly lonely at home, what with my father being at work and my mom's "absence" due to her inebriation, I at least gained a semblance of normalcy and company with my neighbors. It was during this period, when I was seven or eight years old, that the realization that something was very wrong with my mom dawned on me. On a day that she had consumed too much alcohol and taken too many sedatives, she suffered dangerous complications and had to be rushed to the emergency room.

In order to help out around the house and to care for me and my brother, Gammy came to live with us for a while. Because the house was in such disarray, Gammy knew that my mother had experienced quite a downturn. While pulling the home back together, she knew she had to teach me how to clean, cook, and manage a household. By the time I was eight years old I could keep the house going on my own.

The difficulties with my mother continued and the absence of my dad during the workday found me developing a close bond with my brother. He was very protective of me and spent a lot of his time making sure my mom didn't hurt me. I think that it was around this time that he also began to realize that something was really wrong with Mom, because even though my mother was at home, we often felt it was only the two of us. My mom was in a stupor much of the time, leaving us to tend to ourselves. At that time, my Aunt Mary and Uncle Jim also lived in Tucson, not very far from us, and so my cousins, Jason and Tara spent a lot of time with my brother and me. Aunt Mary was a refuge for us when Mom was out of commission, which was much of the time. Soon afterward, Mom had her first of many stays in a rehabilitation center.

My attendance at Schumaker Elementary School also helped to dissipate my loneliness. I played with neighborhood kids after school and also became an avid reader. Still, I found myself hanging out with increased regularity at my neighbor's residence across the street. I very much enjoyed the company of Mrs. C. and her two girls. That is not to say that there weren't times when my mother was sober and we would engage in lots of fun mother and daughter stuff; it was just that, sadly, those occasions were too few and far between. Nevertheless, Mom did try to take good care of my brother and me; when she was sober, she ensured that we had clean clothes and hot meals on the table.

During the holidays my mother tended to fall off the wagon. As the years passed by, she consumed increasing quantities of alcohol and prescription pills, which she managed to obtain from several doctors. Every year at Christmas time, my grandma and I would bake lots of Christmas cookies, enough to pass out dozens to neighbors and elsewhere. One Christmas, when I was ten years old, a Christmas party was planned for a dozen or so family members. However, when the time came for beginning the actual preparations, my mother was too inebriated to participate. I called Gammy, and over the telephone, she coached me through the preparation of the entire Christmas meal; at the age of ten I cooked and served a feast for over a dozen people all by myself.

At around this time, Gammy had begun to manage an apartment complex of about ten units for her nephew, while she herself lived in the house that was on the property. I began to spend every possible moment with my beloved Gammy. It was where I felt safe.

It seemed that my childhood summers were usually filled with drama, and one particular summer was no different. Our next door neighbors were older and spent summers in New York. As a result, they would ask my mother to keep an eye on their house and water the few plants they had. These folks also had a plethora of alcohol, which is why my mom "volunteered" to watch their home. When the Richlings returned home, they found their liquor cabinet virtually bare! They approached my dad about this and he had to reimburse them for all the booze my mother had consumed. This was such an embarrassment for us, and I'm sure the entire neighborhood knew about it.

During the summer of 1973, when I was just turning eleven, I pulled off the masterpiece of my elfin antics. Perhaps it was my way of gaining a moment's attention, given the lack of attention from my mother, but I meant no malevolence when Mrs. C. and her family were on vacation that summer. You see, I somehow got it in my head that it would be great fun to call several furniture stores and order the delivery of various household furnishings; I gave sizes, colors, and everything. I must admit that I had always dreamed of decorating a home, and this minor antic made me feel incredibly grown up. But boy, did I ever get into big trouble! My impish nature, which persists (albeit, less intrusively) to this very day, apparently was not at all appreciated. Upon their return home, my dear neighbors discovered several "attempted but unsuccessful delivery" notices on their front door. So, Mrs. C. called my mother and the proverbial fur flew. In the aftermath, I not only received an indeterminable term of restriction, but also had to see a psychologist, to whom I recall having expressed my enmity toward my mom for her substance abuse. This was the first time I had been able to tell anyone of my dislike for my mother and her behavior. I think I was trying to hurt her the way she had hurt me.

With the passage of some time, things calmed down. In June of 1974, I graduated from elementary school and entered my junior high school years at Magee that fall. Initially the transition from elementary school to junior high was rather disconcerting. The change from classes in one room with one teacher and the same students, to attendance in various classrooms with different teachers and pupils was challenging, but I adjusted quickly. At the same time, I began to assume more and more duties at home as my mother's alcoholism worsened, which, in turn, only deepened my dislike for her. Often my brother or I would discover some of our mom's corrosive lubricant and promptly deposit it into the toilet, but for the most part she consumed her poison without interference and with unabashed indifference. Thunderbird was her choice of poison.

All the while, my dad persisted in his slavish toiling in order to bountifully provide for all of us. He was unavailable during weekdays, while my mother was simply "absent" due to being in such frequent alcoholic fogs. There were many evenings when Mrs. C. would see me on the front porch waiting for my dad to come home. She would take me to their house and feed me. My brother would seek refuge at his best friend's home a few streets over from ours. Still, I adapted, and busied myself with school and managing the household; besides, I was always able to enjoy safe harbor at Gammy's... that is, until October 8, 1974, when, at the age of twelve, my refuge was forever lost.

Edna, Rachel's Grandmother (Gammy).

Chapter Three

Frank: the Middle Years

To this very day I remain shocked over how rapidly my life plummeted out of control. One moment I was an accomplished athlete from excellent stock and succeeding as a cadet at a prestigious military academy prep school; the next, everything spiraled downward at lightning speed.

It was with feelings of great excitement about following in my father's footsteps that I began attending Brentwood Military Academy. Certainly, the new adventure in my young life engendered a real sense of enthusiasm, just as wearing a uniform and participating in military drills was intoxicating. Moreover, I felt an increased sense of belonging. The comradery I had known as a member on a team was an attractive aspect of athletics, but to be on a collective journey toward a common purpose with so many students was a unique and intense experience for me. We were not merely attending school, but instead marching as one toward honor, duty and country. Perhaps not all of the cadets had assumed the same feeling of purpose and service; I however, had a degree of comfort with academy life. The disciplined regimens, coupled with the definitive moral code that had been deeply instilled within me from religious training and the instruction of my parents were reinforced by the structure and strictness of the military academy. My inaugural semester went well.

Early in 1970 I began my second semester of military school at the ripe old age of fourteen; however, there was a sudden and discernable difference. Seeking to increase student enrollment, the academy had permitted the admission of problem kids during the Christmas break. During my first semester I had not really made any close associations with other cadets. My feelings of cohesion were more of a universal sense and were bolstered by the determination to excel in the classroom, where my efforts and diligence were frequently rewarded by many upper classmen.

As it turned out, the seemingly innocuous enrollment of less driven students became both a temptation and an obstacle. Up until that point in my life my every desire and goal had honorable intention, so I found myself ill-prepared to be suddenly confronted with kids who routinely cut school, acted up in class, smoked, and even used drugs. The disciplined manner in which my parents had taught me to conduct myself, along with the religious training, had insulated me from this breed of character. It would seem that the straitlaced environ of a military academy would be the last place to find such pupils.

Looking back now at this momentous juncture, I can observe the slow progression of an insidious temptation to competing interests. One of the more distinct dissimilarities between my life up to that point and that of the new students was the fact that my pursuit of academic prowess and military excellence was hard work. I had always prided myself on my tireless efforts toward achieving success in any endeavor, so the lifestyle exhibited by the problem kids seemed so particularly lackluster and carefree. I had always enjoyed the process of laboring devotedly toward an intended purpose and had never even contemplated an existence based on laziness, apathy and non-conformance. I remain at a loss as to what caused my gravitation toward that group of miscreants. Perhaps the mysterious nature of something new and forbidden was what had captivated me. Looking back, the one thing I can say with certainty is that the deviousness of the devil was afoot.[2]

It was with a sense of naive curiosity that I began to casually associate with those new students. At first we did not meet on an everyday basis. I perceived my association with them to be a harmless new adventure, an innocent hanging out between classes to perhaps sneak a cigarette or engage in some other minor antic. (Nota bene: No participation in miscreant behavior, casual or otherwise, is innocuous!) Unfortunately, I failed to heed my sense of caution and initially thought of it all as boyhood mischief, as a minimal and temporary descent into the excitement of the taboo. My failure to immediately cut off what proved to be demonic prompting at its very inception soon evolved into keeping company with dangerous persons and adapting their perverse concepts with increased regularity. Although I had previously followed godly directives, I began not only engaging in the simple occasional lapse, but had become inundated with deviant enticements. These were lures that I eagerly soaked in and which inevitably revolved around ungodly attitudes of disrespect toward authority. The bedrock of honor that had been so carefully cultivated was being undermined... and I was not even aware of it!

It must be said that these current observations are in no way intended to excuse my abandonment of the training that my parents had so painstakingly and lovingly provided. By tracing how the casual bad choice can so rapidly lead to more frequent indiscretions, I hope to create a consciousness of the danger of keeping bad company. Inherent in my decline was heeding those who were already well-versed in disrespect for authority. The outgrowth of my once casual acquaintances was the onset of indolence toward school work, the cutting of a few classes, and

---

2   For more information on demonic tactics, see Frank and Rachel's *Noetic Jerusalem*, published by Amazon.

an escalation of these antics, coupled with the contemplation of criminal activity.

Consequently, as the school year progressed, so did my decline. Rather than striving for excellence as a dedicated cadet, I sought to impress my new found nefarious associates. The consideration of illicit endeavors became a reality as I cut classes in order to visit local markets where I would shoplift cigarettes and then dole them out to my dutifully impressed companions. The diligence and effort that had served as the cornerstone of my existence as an obedient son and faithful adherent of God crumbled. Rather than enthusiastically participating in classes or military drills, I cut school with alarming frequency in order to hang out with my new pals under the Santa Monica pier, where we wasted away the hours. In spite of the drastic alteration of my goals, I must vehemently declare that the sole impetus for my tragic descent is the failure to have cut off what I today know to have been demonic attacks at the very moment of provocation.

The loss of respect and admiration by upper classmen did not function as much of a deterrent... how could it? I had taken the proverbial bait of temptation – hook, line, and sinker. I racked up demerits and was assigned quite a bit of detention. (At the academy this involved extra drills after class.) Then I simply started to skip detention. Of course, my "buddies" cheered me on and admired the development of my nonconformist attitude.

I don't really recall the impact on my parents during those early stages of my devolution; assuredly they were heartbroken. What I do remember is nearly overdosing on barbiturates. It was an especially hot day and the oppressive heat acted like an invitation for my new friends and me to sneak off after the noon drills. We had earlier decided to meet at a bushy gully adjacent to the school because one of the guys said that he had something to show us. This pupil had stolen some bottles of pills from his father, who was a doctor, and he proudly displayed them to us. Without really knowing what we were doing, we began taking pills, each one of us trying to outdo the others. After a while, my friends began staggering off, one by one, until I was the only kid left in the gully. Suddenly, several upper classmen burst through the bushes in front of me and I was dragged off to the Commandant's office. Apparently some of my comrades had been seen stumbling around the hallways, and under questioning they indicated that I was perhaps still in the gully.

Boy, was I ever in trouble! There I was, doing my level best to sit upright in the chair and not really succeeding, while the Commandant spoke to my mother. Then, I was instructed to stand up, a feat that proved to be impossible. I fell out of the chair and had to be helped to my feet and out the door to my mother's car. I was suspended, of course, for the remainder of the school year. Initially the shame of having disgraced both myself and my parents was overwhelming. Had I, at that point, returned to honoring my parents and resumed godlier pursuits, perhaps my life would have turned out very differently. What I opted for instead was to seek consolation from the same so-called friends who had encouraged my decline in the first place. The embarrassment and the shame still hurt, for it was not just my parents who had been disappointed in me. Everyone we knew (family, friends, shopkeepers) was acutely aware of and disappointed by my behavior. Even while I was on suspension I continued to flee to my cohorts, who would cut class and hang out with me. In their presence, I felt neither humiliation nor guilt, but acceptance. Their acceptance fostered misdirected anger over my plight. It has been said that a consequence of participation in demonic engagements tends to diminish any sense of responsibility. That is precisely what I began to experience. Rather than regret my transgressions and work at preventing a similar lapse, I only focused on how "unfair" my situation was. With the help of my compatriots (all of whom had acquired a wealth of experience in escaping responsibility), I began to misperceive shame and punishment as unjust. Thus, in the spring of 1970, at the age of fourteen, susceptibility to temptation had taken a firm hold of me.

Although I could have easily returned to the model of ethics that my parents had consistently displayed and taught, I considered my ejection from the military school as a personal affront (which is what I now know to be the sin of pride). Rather than draw upon my parents' instruction and my remnant faith in God, I instead gravitated toward activities that were the antithesis of society's established mores. With even more free time on my hands and relatively little inclination to resume my status as an aspiring cadet, I not only maintained associations with the very kids who had encouraged my fall, but also began to spend my days in the company of counterculture advocates on the nearby UCLA campus. Like my school pals, they were also all too willing to assist me into further separating from the godly. Once again I felt excitement simply by turning my eager attention to vile ideas – especially those that assured retribution against what I by then regarded as an unjust and abusive society. Looking back upon those times I can so clearly see how I departed the struggle for staying on the straight and narrow road with such relative ease, may God forgive me, as I caved in to temptations and permitted my heart to be taken captive.[3]

At that time, my cooperation with what I today know to have been demonic provocations led to trying marijuana once, using sleeping pills a handful of times, and an inclination toward misbehavior. Then, one summer day in 1970, I set out to reacquaint myself with marijuana, but in no way could I imagine the devastation it would inflict. No sooner had I begun to hitchhike when a young man picked me up. We stopped off at a liquor store for some wine before ending up at his house. At that stage in life I had never even kissed a girl. At the age of fourteen, that man took advantage of my innocence and inebriation and proceeded to sexually assault me. Attempts to deal with the shame and emotional trauma were a terrible struggle for me. I just could not

---

3   Church Fathers define a five-step cycle towards sin, which consists of: 1) provocation, the demonic thought; 2) interaction with the provocation; 3) assent, or participation in the provocation; 4) captivity, or onset of habit; 5) passion, the entrenchment of sin in the soul.

comprehend what had occurred. It wasn't until recently, in about 2012, that doctors have pointed to post-traumatic stress disorder (PTSD), a serious and debilitating mental illness resulting from having experienced a traumatic event, in order to explain how my sexualization, extreme substance abuse, and risk-taking behavior were all due to that assault in 1970. The differences between my life prior to having been raped and subsequent to it display the destruction caused by the mental illness and a life adrift from God.

After I had been raped, my parents sent me to a psychologist (for individual and group therapy), but I continued to flounder. Eventually I gravitated away from the role of sexual assault victim; it had become too painful. Instead, I sought to "normalize" what I had experienced by attempting to convince myself that sex between an adult male and a child was typical. Absent healing from God, this impression continued to fester.

Many of my life choices can be characterized as extremist. This can especially be seen in how quickly I adapted to perpetrating anti-establishment objectives. Apprenticed to campus radicals, I gained an extensive education in "direct action" and urban guerrilla warfare. I learned how to set fires, construct and explode pipe bombs, recruit more soldiers, and to both manufacture illicit substances and establish distribution networks. It felt satisfying to have been befriended by older activists and to have even been included in their plans. On many occasions I was invited to a dorm room or to an off-campus apartment where ideas for far-reaching schemes were fleshed out. On one such occasion, discussions ensued over strategies on how to most effectively disseminate the LSD that they were manufacturing. On another occasion, BLA members (the Black Liberation Army, the radical, violent faction of the Black Panther Party) contemplated the robbery of an armored truck, or, as they called it: the liberation of funds for "the cause". Obviously, my desire for inclusion possessed no moral compass.

At around this time, together with a very close friend

(Jimmie, my trusted confidant and crime partner from late 1970 until his death in 1982), I founded a loose-knit group, named the League for Social Destruction (the LSD). We carried out assaults on establishment installations such as bank buildings, water and power outposts, construction sites, telephone equipment centers, and other vital bases of societal operations. However, what still really makes me cringe today is the change in how I thought, and worse – how that led to even more extreme crossroads.

The one-time church-attending kid, the all-star athlete, the good student and aspiring cadet who had come from loving, well-to-do parents, had, within a few months after having been raped, become an enemy of the state. The impact on my thought process, as a result of PTSD and having turned away from religion, included the substitution of all-American ideals for the utterly insane ambition of intending to disrupt the society that I had somehow come to see as having mistreated me. These obviously deranged and indefensible new aspirations profoundly affected my stream of consciousness. For instance, rather than recognize that I had not only fallen in with a bad crowd but had actually become part of that bad crowd, I concocted ridiculous scenarios in my mind. I believed that those scenarios absolved me of blame because I considered myself to be the victim of a cruel and uncaring society.

Prior to having been raped at age fourteen, as well as departing Episcopalianism along with my parents' teaching, I would have immediately understood the dangers of having adopted evil ways and would have at once fled into the protective arms of Christ Jesus, my mother, and my father. Instead, I blinded myself from any recognition of what a degenerate I had become. My unwillingness to accept reality caused me to rely on drugs to reinforce my self-induced ignorance. I also began to act according to the PTSD that had been inflicted upon me by permitting older men to sexually use me in exchange for drugs or money. I began to turn the world upside down. Good (honor, purity and self-discipline) became undesirable; I craved what was evil (hedonism, lawlessness and irreverence). My abandonment of all religious training led to an increase in the mad cycle of sin. Having been sexualized, I prostituted myself; the shoplifting of cigarettes became random burglaries; minor participation in drug activity turned into the manufacturing of drugs and burglarizing pharmacies.

I have written of the shame I endured as a consequence of having been suspended from the military academy, as well as the destruction of my overall well-being by having been a sexual assault victim. The anguished despair and heartbreak I inflicted on my loving parents must also be recognized. It remains the most evil, vile abomination I have committed in my entire life. Having poured their hearts and souls into my welfare, they then had to observe their only child's involvement in utterly beastly pursuits... They were devastated. I beg God's forgiveness for the horrible distress I inflicted on my precious parents every day.

I never did return to the Brentwood Military Academy. Nor did I ever again pursue my dreams of following in my father's footsteps. Instead, I more firmly entrenched myself in the degenerate life I had adopted as my very own. At the time I did not really consider the road upon which I had embarked. Focus had shifted to desperate attempts to mask my shame. To recognize my failures was simply no longer part of my agenda.

Obviously, my parents frantically tried to help their wayward son to be healed of sexual trauma (PTSD). Once a return to military school had been foreclosed, my parents proceeded to enroll me in a series of private educational institutions. The hope was that the more individualized attention I could receive at such facilities would prompt a retreat from my moral decline. The first of these private establishments was the Melrose School in Santa Monica, recommended by my psychiatrist, Dr. Brandt. It was a learning center for emotionally disturbed children that offered very small classes and personalized instruction. However, my interests no longer included educational goals. Unwilling to give up, my folks then arranged for me to attend an exclusive private school in Beverly Hills. It seemed however, that many prestigious private schools had gone the way of the Brentwood Military Academy by catering to more and more rich kid problem students. Of course, being a troublesome pupil myself, I knew what it felt like to be perceived as a disruptive and unwanted force. It hurt, and it compelled quite a bit of anger. At the Beverly Hills School one teacher was assigned to three or four students. This available extra instruction was not the solution, because I merely wanted to hang out at a nearby park with a few other like-minded students and smoke dope. About a handful of us had become pretty close. We would spend time together at one another's houses or go to concerts, but all of us lasted only a semester at Beverly Hills.

Still dedicated to helping their son, my parents even tried an alternative school in the San Fernando Valley called You & Me High School that was managed by "free-thinkers". While this experience initially provoked some interest, I soon found that even the relaxed curricula and company of fellow counterculture types failed to retain my attention. I invested more and more time in taking LSD and spending days in the school's back field caring for the goats and chickens.

Actually, the straw that broke the camel's back at You & Me High School was another near overdose. The entire school assembly at You & Me was made up of several dozen kids. We went on a field trip to a mountain resort near Idyllwild. I had become pretty good friends with one of the girls – there were no sexual relations and I had still never had sex with a female. Upon our return my parents had arranged for me to stay at her house in Topanga Canyon while they vacationed in San Diego. The next morning I woke up late and found a note saying that Cindy and her mother had gone shopping. I wandered into their bathroom to investigate the medicine cabinet (Yes, when visiting other people's homes it had become my habit to check their medicine chests for drugs). I found a half full bottle of Valium and on the way to the kitchen located an unopened fifth of Royal Canadian liquor. About an hour lapsed. All I remembered was being thirsty, taking swigs of alcohol, and continually popping a few pills. Then I noticed that both bottles, the whiskey and the Valium, were empty, and I called a friend in Santa Monica for help. Santa Monica was not far, and even though my rescuer rushed right over, by the time he had arrived I was barely conscious. I recall being taken out to the backyard and forced to hike up a steep hillside, strenuous exercise being an antidote for drug overdoses. The next thing I knew I was tumbling down the hill. Twelve hours later I woke up in Santa Monica at the residence of a You & Me teacher. Everyone was asleep and some car keys were on a table. I snuck out and took off in the teacher's Toyota. The combination of still being incredibly wasted and never having operated a stick shift had its predictable result: I wrecked the car. Of course, I was no longer welcome at You & Me High School. Once again my misdeeds had ended in rejection; yet I still failed to recognize that my life had been spared.

My family was running out of day school choices; so when they finally decided on a boarding school, I reluctantly began packing. The Catalina Island School was an exclusive establishment situated on Catalina, an island across from Santa Monica. While initially it was quite a novelty, I didn't really fit in with any of the students and became somewhat of a loner. There was one teacher, Morty, who took an interest in me. Quite frequently, once classes were over, we would hike to secluded areas, smoke a little hash, and then Morty would either give me counseling or teach me American literature. The close association with this unique educator led to a redoubling of my efforts to be sociable. I even joined the school's soccer team. Still, I did not take to life on Santa Catalina Island and began the practice of hiking the few miles along the rugged coast to Avalon. This was a wild and dangerous trek since there was no beach and my journey through the thick brush at water's edge was hampered by crashing waves. The Catalina Island School did its best to facilitate my adaptation, even inviting my dad to spend a few days with me in the posh lighthouse when homesickness seemed to have been the problem. Nonetheless, I continued my treks to Avalon, where I would then take a sea plane to Long Beach (near Santa Monica). My parents always returned me to Catalina Island (again by sea plane), until the school no longer welcomed me back. That was in 1972. I was sixteen years old and my parents were running out of options.

Many people, entirely unfamiliar with the details of my home life, have suggested that my parents must have been lax in discipline. They fail to place responsibility on the sole person who was accountable for my depravity: me! In retrospect, such accusations wagered against my parents causes me significant pain and consternation, because my mother and father consistently applied a plethora of disciplinary measures. I simply remained unpersuaded that altering my course was in my best interests. Over the years I received corporal punishment on a fairly routine basis; however, the brevity of its discomfort resulted in my discounting it as an effective deterrent. In conjunction with corporal punishment, other behavior modification tools were utilized, among which was the withholding of my weekly allowance. Whenever that tactic was used, I simply figured that a single burglary or a few drug deals would nicely replace the missing weekly stipend. I was also assigned extra chores. However, these correctional measures were of such short duration that, like the spankings, they also failed to be persuasive. Moreover, whenever I was grounded, I would usually run off and by the time I returned, a day or two later, my mom and dad would have been so worried about me that their relief usually culminated in a change of schools or counseling, rather than additional punishment. Unfortunately, none of the weapons in my parents' far-reaching arsenal ever produced the desired long-lasting effect. There were actually some occasions which induced a reversed impact, as I twisted what had been intended for correction into examples of how unfairly I was being treated.

My father even invoked the extreme approach of soliciting law enforcement assistance. For example, I had been placed on probation for a string of delinquencies yet continued to retain an unrepentant demeanor. In fact, my attitude grew even more disdainful. At wit's end, my father had covertly arranged for my probation to be violated (for me to be sent to jail) and, under the guise of a routine meeting with my probation officer, I was driven to the Santa Monica office. As soon as I entered the building, what was occurring became readily apparent. Rather than recognize that my misdeeds had led to his choice of action, I distorted my father's desperation into my having been outrageously and unjustly abused. Years later I spoke with my dad about that event. My self-centered focus had always revolved around how the experience had affected me; I had never before considered the impact on my father. To listen to him express his utter despair as he walked across the parking lot toward his car, turning his back on the son who was wrestling with authorities and pleading for his help, was heartbreaking. The father, whom I at one time had wanted to emulate, whom I adored, had had to endure unimaginable sorrow at the hands of his own son.

Another example of my dad having importuned police intervention occurred after he had warned me about smoking marijuana. Having asserted a need for some independence, I had turned the garage into a "guest house". I laid shag carpeting on the concrete floor; moved in my bed, sofa and other bedroom furniture and declared that locale as my new, separate residence. One evening when my dad had returned home from work, he knocked on the garage door to greet his son, but when I answered my "front door" the pervasive odor of marijuana nearly knocked him over. He then informed me that if the activity recurred, he would call the police. The very next day he came home for lunch, knocked on the door, and when I opened it a visible cloud of marijuana smoke enveloped him. He promptly summoned the police. The next thing I knew, the garage door (that is to say, an entire "wall" of my "house") flew open and about a half dozen detectives were lined up across the driveway, with guns drawn. I was carted off to jail.

In light of the overwhelming evidence regarding a strict application of a wide range of disciplinary tools in their efforts to rein in the son who had, as a consequence of PTSD, become sexualized, abused drugs, and continuously chased risky experiences, it must be clearly stated that my parents were in no way remiss... in no way.

The tireless efforts exerted by my parents through enrollments in private schools, through disciplinary measures, through summoning law enforcement also included my being admitted to psychiatric hospitals. My increased usage of drugs, both in terms of variety and quantity, caused my parents great concern. A crisis intervention also took place. I had ingested a handful of sleeping pills and my obvious "condition" caused my mom to take me to the family doctor, where I gave a urine sample. Once the result came back as positive for barbiturates, I was admitted to the Los Angeles Children's Hospital for observation and additional tests. Since it was not a secured facility, I easily absconded and upon having arrived back home, began to ingest sleeping pills, which I washed down with alcohol. A cousin from Cleveland had shown up for a visit with my mom, while I was supposed to be hospitalized downtown. When my mother's pleas for me to stop drinking fell on deaf ears, this cousin took it upon himself to intervene and an altercation ensued. Of course the police were called. When they arrived, I continued brandishing a knife because I was too stoned to comply with their instructions. I was beaten and arrested and emergently admitted to the Cedars-Sinai hospital's psychiatric unit. There, in a frenzied state, I began kicking the door of the room into which I had been locked. When that failed to receive the desired attention, I set fire to my bedding. They had left me in underclothing and socks, so the lighter that I usually kept in my socks had not been detected. I then picked up a metal cot and started trying to break a window that faced the street. It was soon determined that I was not suited for that facility and after a brief stay at home, I was transferred to the Resthaven psychiatric hospital. Once again an attempt by my loving parents to help me produced few, if any, results. A common practice for me during my time at Resthaven was to use my walking pass time (an occasion during which we could walk around outside) to sneak down the hill to Chinatown where I would talk strangers into purchasing liquor for me. It was the only period in my life when I drank consistently, consuming at least a fifth of Boonesfarm wine and a half pint of vodka almost daily... and I was only fifteen at the time. My antics went unnoticed for the most part, but there were those occasions when I really overdid it and was placed in the lock down ward, where inevitably I would end up rolling around in my own vomit.

It was also at Resthaven where I first fell in love. There was a stunningly gorgeous fourteen-year old Native American girl, Amanda, at Resthaven. We quickly became friends, but she did not feel romantically inclined. The closest I got to a relationship with Amanda was when we played the leads in Romeo and Juliet and I imagined that we were truly young lovers. That drama class was quite an experience; the rehearsals were great fun; the night we would perform publicly approached rapidly. On the evening of our big show another patient at Resthaven suggested a journey across town. We made it back to Resthaven, a little late but in one piece, and I attempted to perform the lead role of Romeo after having ingested LSD, hash, and opium. It proved to be quite a challenge, but one that I managed. Amanda was utterly disgusted by my behavior and we were never again very close.

Eventually I returned home, but not much in my behavior or attitude had changed. What was soon to change was my neighbors' tolerance for my continued presence in the community. In 1972, I had ended up in juvenile detention for several weeks, and absent some dramatic change, it appeared that the judge had no intention of permitting my release. My parents were therefore confronted with the terrible choice of either losing their son to the state penal system, or departing the home they had known in Los Angeles for eighteen years. Their decision was made even more emotional by the fact that I was brutally gang-raped while in juvenile hall.

So many people have suggested that my parents should have simply abandoned me, either by kicking me out of the house or letting me rot in jail, but that would have meant abandoning their Christian precepts. My mother and father always saw a child as a labor of love. Having observed their patience as well as their unconditional love for me has been an incredibly poignant lesson in Christian love (the love of God). I only wish that every child had parents who never quit on them.

Anyway, my mom and dad not only wished to liberate me from the clutches of juvenile "justice," but also hoped that a change in residence would stimulate my return to normalcy; so they uprooted the family home. Our new locale was a mile or two down Sunset Boulevard, not far from the home of O. J. Simpson and that of his murdered wife, Nicole. While it was an extremely nice area, it tragically turned out to be yet another failed endeavor.

Considering the number of private schools, the amount of therapy, confinements in psychiatric hospitals, types of discipline, and police intervention, I simply cannot fathom how anyone could interpret my parents' actions as negligent. My abject unwillingness to pursue responsible objectives; my absolute failure to seriously deal with having been raped several times; and my purposeful turning away from God and godly pursuits are the multi-pronged source of the evil perpetrated against me as well as of those evils in which I willingly took part. In addition to the sexual assaults (the 1970 molestation and 1972 gang rape), I was again attacked in 1972 while my parents and I vacationed in Aspen. A local musician had taken me to his home and sexually abused me.

During the early 1970's, although I was only in my mid-teens, my life was one continual downward spiral into increased crime and drug use. Nothing that had been important in my earlier life – neither my parents nor God – appealed to me. It was during that period of my life however, that I had my one and only girlfriend, Sophie (prior to the woman who became my wife many years later). In January of 1973 I had ended up in jail on a charge of incorrigibility that my parents had lodged in yet another loving attempt to rein in their wayward son. My release occurred on my seventeenth birthday. At that time, I was enrolled in the extension program of the public high school; University (or Uni) High School, what we all called "Stoner High". Probably every public high school has one, a spot on the fringes of school property where problem students are exiled, and that had become my fate. Soon after the onset of my attendance at this facility for losers, a beautiful girl showed up, Sophie.

A week or two after the appearance of Sophie, some of my friends – we were a group of stoners who usually ditched school so we could hang out and get high – mentioned that a great party was going to be held at the house of some girl, who happened to be the daughter of a very famous Hollywood movie producer. I eagerly agreed to accompany them. Entering the sprawling ranch-style home, my jaw dropped; it was Sophie's house. We spent the evening together and as the shindig came to a close, Sophie indicated that I should stay. At age seventeen I experienced sexual relations with a female for the first time in my life.

Over the ensuing months we were inseparable, but she had some drug charges pending from before we had met, and in the summer of 1973 Sophie went to a juvenile detention center. In an attempt to keep us together, my mother petitioned the court for custody, so that Sophie and I could be married and reside with my parents, but the judge denied the request. We had to content ourselves with letters, until she began getting furloughs every month or so. Her father never really liked me and the last time I saw Sophie was after having sex in the back of her car, when her dad showed up and I fled on foot with him chasing me down the street. By the time of her next furlough, my eighteenth birthday was approaching and I was in jail myself... but that's another story.

It was while Sophie was in jail, during the summer of 1973, that I dabbled in the music business when my dad landed me a job with his cable radio station. In 1972 my father had retired from the United States Army as a one-star general. At around the same time, his prowess as an executive with Hughes Aircraft resulted in his having become a highly sought after communications expert. A company known as Teleprompter had begun a cable television station that was based in Los Angeles called Theta Cable, and my father was approached about becoming its president, a move that Hughes Aircraft endorsed by loaning him to Teleprompter and Theta Cable.

Even in my relatively depraved state, I still adored my father and admired his example of honor and integrity. Prior to my having worked at the radio station I had been temporarily employed at the cable company as an installer, an experience during which I had occasion to observe my dad's management style. Dad was an extraordinarily accomplished man; yet he was so humble and treated all employees with utmost respect. During his regular tours of the station, he would engage all levels of staff (from line workers and camera operators to upper management) in candid discussions about their opinions and concerns. Despite my evil involvements, I always prized the model of honor that my beloved dad perennially evidenced. May God guard and perfect his soul!

As an innovative master in communications my father expanded Theta Cable's services to include a premium movie station (the Z-Channel) and a rock radio station. My penchant for rock music led to my having successfully petitioned my father and the KBLE radio station owner/manager for a position as the station librarian. Initially I intended to pursue a career in the music industry – the ability to watch noted guest broadcasters such as Barbara Birdfeather and Wolfman Jack, as well as to secure the latest releases from record companies would provide the requisite education and connections for success. In virtually no time, as had unfortunately become my habit, I corrupted good ideals into ungodly ones. I misappropriated my duties as station librarian by warping interactions with the Hollywood record companies into illicit enterprises that involved band members and their managers.

My new ambitions included attending parties in the Hollywood Hills with superstars – Keith Richards, Jimmy Page, Joe Perry, Lou Reed, David Bowie, Iggy Pop, Sly Stone, John Kay, et al. To further my involvement with these superstars, I increased the frequency of my pharmacy break-ins. I had discovered that a consistent stockpile of narcotics would increase the likelihood of my popularity, because most of the early 1970s rock bands were heavily into drugs. Since I owned the best dope, I commanded much attention... proof positive that once the devil gets his claws into you, the pit truly becomes bottomless.

Having already increased my involvement in drugs (via felonious pharmacy break-ins), I then furthered my putrid agenda by expanding into occasional theft. My old League of Social Destruction co-founder, Jimmie had joined me on burglaries in the ultra-rich Bel-Air section of Los Angeles. Our intent was to requisition the proceeds from our criminal enterprises to facilitate our ability to routinely keep company with some of the world's most famous rock bands.

Looking back, my pursuits clearly furthered my abandonment of God. It was in that despicable condition – absent God and religion, a slave to demons, ill from PTSD, having absolutely devastated my parents, clothed in profound dishonor – that I approached my eighteenth birthday.

Chapter Four

Rachel: the Middle Years

I arose early on the morning of the eighth of October, 1974 to the sound of the constant ringing of the phone. I heard my mom talking to many different people during those telephone conversations and knew at once that something significant had happened. Furthermore, even though it was much too early for my dad to have left for work, he was not home. Eventually, my mother got off the phone and retreated to her room in a state of despair.

The unfolding of those circumstances had frightened me to the point that I actually thought that something had happened to my dad. I went into my mother's room and in a shaky voice asked her what was occurring. As soon as she uttered the words, "Something bad has happened." I screamed, believing that it was about my beloved daddy. Continuing, my mom told me that my father had received a call late in the night about something being wrong with Gammy. So he had gone to Gammy's house and then accompanied her to the hospital. And then came those god-awful words that continue to haunt me, even today. My mother told me, "Gammy has passed away."

I was devastated, and initially reacted by grabbing a picture off of my mom's wall and dashing it to the floor. I then ran out of the front door in hysterics. I simply could not conceive of life without my Gammy.

I soon returned home and found my mother on the telephone again. Screaming, I pleaded with her to take me to the hospital. I wanted desperately to see my beloved Gammy. At the hospital I learned that Gammy had suffered a massive cerebral hemorrhage and had been placed on life support. The doctor stated that were she to ever come around, she would be a vegetable. Moreover, Gammy had signed a "Do Not Resuscitate" document, so she had to be taken off of life support. This was not at all an easy development for Gammy's doctor. He had met her when he had been a guest at the El Corona Ranch in the 1950's and had been her physician for nearly as long. Unable to do it himself, he had one of the nurses remove Gammy's life support. I was pretty much inconsolable, so the doctor ended up giving my mom a prescription for Valium for me. The following day a touch of reality tinged with fear began to sink in; my refuge, my Gammy was gone.

The funeral occurred a few days later. Afterward, many people from church stopped by our house with some food. As soon as we had arrived home, my mother drove off. I knew exactly where she had gone... to the nearest store for a bottle of alcohol. So it was that when my dad and I needed her most, Mom abandoned us. Later on that day, she disappeared into her room in a drunken daze.

Although Gammy had been my paternal grandmother, she was loved and adored by all of my maternal kinfolk, especially by my mom's twin sister, Mary. At that time, Aunt Mary and Uncle Jim were on a military base in Greece, where Uncle Jim was stationed. It really upset them to have not been able to attend Gammy's funeral.

My return to school in the fall of 1974, when I was twelve years old and in my first year at Magee Junior High School, was extremely difficult after Gammy's passing. Class attendance, the

attempt to study math, social studies, and so on, seemed so unnecessary. I had a hard time coping, and at times, even had to
leave class and go home. It took quite a while to edge back into
the school routine. My mother's drunken behavior made my adjustment even more of a struggle.

Then came the holidays. So many cherished memories of
preparing the Christmas feasts with Gammy made that 1974 celebration of Christ Jesus' nativity such an unbearable experience.
Typically, as at almost every Christmas, Mom was drunk.

In 1975, my brother, who had begun to run track in his
freshman year at high school, was then in his sophomore year.
That spring, my brother had a big track meet and my mom, who
was in a highly intoxicated state, intended to attend the event.
When I returned home from school that afternoon, she insisted
that I accompany her in the car – something that often occurred
when she had been drinking. I desperately tried to think up an excuse, and even visited my neighbors to inform Mrs. C. about this
dire development. Mrs. C., bless her heart, then told my mother
that I had an important exam the next day, and therefore required
the aid of her elder daughter to prepare more effectively. Thankfully, my mom agreed to let me remain behind. She embarked
upon her drunken journey on her own, and I was exceedingly
grateful to not have gone.

The family expected Mom home at around 5:30, but as
supper time approached, her continued absence became a cause
for concern. Mrs. C. knew that I would be joining her clan for
dinner, an occasion that had become a common occurrence as a
result of my mother's alcohol abuse. Finally, my dad called Mrs.
C.'s house at about 7:00 pm with unwelcome news. Predictably,
Mom had been in a really bad accident. Apparently, in a drunken
stupor, she had veered off the road and crashed into a metal pole.
Thank the Good Lord that no one else was involved. As for my
mother, although she had completely totaled the car, she had only
suffered some minor bruising. However, she did end up in jail.
When the topic of bail arose, I begged my father to leave her in-

carcerated. He couldn't. He loved her and went off to secure her release.

During the ensuing days my mom acted rather reclusively, spending much of the time in her room. When my dad purchased another vehicle for her, it seemed to brighten her mood. My mother even went back into the rehabilitation center. However, my brother and I had a very disappointing experience with the rehab director, one that perhaps explains why my mother's recovery endeavors never enjoyed lasting impact. During a visit to my mom at rehab, my brother and I spoke with the director, a character who was an avid apologetic for our mother's substance abuse. She suggested that my brother and I were at least partially responsible for Mom's substance abuse! I may have been only twelve, and may not have displayed the best of manners, but I informed that woman, in no uncertain terms, that my brother and I were not to blame for my mother's alcoholism. I went on to give her a piece of my mind before my brother and I stormed out of her office.

My mom stayed at rehab for approximately sixty days. As bad as it may sound, I must admit that it was nice to not have her stumbling around the house. We (my dad, my brother and I) occasionally visited Mom at the center. Each time we returned home, it was a return to a less stressful home environment for all of us.

Gigi, my mother's mom, and her mother (my great grandmother) were in Tucson, so I visited them frequently. Those visits were not like the ones I once had enjoyed with my Gammy. Gigi worked, and I'm sure the last thing she wanted to do at the end of the day was entertain a kid. Thus, the summer of 1975 was a bit troublesome, as were most of the summers of my childhood. We made some plans to have lunch with my mother at the rehabilitation center for my birthday, but I was skeptical of a joyful result.

I was aware that my mother had engaged previously in surreptitious trysts with other men – knowledge that no twelve-year old daughter should have to endure. At that time, I strongly suspected that she was involved with another resident at the rehab clinic. My relationship with my mom was fraught with perennial suspicion. I distrusted her, so I always thought that she was up to something. My suspicions were usually confirmed by discovering her many dishonorable deeds. On the occasion involving my thirteenth birthday in August of 1975, my dad and I were late for the scheduled lunch. When we entered the rehabilitation center, we noticed that my mom was seated with a man at one of the tables. While there were other patients around, it just seemed odd to me. I sensed that something more than a casual acquaintanceship was afoot. My mother was especially cavalier in demeanor and grumbled, "You're late. I've already eaten." This took place on my birthday. We had thought it would be a nice treat for my mom, and believed that she desired to spend time with me on my birthday. We remained only a few minutes. I was very hurt.

My mom was released from rehab a few weeks later. Once home, her behavior seemed quite strange; she hardly ever left her room. Actually, she really didn't seem to be happy to be home. That fateful premonition turned out to be accurate, once my mother's relationship with Ed became known. It was almost time for me to begin my second year at Magee Junior High School, when my mother announced to my dad that she intended to go on a camping trip with some friends from the rehab center. My mom had never been camping, nor had she ever had a whit of interest in the outdoor life; huge red flags went up in my mind. A few days later I found my mom packing all of her clothes (and some of mine, as we wore same size), jewelry, everything. The man that I had seen with my mother at the table in rehab was in the house, and immediately I knew that something was amiss. My mom tried to pawn him off as an innocuous friend, while Ed tried to assume control of the situation by ordering me to serve him a cup of coffee. Of course, I refused. My mother was furious, but she kept packing her things. Then my mom left with Ed in the car that my father had purchased for her. I knew that she was leaving us. It fell to me to notify my dad, who was at work.

It was one of the hardest things I have ever had to do... to call my precious daddy and tell him what had happened. He returned home right away and noticed that all of Mom's things were gone. All he could manage to do was to sit on the edge of the bed, in tears, as he realized that Mom had left him for Ed, a heroin addict.

Not long after my mother's abandonment of us, my dad learned that she had pawned all of her jewelry, even her wedding band. Then, divorce papers were filed. I was in abject fear over the prospect of my mother gaining custody of my brother and me. This potential threat hung over our heads as my brother and I took the city bus to an attorney's office to declare that we wanted to live with our father. Earlier, my mother had telephoned us in an attempt to persuade us to live with her – probably so she and Ed could receive government assistance money for having dependent children – but I told her that that would never happen. We categorically informed the attorney that we desired to remain with dad. I even told him that if he separated my brother and me from our dad, we would run away. My brother was 15 and I had just turned 13. He was old enough, by law, to decide who to live with, but I was not. The lawyer assured my dad that he would get custody of both of us.

Dad did get custody of us and also retained the house, since he had to pay off my mom's debts. Still, all he wanted were his children and his home. Soon after being denied custody of her children, my mother took off with Ed and moved to Farmington, New Mexico. I would not hear from my mom for over a year, until Christmas of 1976.

It was also in the fall of 1975 that some new neighbors moved in a few doors down, a pastor, his wife, and their three kids. I became their babysitter, both in their home for their children and at their church's nursery. Although the new family was non-denominational (a fact to which I will later return), it did not trouble them that I had been raised in and continued to attend the Church of Christ.

It was during the summer of 1976, when I was nearly fourteen years old, that I began competitive running. I was encouraged by my brother, who had begun to run as a freshman at Sahuaro High School and was then about to enter his senior year. We were very close, and did much of our training together. He was pretty good. In fact, in the fall of 1976 my dad and I attended one of my brother's cross-country meets in Paradise Valley and my brother did well enough to place ninth in the entire state. We were so proud of him.

Another significant fall of 1976 event, although one that was not at all joyful, occurred when the quarterback for the Sahuaro High School football team passed away in a horrible automobile accident. He had been a very popular and extraordinarily nice kid, and most of the school's assembly attended his beautiful and moving Catholic funeral. However, during one especially poignant moment, the deceased's mother attempted to pull her son out of his casket. I became extremely frightened and began to contemplate my own mortality.

I had previously engaged in some discussions with the new neighbors (Pastor Jeff and his wife, Janice) about their church's views on salvation. With the sudden death of a young, vibrant athlete, I found myself in a more profound struggle for the truth about salvation. I rushed home after the funeral, hurriedly changed clothes, and then scampered off to Jeff and Janice's residence.

Janice was at home and ushered me in. I explained what was occurring; my fears, questions, etc. After having brought her up to date, I then posed a simple question to Janice: How could I go to heaven?

Generally, in non-denominational practices when inquiries regarding salvation are posed, there are two questions they will ask: 1) "If you were to die today, would you go to Heaven?" and 2) "When God asks, 'Why should I let you into My Kingdom?', what would you say?" These interrogatories are a preamble to what they call the "Sinner's Prayer," and Janice posed both. My replies were: "Yes, I would go to Heaven." and "Because I have been a good person." Janice instructed me by telling me that good works (like being a good person) will not guarantee an individual's entry through the gates of Heaven. She continued by adding that only by accepting Jesus Christ as one's Savior was entry into God's Kingdom possible. Right then and there I informed Janice that I wanted to go to Heaven and that I accepted Jesus Christ as my Lord and Savior. We immediately kneeled and then, Janice led me in praying the "Sinner's Prayer":

> "Lord Jesus Christ, I acknowledge all of my sins and seek forgiveness from you for all of them, and I accept You as my personal Lord and Savior. Amen."

At that time, I was no longer babysitting at their church nursery, although I had remained as the babysitter for their children. Upon having uttered the "Sinner's Prayer" with Janice, I also became a member of Jeff's local church in Tucson, a membership that I would maintain for the next few decades.

Clearly, my brushes with the concept of death over a relatively short period of time – my Gammy's passing in October of 1974, my mother's near death car crash in the spring of 1975, and the death of a vibrant high school quarterback in the fall of 1976 – incited my profound awareness that the Good Lord was calling me to Him. My attendance at Jeff's church was far more intense than that of my previous, cursory attendance at the Church of Christ. By the fall of 1976, a heartfelt and utter commitment toward the working out of my salvation had resulted in my being a neophyte congregant at Jeff's Bible church. There were two weekday and two Sunday services. I went to all of them.

My dad had continued to work at Skagg's drug store, which had become Osco. When a new store opened near Sahuaro High, my father was transferred there as the assistant manager. This turned out to be quite convenient, since it made it easy for my brother and me to drop by. Actually, there even came a time when the manager would let me occasionally work there if I didn't have any chores at home, which meant that I didn't have to spend too much time alone in an empty house. It had fallen to me to do the household work – the cleaning, laundry, cooking, marketing, and so on – so I had little time for friends and activities. I did still do cross-country running which was a tremendous outlet for me.

My brother was good about taking me places, such as on shopping excursions for family needs. Occasionally we took those excursions in the elderly 1964 green Volkswagen Beetle that my dad had been left with after my mother had abandoned us. The vehicle was on its last legs; it had no passenger seat and needed to be push-started most of the time. We always joked that it was probably the reason why my brother had gotten so good at running, especially since on many a morning dad would walk up to my brother's door and knock on it gently while whispering, "son... son."

As Christmas of 1976 approached, my mom called. It was the first we had heard from her since the fall of 1975. She announced that she had returned to Tucson with Ed, the heroin addict and were staying with some of Ed's kinfolk. While Ed's sister-in-law was a strong Christian woman who had really tried to help my mother, things did not turn out well between them. Learning that my mom was again living in Tucson was a disturbing development. The reprieve from her insanity was over.

Part of the divorce decree entitled my mother to seeing my brother and me. We tried to refuse, but were unsuccessful. I was very apprehensive about that first time that I was to see her again after such a long time, and my brother graciously accompanied me. I was very afraid of Ed, a man over six feet tall and much larger in girth than one would expect from a career junkie. It didn't help that his chronic drug abuse had made him extremely unpredictable. I was stunned at my mother's appearance and also noticed the bad scars on her arms. Apparently, she had been in a car accident in New Mexico when the car had run into two horses, one of which had gone through the windshield, which had resulted in the scarring on her arms. In fact, bits of glass remained in her arms for several years. It seemed to be poetic justice that my mother had left in the car that my dad had bought her and soon thereafter totaled it.

I had somehow come to the belief that my mom's return to Tucson meant that she was sober. I immediately knew, however, on the day of that first visit that she had in fact continued to abuse alcohol. At that time, I had thought her behavior was due to alcohol and perhaps prescription medication abuse; but to my dismay, I later learned that Ed had led her into the netherworld of heroin.

Christmas of 1976 came and went without incident; gifts and pleasantries were exchanged, but my mother's return to Tucson meant that I had to see her more often. This was difficult for me. Whenever I saw her, Ed was present. He tried to be chummy, but I rejected his niceties; he made me sick. How could it have been otherwise with his having taken away my mom and my being so afraid of him? Moreover, it was incredibly hard on my father, a kind and hard-working man, to live with the reality that my mom had left him for Ed, a criminal and heroin addict. My mother had even taken Ed's last name.

My stomach began to trouble me, a condition directly related to the turmoil of having my mother around. I went to the hospital for tests, and when all was said and done, the doctor told me to stay away from my mother and that I'd be fine. I really think my deep-seated suspicion of her, coupled with a complete lack of trust in her was just too overwhelming for me.

Things worsened in the spring of 1977. My brother's high school graduation ceremony was scheduled for early June. On the very day of the commencement ceremony my mother called to tell my brother that she would not be in attendance; she was in jail. Apparently, she had passed some bad checks and been arrested. Although my brother was devastated, neither of us were surprised.

Later on, in the summer of 1977, after my mother was released from custody, my mother's mom (Gigi) began to support my mom and Ed. Gigi had worked at the same dress shop for a few decades. Living on a meager income and having to subsidize her daughter's existence in a seedy motel was a significant drain for her. At least we did not see my mother as much that summer. In fact, my dad had purchased a conversion van and we (my dad, my brother, and me) enjoyed a fantastic vacation! We journeyed west to California and the ocean, and then north, all the way up to the state of Washington. That was a glorious excursion.

By the end of summer vacation 1977, I was fifteen years old and entering my sophomore year at Sahuaro High School. My mom continued to sponge off of Gigi and maintained her co-dependent relationship with Ed. There were times when she was not with him. It was during one of those occasions that my mother had even talked my dad into permitting her return to our home, in the guest bedroom. Of course this did not turn out well; my mom had continued her drinking and had somehow gotten a hold of about two dozen Valium, which she decided to take all at once. The result was awful. My mother began to hallucinate and thrashed about wildly in bed. We had to hold her down during the fifteen mile trip to the Kino Hospital emergency room. By the time we arrived, not even the orderly, a one-time Mr. Arizona title holder, could control my mom. She was treated for an overdose and then spent several weeks in the psychiatric ward, where I visited her a few times. Once she got out of there, my mother stayed at Gigi's for a while and actually did fairly well, even though she worked several jobs and was not successful at any one of them. My great grandmother was living with Gigi too, so my mom was a great help with the house and meals. As far as we knew, Ed was not around during that time, which is probably why she fared better.

Such were events for the rest of 1977 and throughout 1978. But I did have my running and I did well in school. I adjusted to the difficulties in my life. I held on to my faith in God to get me through.

During my senior year at Sahuaro High, classes were for only half a day; so I would go to school in the morning, then do household chores and run in the afternoon. I must say that my mother outdid herself for my graduation from high school in June of 1980; she bought me a beautiful dress and she attended my graduation.

Rachel with her mom, dad and brother, 1970.

Chapter Five

Frank: Adulthood

I turned eighteen in a predictable place: Prison.

In the months leading up to January of 1974 and my eighteenth birthday, my parents' efforts to dissuade my continued abhorrent behavior never wavered. By the fall of 1973, I had eased up on many of my more extreme pursuits (armed robberies, attacks on Department of Water and Power outposts, etc.), out of a sense of responsibility to Sophie, who was imprisoned at that time. I was still heavily involved in drug trafficking and other felonious enterprises. My mom and dad had, unfortunately, become all too well acquainted with my penchant for such pastimes. They endeavored, as always, to orchestrate a strategy for straightening out their wayward son. Their new plan of action allowed for me to accompa-

Frank 18 standing in juvenille detention facility garden.

Frank 19, with his dad.

ny my father on business trips around the country. My father's presidency at Theta Cable was very much a hands-on operation; he had taken on the responsibility of expanding the company's services nationwide by personally attending board meetings and city council hearings in different states. The idea behind my accompanying him on some of those excursions was to keep me out of trouble. We traveled mostly along the eastern seaboard, but there were also trips to Idaho, Colorado, Hawaii, and elsewhere. For the most part I was quite well-behaved; in fact, during those times with my dad I felt, well, normal again.

Of course those trips did not last forever. Once I returned from those momentary reprieves from lunacy, which were rather like forays into the brief twinkling of childhood innocence, I seemed to lose no time in re-submerging myself in decadency. My lifestyle of reckless abandon produced nothing other than several arrests in abrupt succession. Some of the detentions were for relatively minor infractions, such as being collared for simple drug possession (small amounts of marijuana). However, I also accrued a few more serious charges.

Although I had finally realized that fraudulent entry into drug stores was overly dangerous, I decided to violate my maternal grandmother's abode and sense of security in an effort to obtain prescription drugs. I considered such a violation to be a less dangerous and injurious endeavor. After having broken into her premises, I made my way to a large chest of drawers which I knew held a cache of pill bottles that had accumulated over the decades. My dear grandmother, who had always lovingly nurtured me, had to endure the indignity of having her home broken into by her own grandson. I soon thereafter added injury to insult by stealing her car so I could go on a joyride to Oregon.

On another occasion, I stole some property from the roof-top of a business establishment. My accomplice informed on me and I was subsequently arrested and charged. The usual routine that accompanied captures for such offenses involved a trip to the nearby West Los Angeles police station, where I would be offered my freedom in exchange for a written confession. This "arrangement" with local law enforcement enabled my liberation from custody and a return home while police secured incontro-vertible evidence of guilt, quid pro quo.

In December of 1973, just prior to turning eighteen, I had several pending court appearances. Generally, a pending court date for a previous offense would be postponed when new charges were lodged for subsequent crimes. Such a situation permitted me to temporarily delay the inevitable while enabling the pros-ecution to stack up the charges, so that once I finally did appear in court, the mere number of felonious indictments would en-sure a period of incarceration. With my eighteenth birthday mere weeks away, judicial proceedings on accumulated violations that included grand theft auto, drug possession, attempted grand theft, receiving stolen property, and even a charge of incorrigibility that had been lodged by my parents, could no longer be suspended. So, I recruited a few buddies, stole my father's car, and embarked upon what was intended to be one last lost weekend in Las Vegas. We did not get very far. A carload of long-haired stoners tooling down the interstate in the middle of the night rapidly attracted the attention of the California Highway Patrol. In no time at all I was treated to the less than desirable accommodations of a small town jailhouse. The end result of that escapade was a return to the Los Angeles County Juvenile Hall and a plea arrangement, wherein I pled guilty to a couple of the charges in exchange for a six-month sentence in one of California's roughest prisons, the Youth Train-ing School (YTS) in Chino.

The advantageous environment in which I had been raised

had shielded me from blighted neighborhoods and the gang activity that so often characterizes many impoverished areas. Upon entering YTS I experienced significant culture shock and encountered a whole new breed of character. Up until that point in my life I had been the product of well-to-do society and immersed myself, during my teen years, in the drug scene. To suddenly experience youngsters who advocated racial supremacy and employed violence as the answer to all problems was quite disconcerting and very frightening. I felt overwhelmed by a sense of distressed disorder which arose from having not previously been concerned about my racial constitution to having to even contemplate interaction with non-white kids. For me, this was something akin to a capital offense. A crisis stage of disquietude erupted when I experienced my first riot.

As in most prisons, there was a communal athletic field at YTS. Several months into my sentence, there came a day when several hundred prisoners were milling around the centralized recreation area. Some of us were readying ourselves for a pick-up baseball game. All at once there was a collective sensation of tension and then an explosion of activity. I had pretty much stayed to myself during that stint behind bars. Having not really fit in with the other prisoners, I was unsure as to exactly how friendly I should become with already hardened criminals, so I had made only a few casual acquaintances. My status did not allow for my being privy to insider information, so I had no idea that a riot was in the works. In my brief tour as a state prisoner I had become aware of two general jailhouse rules: 1) mind your own business and 2) always stay alert. So, once everybody began to run everywhere, I kept watch, or so I thought. Unbeknownst to me, a Black guy crept up behind me. By the time I became aware of his presence it was too late to block a strike or to even duck; the next thing I knew, a baseball bat crashed into my lower lip. Somehow I was not seriously injured, although several lower teeth became permanently misaligned. As a young teenager I had learned some martial arts, the basics of which I had picked up on the UCLA campus. Those basic skills enabled me to rapidly disarm my attacker before he could get off another swing. Then I heard several voices in the background yell, "Hit him!" and "Do it!" I wasn't really sure, but I figured out that I was supposed to retaliate. At that time in my life my martial arts abilities served as a means of protection. To inflict willful injury on a human being was an alien concept. Nonetheless, I smashed that kid's knee with the bat. I guess my "bravery" in combat had impressed some of the higher-up White gang leaders, because from then on, I was pretty much accepted as one of them and therefore privy to insider information. Not only had my initiation into violence been secured, but my admission into White supremacist activity and prison life was also under way.

The six months at YTS passed with relatively little other uproar. My inclination for the countercultural resulted in my be-friending another prisoner who happened to have some extreme and unpopular beliefs. He was a satanist and I found myself dab-bling again, in the occult. Several years earlier, I had also had some brushes with the occult with UCLA campus radicals. Those brushes had included tarot, astrology and Eastern philosophies such as Taoism. During that period, I had pretty much shunned any religious involvement, having just escaped the church and wanting to be a "free agent". I did not become an ardent prac-titioner of the dark arts at that point, but several years later, and with fewer competing interests in prison, I became quite involved in a variety of demonic teachings.

Those brushes, in no uncertain terms, exacerbated my abandonment of God, in spite of opportunities for involvement in Christian precepts. Soon after I had been locked up in Decem-ber of 1973, the reverend from St. Alban's Episcopal Church, Father Norm, came to see me several times. Father Norm was an interesting man of Japanese descent; discussions with him were enjoyable. However, I steadfastly ignored calls to return to God. I did initially contemplate "making a deal" with God (the "I'll be good if you get me out" scenario), but ultimately I determined to pursue my own agendas... like my soon-to-be involvement with the satanists while in the YTS.

Participation in the occult seemed, at the time, to be a rather innocuous pastime; of course, was I ever wrong! I turned a blind eye to all godly pursuits and descended into what was societally frowned upon: my fondness for countercultural agendas. I did not recognize that I was involved with something of a far more insidious nature. Incredibly, I deceived myself into believing that I still believed in God, but had merely decided not to obey Him. What I am pointing to is my own fall into the sin of pride; I believed that I was my own master and could "do my own thing"... or even become like God! Moreover, seeing God as good, satan as bad and the occult as harmless placed me directly on the stage of sinful pride. I pondered the "benefits" of magic, believing that I could exert some control over the material world. I fooled myself into thinking it was perfectly fine, as I had always only performed what was considered "white magic" that is, so-called benign rituals intended to help others. I actually thought that anything involving magic and the occult was harmless and okay. There I was, an imprisoned youth who had lost his childhood love for God and who, rather than returning to that love, increased his interest in demonic pursuits.

Ironically, at the same time that I was immersed in being the "good prisoner," I also fell into violence, racism and other demented activities that seamlessly agreed with my much-later diagnosed PTSD. As the practice of witchcraft demanded secrecy, the ungodly alliance that I had developed with evil became more firmly entrenched within me, since there was no counterbalance to that pathway in my life then. As I look back in horror, I now realize how fully I had linked myself to the underworld. The occult is absolutely not some innocuous pastime. Had I only heeded Father Norm's pleas to lead a godlier life, then I would have opened avenues toward the love of God that would have led to my incarceration becoming an experience that would have incited purification. In other words, if I had sought out the love of

God while in juvenile hall, then those circumstances would have resulted in my having been healed of PTSD as I would have been working out my salvation.

My release from prison in June of 1974 found me in even more dire straits, steeped in the filth of the occult, trained in violence, and mired in racial supremacist delusions. Nevertheless, I still owned the choice of recognizing what my many poor decisions had done to me; I still had the ability to repent from evil by restoring the precepts instilled within me by church and by my loving parents. Sadly, I took the coward's way out by refusing to return to a godly lifestyle.

The daily activities of the boyhood that I had once enjoyed with my precious mother were no more. When I was a youngster my mom had involved herself in the PTA (Parent and Teachers Association) at Brentwood Elementary School, and had been the den mother of my Cub troop (she oversaw our gatherings and

Frank 19, with his mom (Jan. 1975).

planned our activities). My mom also took me to Little League practice several times a week and faithfully stayed to cheer me on. Our home had been the place where all of the neighborhood kids played. If no playmates were around, my dear mother would do her very best to play catch or shoot baskets with me. The wonderful family vacations to resorts or to fish for rainbow trout, or to various ski lodges were also no more. Instead of working to enjoy more of those joyous, loving times, I continued what had become a cruel, merciless habit; I would steal one of the family cars and take off for several days.

My new way of vacationing would begin by either creating an altercation out of nothing with my mom, or by blowing a minuscule dispute completely out of proportion. Then I would declare that it was impossible to live in such unfair conditions and claim to have been a victim of the very argument I had fabricated. Finally, I would assert a specious right to escape such a "hostile" environment and then, steal a family car. I would frequently go to Hollywood and hang out with derelicts, consort with drug addicts, and mingle with homosexuals for several days. Another common escape was to take a trip up the coast. I would travel north, up the Pacific Coast Highway to Malibu, where I picked up a few hitchhikers, and then continued up the coast to Big Sur or San Francisco. I recall one such incident where I instigated the usual uproar and located where my mother had hidden her car keys. When I got to Big Sur, I steered the car off to the side of the road and came to a halt, in what I thought was a designated pullout by the roadside. As I was lighting up my hash pipe, I heard a sharp tap on the window. Without thinking, I rolled down the window and saw a uniformed man with a badge on his shirt pocket standing next to my car. The officer was waving his clipboard around in a fervent attempt to escape the cloud that had emerged from my window. He began to speak and although I could see his lips moving and faintly hear some sound, I in no way comprehended what he was saying. Then, suddenly, I figured out from his gestures that rather than having parked in a pullout, what I had actually accomplished was to have parked across the entrance to a campground. A long line of cars not so patiently awaited my departure so that they could enter the camp. As I turned my gaze from the line of cars to the officer, whom I had by then identified as a forest ranger, I heard him say "Move along now and have a nice day."

I should have recognized the obvious detriments to those nefarious excursions as they included: the crime of grand theft auto, an extremely serious atrocity against my own parents; associating with dangerous deviants and operating a motor vehicle while severely intoxicated. Sadly, however, I did not. What I have long since recognized is that the single greatest tragedy of my actions constituted the emotional devastation of my parents. My selfish desire for excitement required them to endure dismay while their only child stole one of their cars. I inflicted incredible distress on them with my prolonged absences. My heart breaks as I think of my parents being unable to sleep at night, desperately phoning local police stations and hospital emergency centers in search of their son. I now see what I had done as an example of how utterly depraved a person can become by leading an ungodly life.

My freedom from incarceration in 1974 was not long lasting. While I was in prison, Sophie had been released and gotten a new boyfriend. She was the only girlfriend I ever had, and the only girl with whom I had sex. Many mental health professionals have suggested a direct link between her rejection of me and what I did in the ensuing months, especially when considering my having been sexually assaulted and the fact of my PTSD.

Within two months of my release I was back in jail on a very serious charge. I was riding my motorcycle one day in July of 1974 when I noticed a young girl (she was only ten years old) staring at me with a look of revulsion. Her look had angered me. At the time I had not yet developed any desires for sexual relations with children; however, rather than to accept that kid's legitimate reaction to a scruffy-looking criminal, I instead drove up to her and kissed her before speeding away. Given the fact that I had offended a much weaker victim, I was back in custody within days.

Finding myself yet again in the Los Angeles County Jail, my indoctrination into prison gang involvement continued. I was placed in what is called "high power," or maximum security. That section happened to be where several Aryan Brotherhood members (the AB was the main White prison gang) were housed. My naiveté and youthfulness inclined them to watch over me while my efforts to be one of "the fellas" (a euphemism for AB members) impressed them. In a relatively short time, I became their protégé and learned my lessons well.

I also began to suffer more severe psychiatric symptoms while in the Los Angeles County Jail. These manifested as both auditory and visual hallucinations, along with acute bouts of disorientation. The mental health care in the Los Angeles County Jail was atrocious and the medications I had been placed on were ineffective; it was a frightening experience.

After having spent the remainder of 1974 in the Los Angeles County Jail's high power housing unit, hallucinating and learning how to be a veteran convict, I felt that confinement for psychiatric treatment in a mental hospital would be in my best interests. I instructed my attorney to pursue the possibility and eventually was able to plead guilty to lewd conduct (the unlawful kissing) and was sent to California's maximum security mental hospital in Atascadero. I intended to undergo treatment for PTSD,[4] however that initial good intention did not last long.

Soon after my arrival at Atascadero State Hospital, I attempted to fulfill my intent to engage in treatment by enrolling

---

4   Officially, post-traumatic stress disorder (PTSD) was not listed in the American Psychiatric Association's Diagnostic and Statistical Manual until the 1980s. However, the symptoms suffered by Frank in the 1970s (altered cognition, sexualization, criminality, etc.) were the product of traumatic experiences that were later recognized as having resulted from PTSD.

for a university course in psychology from the University of California at Berkeley on which I did fairly well. Then, I was brutally raped and nothing seemed to matter anymore. I dropped out of university, once again eschewing responsibility for my actions, and immersed myself further in the prison lifestyle. While I did manage to subsequently take and pass a General Equivalency test (GED, an alternative to a high school diploma), it was not long before I sought out and ingratiated myself with Aryan Brotherhood members. What strikes me now, although admittedly my participation in psychotherapy was lackadaisical at best, is that psychiatric treatment simply is not at all an effective cure for the soul; nor is it a replacement for involvement in God's spiritual hospital (the Church).

The Aryan Brotherhood had an extensive drug operation at Atascadero. Initially I was responsible for transporting drugs. As time went on, my responsibilities in the drug ring increased; I collected the money made from dealers and received the delivery of drugs directly from the "horses" (state employees who smuggled contraband to us). I even was, on occasion, permitted to directly negotiate the costs for various amounts of product with "horses".

That period of incarceration (from 1974-1978, between the ages of eighteen to twenty-two) in no way altered my decline into evil. Nor did I receive treatment for PTSD. The vast majority of that prison sentence was spent in learning to become a far more sophisticated criminal. In fact, I even began to train less experienced prisoners in the art of manipulating staff and getting away with misconduct. Moreover, I continued the many illegal activities that I had engaged in while not in prison. Despite my incarceration, I continued to burglarize medicine cabinets in the very mental hospital to which I had been submitted for treatment.

In 1977, about three years into my stay at Atascadero, I obtained what was known as an "A" recommendation. An "A" recommendation indicates that a patient has undergone treatment with success and the court is asked to release him, whereas a

"B" recommendation indicates that the patient is unamenable to treatment, and the court is asked to send the patient to prison. I was moved to the pre-release ward. The recommendation made its way through the judicial process and several months later, the judge concurred with the state hospital. My release papers were signed, and I was a mere few weeks away from freedom. Then I did something really stupid. I had been working in the pre-release unit's kitchen and had a vociferous argument with a staff member one day. She was a psychiatric technician trainee in her early twenties, who happened to be really good looking. During the confrontation I uttered some extremely disparaging remarks and, since she was sleeping with a program director at the hospital, she solicited that supervisor's intervention. The judge was contacted and my release was rescinded. I was transferred to a regular ward for further treatment.

That obviously crushing development was a cause for my growing disenchantment with the system. Although I had routinely manipulated and abused establishment's constructs, I still expected that the judicial and penal processes would function fairly when applied to me. Therefore, the verbal abuse I had hurled at the program director's mistress had resulted in the cancellation of my release, which only furthered my anger at the system. Moreover, the same staff members who were smuggling in drugs began to enter highly detrimental progress assessments in my chart, some of which pertained to suspected drug use and drug sales. Additionally, at approximately that time, the California legislature altered many of the sentencing laws. For instance, lewd conduct had been a one-to-life sentence that then became a term of three, four, or five years under the new guidelines. I had been originally given one-to-life, a term that had been suspended so that I could be sent to the Atascadero State Hospital for treatment. Once California adjusted their sentence structures, I was re-sentenced to the upper term of five years. However, since I was in the mental hospital, there was a significant caveat; unlike prison (in prison once a sentence has been served, the inmate must be released), I could be returned to court every year, such that my stay at Atascadero could be extended for a year upon the hospital's request. Several staff informants let me know that the administration at Atascadero intended to make full use of those annual extensions, and that I should not expect release for a long time. I knew that if I were in the prison system that I would be very close to a mandatory release, so I immediately set in motion plans to secure a "B" recommendation from Atascadero in order to be returned to court and sent to prison. I was successful in obtaining a "B" recommendation in the summer of 1978.

After having been imprisoned for four years, I reappeared in a Santa Monica courtroom. The judge carefully scrutinized all reports from the hospital and expressed great concern over all of the references to my involvement in drugs. Consequently, rather than impose the five-year term and send me to prison, he instead ordered me into a residential drug program in Pasadena. The Gateway Center was near the Pasadena Rose Bowl and was a well-known treatment facility. The program there required a minimum nine-month residency, during which there were a handful of daily meetings. When not attending one of those sessions, residents were assigned chores, such as sweeping the parking lot for an hour or two. At that juncture in my life I had no desire whatsoever to cease my involvement in substance abuse, so it seemed silly to spend nine months of hell in Gateway when I could go to prison and be out free and clear in two or three months. I lasted ten days there.

A court-ordered resident at Gateway had no choice but to remain there; to leave would result in an arrest warrant being issued and a subsequent return to custody. So I planned my leave-taking for a Friday evening, once courts had closed for the weekend. At that point, all Gateway could do was to inform the court of my desertion so the judge could then issue the warrant. I had until Monday before the law would be after me. Since my desertion from the drug program residency occurred after four years of incarceration, I immediately set out to obtain narcotics.

Once I had sufficiently "medicated" myself, I headed off to my parents' house. Obviously, my parents were very surprised to see me and very disappointed that the drug rehabilitation had not been successful. The following day, a Saturday, I took a taxi some sixty miles to a girl's house. We had attended You & Me High School together and had stayed in touch over the years since we were both heavily into drugs. She was able to arrange my purchase of myriad substances. Initially I had no intention of returning to Gateway, but my parents pressed for my re-entry. I finally acceded to my dad contacting the facility to inquire about my return; they agreed to accept me back. My dad drove me back to the Pasadena facility on Monday and dropped me off in front of the grounds. Prior to announcing my re-entry, I detoured to the bushes and deposited my stash therein. However, from that point on my scheme went terribly wrong.

When I was in the Los Angeles County Jail awaiting court hearings after my return from Atascadero, I had purchased a few ten-dollar packets of marijuana, some of which I had hidden in a toothpaste tube. I had forgotten all about it until the container found its way into the toiletry kit that was at the time being thoroughly inspected by Gateway staff. The remnant half a joint or so was discovered, and I was ejected from residency at the program. Since my return had occurred in the late afternoon, an informatory call to authorities would not be placed until the following morning. So, after having retrieved my stash from its resting place, I headed off for a new escapade. At the first gas station that I came across I locked myself in the bathroom and began to sample my abundant treasure. I was still in Pasadena and began to navigate the journey to Brentwood, a destination of approximately twenty to twenty-five miles. After having covered several miles on foot, during which I occasionally ducked into bushes to consume more substances, I took a bus to West Hollywood and then ambled onward toward Beverly Hills.

I had veered onto a side street off of Sunset Boulevard, when I at last determined to call my parents for a ride home.

Consequently, I went to the nearest house and began knocking on the front door. I heard two girls hysterically screaming, "Who is it? What do you want?" I was so high that I not only failed to connect their alarmed cries with my pounding on their door, but I was also unable to articulate my desire to use their telephone. It was not long before the police showed up. After they searched me, a process that turned up most of my supply, I was on my way back to jail for burglary and drugs.

As was often the case, during my experiences with the revolving door justice system, I secured my release from custody within a day or so. However, in addition to my departure from the Gateway Center, I would also have to answer to several felony charges. I again appeared before the judge in Santa Monica, and the sole consequence for everything – leaving the court-ordered drug residency program, burglary, and possession of drugs for sale – was a return to another drug rehabilitation clinic, also in Pasadena. I did not plan on spending a minute more than was necessary in my new surroundings. As soon as I had completed orientation and been dispatched to my room, I went to the window and let myself out. I spent about twenty minutes in rehab.

That took place in August of 1978, and I immediately left the jurisdiction to visit kin in Austin, Texas. That venture turned out to be quite profitable, at least in my eyes at the time, since I ended up with connections to a Mexican marijuana cartel, as well as to a large methamphetamine lab. Eventually, the law caught up with me in November of 1978, and I appeared yet again before the Santa Monica court judge. During his inquiry I reiterated my desire to be sent to prison, since nine months of unwanted drug treatment could not compare to two or three months in prison. Reluctantly, as he already had lined up a third residential substance abuse program, in January of 1979 the judge sentenced me to prison, where I completed the five-year term for lewd conduct.

I was not long for the free world, because I violated parole in May by having been arrested for assault with a deadly weapon. Having been returned to prison, I met a man from my neighborhood. Marshall was well known to law enforcement so, of course, we became acquainted.

I was released from custody in November of 1979. Over the next few months my involvement with more organized forms of criminal activity increased dramatically. From November of 1979 to June of 1980 I was out of prison and providing favors for those still inside. These included several journeys to northern California, which involved the transportation of methamphetamine and meetings with manufacturers of speed like outlaw biker gangs. I also pursued my own agendas during those northern forays by seeking out several growers of sinsemillia (an extremely high grade strain of marijuana) in Humboldt County. I would purchase several pounds of product, and break it up into quarter ounce and ounce packets for sale. Of course much of it was smoked by me.

Contacts from prison introduced me to several different people who had interacted with Mexican drug cartels who were traffickers of cocaine, large quantities of marijuana, and black tar heroin. One contact was responsible for the transportation of those commodities from south of the border to Los Angeles, while my involvement included bartering weapons for drugs. My colleague's ties with Mexican rebel factions who were desperate for arms encouraged me in my trade; I either swapped cheap street drugs for guns or stole firearms out of homes. My proficiency at exchanging weapons for pure narcotics at bargain basement prices not only permitted the procurement of chemicals, but also enthralled me; I was very proud of having provided weaponry to Mexican revolutionaries.

Speaking of prison contacts, one of my closest associates, the aforementioned Marshall, and I were released at about the same time. Shortly thereafter, we organized a theft ring operation. We utilized thieves who stole jewelry for which we then paid twenty-five cents on the dollar, at most. Then, we would melt down the gold and create new rings, pendants, etc. into which we could reset stones. Those refurbished items were then sold at retail prices at a friend's galleria on Hollywood Boulevard. It was quite a nice operation until some of Marshall's other endeavors resulted in several law enforcement agencies implementing surveillance on us. So, I became involved in other interests. One such undertaking developed upon my return to the Lone Star State of Texas where I reacquainted myself with the Mexican drug cartel. The result was that I began transporting marijuana from Texas to Los Angeles in addition to arranging sales of large shipments of marijuana. For my services, I received some pay and all the weed I desired.

In looking back upon that period of my life, I can only conclude that I had really self-destructed and was awash in discontented rebellion. I endeavored to inflict upon others, via a myriad of drugs and crime, the same state of discontent and self-destructive tendencies. I excused the evil I was perpetrating and inflicting upon others. I eschewed the standards my parents had taught me; I disregarded the lessons I had learned in church and school; I justified the manufacture, transportation and sale of drugs, and, in fact, considered those options to be acceptable; finally, I induced others to engage in the same poisonous pastimes. By the spring of 1980, I had recruited several fourteen to fifteen year-old kids to peddle my wares. They were my inroad to the huge, untapped customer pool in local junior high and high schools. It was exactly those convoluted attempts to legitimize my life of sin that soon led to one of the most tragic events in my life.

I have previously referred to my having been sexually molested in 1970 at the age of fourteen; gang raped in juvenile hall; orally sodomized in Aspen; sexually assaulted at Atascadero, as well as my unsuccessful efforts over those years to overcome PTSD. In general terms, I had failed to address the initial shame, despite having had recourse to immediate opportunities for treatment with psychotherapists, several months at a private residential psychiatric institution, as well as subsequent time in the state mental hospital. I made many attempts to transform my guilt and disgrace into a vehicle wherein I was less compelled to feel humiliation. Such endeavors included normalizing variant strains of misconduct (drug abuse, crime, countercultural involvements, etc.) in my mind. Today, I understand that those endeavors were actually the adaptation of very irregular, even demonic, patterns of thought; I conceptualized sinful behaviors as perfectly legitimate courses of conduct. My efforts to transcend the emotional shock of having been sexually assaulted as a child had developed into seeking to mutate that terrible experience into something that was somehow acceptable.

For instance, after having been molested by an adult male, I then began to engage in homosexual activity on what I perceived to be a casual basis. This particular activity fit in well with my having eschewed conventional societal norms, as homosexual activity was very much stigmatized at that time. Such forbidden fruit both attracted me and set me firmly on the path toward justifying what had happened to me. It has since become so very obvious to me that my failure to have treated having been a child molestation victim simply led to more and more sin. Merely mentioning that I had been repeatedly molested as a boy fails to wholly present the entire file of my severe trauma. I also had to testify in court against my 1970 attacker and endure continuous sexual harassment from 1973 until the 1980s. Doctors have confirmed that those experiences significantly worsened my PTSD.

Today, looking back, I can see how my having coupled with evil promptings (homosexual conduct, drug use, pride, anger, despair, and other insidious passions) inflicted horribly irregular patterns of thought. A conglomeration of competing evil concepts took up residence in my mind and in my heart. For instance, I suffered from intense guilt over having been sexually assaulted several times, a guilt that erupted not only as a consequence of having been attacked, but which also resulted from feeling at least partially responsible for those abuses. It was I who had decided to place myself in a man's home which culminated in the initial 1970 molestation; I had landed myself in juvenile hall wherein I suffered brutal abuse; I had willingly entered a stranger's residence that led to the Aspen assault; and I had wound up in detention at Atascadero, which lead to yet another assault. Feeling partially responsible for the atrocities visited upon me led me to try to accept those horrible events as somehow normal. I sought to adopt something as abominable as sexual relations between males as not merely permissible but further, as a positive endeavor. That is to say, I desperately attempted to explain away what had happened to me by concocting a convoluted scenario wherein what I had suffered was "okay". My voluntary engagement in homosexuality was a means of sanitizing the forced sexual assaults. When that failed, I sought to deal with the attendant humiliation and anger at having been sexually violated by revisiting the same atrocity upon an innocent child. Somehow, having lost my own innocence had fueled an ungodly desire to inflict the same horrendous fate upon another human being. The dual desires to both avoid guilt and to impose guilt resided within me and erupted in an extraordinary commission of violence.

As I had mentioned, in the spring of 1980 I had initiated a drug operation in Los Angeles with a sales force that incorporated the services of teenagers. Always on the lookout for upscale customers, I also knew a person in the Topanga Canyon area who was smuggling pounds of cocaine from South America. That venture often took me to Hollywood nightclubs frequented by celebrities. One evening I was introduced to a man who was a movie producer from Pacific Palisades. We made arrangements to meet at a neutral site a few days later to discuss a mutually profitable venture. We did meet at Rustic Canyon Park, however, something about his arrogant and presumptuous nature made me realize that business dealings with him would be unwise. I broke off negotiations with him and, traveling by motorcycle, I doubled back along a secluded fragment of Rustic Canyon. There, I espied a young boy who was walking alone. I drove up to that child and engaged him in some trivial banter before forcing him onto my motorcycle. I drove several miles to Will Rogers State

Park, where I got him off my bike and escorted him down a barely discernable path. Once assured that we had not been observed I, God please forgive me, forced that little boy to engage in oral copulation. I was soon afterwards arrested for that abominable exploit and incarcerated in the Los Angeles County Jail.

One of the problems with the justice system of the US involves the predictable result of an accused felon immediately pursuing his release from custody. Justice would be better served were the felon enabled to cultivate shame and sorrow over having injured a fellow human being. Having perpetrated an atrocity against a child while fully realizing the horrendous results this would impose on him, I nevertheless resolved to avoid responsibility for my evil and destructive deed. I know now that even at that advanced stage of perversity, I could have pursued a return to the state hospital at Atascadero as a means by which to resolve both the shame of having myself been repeatedly molested, as well as the guilt caused by having abused a child. Instead, I sought merely to minimize my culpability and punishment. I even attempted to justify the monstrosity I had committed in much the same way as I had tried to explain away the sexual violence that I had suffered. In my mind, the insane mantra of "sex, regardless of age or circumstance, is desirable" was continuously repeated. Satan truly had buried his clutches deep within my heart.

Eventually, I accepted a plea arrangement. I would serve only four years in prison on a charge that was not sexual in nature. This was unfortunate in that, rather than being shunned by the prison population as a child predator, I maintained active participation with hardened criminals. Furthermore, I persisted in my refusal to face what I had become.

While in the Los Angeles County Jail I ran across a prisoner who, although not aware of the circumstances surrounding my detention, was quite willing to further my journey down the dark path. Ned and I had a few acquaintances in common who were involved in the occult, so we struck up an alliance in the cold confines of the jail. Ned introduced me, by mail, to Edwin, a supposed occult master in Oklahoma. My liaison with Edwin would hound me for many years. Not long afterward, I departed for the California prison system and a four-year period of incarceration from June of 1980 until May of 1984. I still recall sitting in a cell in the reception center at Chino (a small town east of Los Angeles) and looking across the fields at the YTS, where a few years earlier I had resided... and I remembered that when I was at YTS, I had gazed over at Chino's reception center hoping that I would never end up there.

Having re-entered the California prison system, I immediately began to reinforce my carefully contrived status as prison tough guy, mostly via trafficking in drugs and other criminal activities. It is common in prison to find that those who

Frank and his crew at California prison Bike Show.

strive the hardest to construct a reputation frequently have something to hide, which was most certainly the case with me. I had smuggled several hundred dollars from the Los Angeles County Jail to the reception center at Chino, an action that enabled me to exert much control over the drug and commissary trade. Chino had some prisoners who did their entire sentence there known as the permanent work crew (PWC), but those inmates rarely did business with the hundreds of detainees who passed through Chino weekly. Nonetheless, I was able to purchase marijuana, heroin, tobacco, and other items from the PWC that I then sold at sky-high prices. I then set out to even more firmly establish my gangster status by arranging a race riot. I planted whispers in the ears of fellow White prisoners over how disrespectful the Blacks had become and posed a solution: a riot. Having successfully instilled disquietude amongst the ranks, I was then able to recruit enough compatriots to implement my scheme with relative ease. Word was passed that as we exited the chow hall we were to kick off a riot. The attack concluded when we put the Black inmates to flight. The White prisoners saw me as a hero; however, the administration "punished" me by attempting to house me in the same cell as a Black man. My refusal to accept what I proclaimed as insufferable accommodations landed me in the hole; so I was again lauded by other prisoners.

The first year of that four-year sentence was spent at an easy going facility in central California, just down the road from Atascadero State Hospital. I quickly set up shop as one of the main players in the marijuana trade. Doug, my supplier, was a heroin addict whose wife smuggled in adequate quantities for him to maintain his habit. (The cost for heroin was covered by Doug's trafficking in marijuana.) He knew an inmate who was responsible for cleaning the visitation area after visitors left; so Doug's wife would leave several packets of pot and a few balloons filled with heroin which were snuck in every Saturday. Doug would return from having seen his wife before supper, but for the entire evening afterward, he was not to be bothered.

In prison yard.

Saturday nights always found him nearly overdosed from heroin. Later, as the night wore on and cell doors were locked until morning, he would make up packets for distribution. Once the doors had been unlocked for breakfast on Sunday morning, I would pass by Doug's cell so he could hand me my order for which I paid every week. He always stood perched in his doorway, usually propped up by the door jamb after a night of indulgence, clad in his bathrobe while passing out his wares.

Selling drugs in a prison provided quite a platform for status, but it was also risky. I was not only in danger of being apprehended by staff, but I also had to provide occasional enforcement. Sometimes I would make sales on credit, such as when someone was expecting money from family. In order to secure a chunk of their money, I would advance him some pot so that once his funds arrived, I was entitled to a portion of them. Frequently, a customer's money would not come when expected, so he had to be informed that the delay came at a price; if I was owed ten dollars, then a late payment would require fifteen dollars to satisfy the debt. Occasionally someone would gripe about the interest rate or would even refuse to pay it. If the latter was the case, I would enter his cell, slap him a few times, look around for something to take (maybe a watch or radio), and then leave with both that item and his promise to pay. Once, after an inmate had talked me into forwarding him a fairly large quantity of marijuana which he then hid, he ran to the sergeant's office to make a false claim that his safety was in danger. His idea had been for him to be put on lock down so that he could ostensibly keep my product without paying. Whenever I discovered that that prisoner had gotten himself intentionally locked up, after having hid a portion of my marijuana without having paid for it, I took a ten-pound weight from the gym and returned to my cell to make a "flash bomb" (a device that explodes in a bright ball of flame but with little danger, since virtually no air is displaced). The idea was to create a hugely visible display, rather than to inflict injury. I made my way to the offender's cell, where I busted out the 9" x 18" window in the door with the ten-pound weight, lit the incendiary device, and tossed it through the broken window. While I never did receive payment for the marijuana, the commotion ensured no future attempts to defraud me, and my reputation soared. I was enthralled with my reputation at the time, but it is clear that the passion of pride governed my life.

Over time, prisoners who had checkered pasts (informants, known child molesters, etc.) were sent to the same sprawling central California facility where I was incarcerated. I felt that staying there would have been detrimental to my status. My sentiments soon reached the administration's ears and I was then transferred upstate, to the violent Soledad Prison. My time at Soledad did not pass smoothly for two reasons. First I did not get along with the Nazis (another White prison gang) and my cellmate was a Nazi. There had been a killing and although the entire prison was locked down, a partner of my cellmate was a janitor and he was allowed out to clean. I involved myself in a drug deal with this same worker and it went very wrong. The second reason for my rough time at Soledad was due to having received a disciplinary report for tattooing while I had been in the California Men's Colony in central California. I appealed the finding successfully, but by the time that occurred I had already served several weeks of confined-to-quarters punishment. On appeal, I was given a new disciplinary hearing. As I was again found guilty, the hearing officer sentenced me to another few weeks of cell confinement, without credit for the confined-to-quarters punishment I had previously served. I ended up in the hole for having attempted to assault the lieutenant, who was the disciplinary officer. The lieutenant instigated plans to have me attacked by officers; so the administration at Soledad then transferred me to the Management Control Unit (MCU) at another especially violent prison in northern California known as the Duel Vocational Institute (DVI, or Tracy, since it was located in Tracy, California).

Once in MCU I again proceeded to polish my stature by inciting another riot. At the small recreation area into which we were permitted several times a week, I passed around word that the Blacks were planning an attack on us. The next time we went outside, it was with the intent of launching an assault. Of course I was in the middle of the fray as canisters of tear gas were detonated by guards and smoke filled the area. Then several warning shots rang out and I saw that moment as the optimal opportunity for eternally cementing my place in prison lore. Thus, despite repeated instructions by the tower officer to cease and desist, I continued stabbing a Black inmate. With a burst from the tower guard's shotgun, I was shot off of him. I do not know if the blast was a bean bag, buckshot, or something else, but I was knocked backwards and landed several feet away.

That incident led to my being transferred to San Quentin Prison. As I think back on my attitude then, I can readily see how my heart had been captured by the passion of vainglory. To attack other prisoners had become honorable to me. I even believed that the resultant discipline was a feather in my cap! I had been sent to one of the worst prisons in the US, proud at having finally made it to the big time! By the grace of God, my stay at San Quentin was short-lived, due in part, to another confrontation with the Nazis. I was then locked down in the Adjustment Center before being transferred to Vacaville, a prison north of San Francisco that was relatively non-violent.

During that four-year stretch in prison I increased my involvement in the occult. I had maintained relations with the aforementioned Edwin, a supposed ranking official in an infamous occult clan, an offshoot of Aleister Crowley's Ordo Templar Orientis. Edwin was able to find me rare books; had sent me LSD a few times and provided a sympathetic ear. I not only increased my studies in satanism, but I also became somewhat receptive to his homosexual advances. I had voyaged quite far down the path of darkness and had few, if any, thoughts about God.

I was at Vacaville from 1983 until my release from prison in 1984. Although my involvement with Edwin had progressed on a personal basis, interestingly, I had still not seen a photograph of him. The facts that he had described himself as tall, part Filipino and part Arabian; that money sent to him for books was lost; that there were some puzzling gaps in his knowledge that an occultist of his ilk should have known; and that he overemphasized sexual relations between us had provoked my suspicion. Throughout that time, I continued to be involved in drug trafficking. In prison I had always preferred to concentrate on the marijuana trade, but the heavy outlaw biker population at Vacaville preferred methamphetamine. I was able to peddle enough of it to keep myself high on a regular basis, but not without some bumps in the road.

The days leading up to the 1983 Fourth of July celebration began with a five-gallon batch of homemade wine, three grams of speed, and half an ounce of marijuana. Over the next couple of days, I stayed awake on methamphetamine. On the Fourth of July when the homemade wine was ready, I began to drink it, injected more speed, and smoked marijuana until an officer knocked on the cell door. I was to report for kitchen duty, but there was no way I could do so without getting caught for being intoxicated. I told the guard that I had been throwing up and was too sick to work. In about ten to fifteen minutes he returned; the kitchen officer had insisted that I show up. Going to the door, I told the guard to leave while pushing him, and then the door hit him in the lip. Within seconds, dozens of guards showed up. They beat me and I was dragged to the hole. That was the first time in about nine years of prison that I had my sentence extended.

Unfortunately, my downward decline continued at Vacaville via increased occult studies and further involvement in drugs. If only during that time of incarceration I had been able to see prison as a means by which God had permitted increased adversity in order to guide me back to Him. Obviously, my abandonment of God foreclosed that potentiality at that juncture. I persisted in a godless agenda, a fateful life course that would necessitate more, future calamities.

I was released from prison in May of 1984 and initially had

Frank 28, after his release from prison.

fleeting intentions toward responsibility. In order to help me adjust to outside life, my parents had invited Edwin for a brief stay at the family home in Brentwood. Just prior to my release I had finally received a picture from him and learned that he was Black (not Filipino and Arabian, just African-American). My parents did not know that he was an occultist and a homosexual. My concerns over his merely desiring a homosexual relationship and not actually being an occult master increased, but I decided to ride things out for a while. Once Edwin left, I started to work with my father in his church organ repair business and also registered for accounting courses at Santa Monica College. I must note that I gave no thought whatsoever to God in any of the endeavors I undertook at that time; I had continued my involvement in the occult and was toying with homosexuality. Without God, nothing (not work, studies or any other endeavor) can yield any salvific results; they all become subject to burning as do wood, hay, and stubble.

In short order, I became bored with working for my dad and, as Santa Monica College had made an error on my registration papers, attendance at classes had been postponed for the semester. Rather than initiate other positive objectives, I decided to travel and visit Edwin in Oklahoma. I embarked on that excursion for the purpose of definitively determining whether relations between us would continue and, if so, in what capacity. It did not take long to find out that he was a fraud. Once I was able to snoop around his residence, it became clear that the checks I had sent to him so he could purchase books for me while I was in prison had in fact been cashed by him (not lost, as he had claimed). Also, there was no doubt that he was a novice occult practitioner who had only homosexual designs in mind. I did not create a scene, but simply returned to Los Angeles as if everything was okay. At least that misadventure had created a sense of disenchantment with occult practice. However, that is not to say that I was discouraged from criminal enterprises; nor did I pursue a return to a godly lifestyle since I had not yet hit rock bottom.

Upon my return to Los Angeles, I decided to travel to northern California and arrange the purchase of some marijuana. Normally buyers procure some early bud (marijuana prior to having reached maturity) as a means by which to assess crop potency, but that year's crop had been planted late. Furthermore, a late frost had occurred, which meant that no early bud was available. At the time, I believed that my fleeting good intentions had been somewhat maintained since I considered the sale of marijuana to upper crust clientele to be harmless. In light of the weather's effect on the crop, I yet again descended into the outlaw biker and methamphetamine netherworlds. The money intended to purchase early bud and to lodge a down payment on that year's late summer crop was, instead, spent on speed. I returned to Los Angeles with several ounces of product. Since my time in Oklahoma had revealed both their poor quality of speed and the high demand, my initial excursion there turned out to be the seeds of a methamphetamine drug ring operation.

Also in my company, as I headed back to Brentwood, was a ragtag band of transients whom I had met in Big Sur. I was traveling in my black 280-Z Datsun. As it was only a two-seater, one of the nomads rode with me, while the other two were in a blue Honda that they had stolen from a woman in Big Sur. Moreover, since they had just ripped off some marijuana from some surfers in Santa Cruz, the trip down the coast was a pleasant one. Although their having left a trail of thefts behind them posed some danger, my endless yarns about prison yard exploits had luckily served their intended purpose of dissuading them from ripping me off.

I only spent one night at my parents' before continuing on toward Oklahoma and my plans to set up a methamphetamine practice. (What my poor parents must have thought as they rose the next morning and were met with the sight of their son and several other long-haired freaks camping out in their backyard, only God knows.) Afterwards, we stayed for a couple of days in Tucson, the apparent home of my friendly transients. Then, one of them (Jack McDonald) accompanied me east on Interstate Ten. Upon my arrival in Oklahoma, I parceled out packets of speed to my dealers and congratulated myself on having fashioned a successful multi-state drug operation. How deviant my ambitions and life had become.

While my relations with the drug culture in small town Oklahoma had flourished, my involvement with Edwin took a bad turn, one that would inflict significant harm in coming years. When Edwin heard that I had returned to the Midwest and was staying with a well-known drug dealer, he came over and asked me to go for a ride with him, a venture that took us to a deserted road along an Air Force base. Admittedly, I had lessened the frequency of contact with Edwin, knowing that a homosexual relationship with him, or any other male, was not to be. Still, I felt terribly guilty over having led him on. When Edwin expressed his concern that I no longer desired relations with him, I confirmed his fear as gently as possible. Edwin then blurted out, "God damn it! I could have had a great relationship with an Air Force sergeant, but I decided to be with you. Now you have let me down and you have ruined my life. You'll be sorry Frank." As we headed back to where I was staying, I attempted to explain how sorry I was about just not being ready for any kind of relationship and re-emphasized how bad I felt about having let him down. In reality, the multiple times that I had been sexually assaulted and the fact that I had visited that same atrocity on a boy made sexual relations, or any intimate involvements, unappealing to me.

Much of the foundations of my methamphetamine business had been put in place, but before returning to Los Angeles I loaned my car to one of my dealers so he could pick up a load of marijuana in Texas. The two of us had determined to include part-time marijuana sales, along with dealing speed. While awaiting his return, I contacted Edwin. I still felt awful about how devastated he had been; so under the guise of wanting to borrow a little marijuana, I made arrangements to see him. I thought perhaps an opportunity to ease his distress would arise. Unfortunately, things went bad as soon as he opened the door, when he again angrily expressed his dismay. I became pretty frustrated, having seen myself as experiencing significant regret over his despair. I had tried to be sensitive to his feelings, but only received venomous attacks in return. I reacted by throwing in his face my knowledge that he had ripped off my family for the book money. Edwin disappeared into his room momentarily and when he emerged several minutes later, he threw the two books that my parents had intended for me on the couch while screaming, "Here's your damn books! Now get out!"

My dealer was scheduled to return my car the next day and I then planned to depart for Los Angeles. While I was waiting for him, I laid down for a while to rest. I heard a knock at the front door and some muffled voices. Apparently Edwin had become so enraged that he had gone to the police department and filed a report that I was dealing drugs. I learned later that detectives had outfitted him with a microphone and marked money and had him attempt to purchase some narcotics from me. I also learned later that Edwin, whose plan to have me arrested had failed, swore to a false report saying that I had assaulted him and threatened to burn down his house when I had visited his home. It was definitely time for me to head back to Los Angeles.

The initial plan was for me to manufacture the methamphetamine myself and then transport it back to Oklahoma for sale. Securing the requisite laboratory equipment became overly problematic however, and attempts to cook a cheaper grade of speed (a process with which I was relatively unfamiliar) resulted in incurring damage to my eye. Since I needed to alter my plans, I contacted my old "business" friends in Austin, and was delighted to learn that the same high-quality methamphetamine was still available. Thus, I intended to leisurely travel from Los Angeles to Austin, where I would pick up the speed, and then continue on to Oklahoma to distribute the product to my dealers.

Jack had accompanied me to Oklahoma and then back to Los Angeles, but he had no idea that I had set up a methamphetamine operation. He agreed to join me for the leisurely travel plans. He thought that we were going to the Gulf Coast to find work on shrimping boats or oil rigs; that way if we were confronted by police, he could not, inadvertently or otherwise, disclose the details of my drug ring. He proposed stopping for a few days in Tucson, which I found amenable to my plans... I could not have been more wrong.

Off we went, eastbound from Los Angeles and headed for Tucson. That was on September 14, 1984; I was twenty-eight years old. Once we got to Tucson, we spent all of my traveling money on narcotics. Our basic plan had been to party all weekend and on that Monday to do some burglaries to secure adequate funding for our journey east. Perhaps Jack did not really want to continue our voyage; at any rate he begged off on the thievery. So I found myself driving alone to Tucson's northwest side on Monday. My intent was to meet up with a cocaine connection to see if he had any interest in making some money. I never did locate him on that fateful afternoon, but I did successfully misappropriate the requisite traveling funds and some cocaine elsewhere, prior to meeting Jack in a downtown park.

My feelings had been hurt. There I was, laying out lots of money, supplying ample amounts of drugs, providing transportation, but Jack had refused to even serve as a lookout while I committed burglaries. To assuage my hurt feelings, I re-asserted my status as the prison tough guy who had to be respected by concocting some story about having stabbed a dope dealer who had attempted to rip me off. We then left the park and went to buy some marijuana. Before leaving town, we went to a bar for a few pitchers of beer and a game or two of pool, and then, filled the car with gas.

The ride toward Austin, Texas, began on the evening of September 17, 1984. We would drive for a while, and then pull over so we could climb to the top of a mesa, where we smoked a little marijuana and did some reading. Within a couple of days, we had crossed the rest of Arizona and New Mexico before finally pulling into El Paso, the western edge of Texas. Once in El Paso, Jack and I decided to enjoy a few hours south of the border. We went to Juarez, Mexico, where Jack sat transfixed before a few nude dancers while, unbeknownst to him, I found someone to sell me a little heroin. Before returning to the US, we bought some "Puro" (nearly pure alcohol) to mix with my pain pills. Thusly fortified, we continued on toward Austin; however, before reaching our destination, my car experienced electrical trouble and ceased running just outside of Kerrville. Thankfully, my mother was kind enough to arrange for the towing of my vehicle to a car dealership in Kerrville for repairs; that was on Thursday, September 20th. Once my automobile had been repaired, Jack and I prepared to leave, but a herd of FBI agents rushed into the garage and placed me under arrest. Initially I thought that someone in my drug syndicate had been apprehended and squealed on me in exchange for leniency. I was therefore expecting to be charged for conspiracy to traffic in narcotics. When the FBI agent in charge informed me that I was under arrest for kidnap, I was absolutely stunned!

Frank at his arrest for kidnap.

Chapter Six

Rachel: Adulthood

When I was nearly eighteen, I graduated from Sahuaro High School in June of 1980. I had no immediate plans to attend college, and continued to maintain the family home and work odd jobs, mostly babysitting. Around Christmas of 1981, my brother began working at a sporting goods store and arranged for me to work there on a temporary basis during the holiday season. I really enjoyed working there and did so well that the manager hired me as a permanent employee. I was so excited; it was my first real job. I began as a cashier, and quickly moved up to head cashier. I very much enjoyed the job, and was thrilled that several young people from Jeff and Janice's church worked there with me. We were like a family. During that period in my life I ran in local road races, mostly 5k or 10k. In the summer of 1982, at age nineteen, I had my first boyfriend; however, it was a very short-lived experience.

Toward the end of 1982 and into 1983 my mother seemed to have been doing well. She moved out of Gigi's home and took up residence in her own apartment; in lieu of rent she did chores around the apartment complex, such as cleaning the units when they became vacant. I enjoyed occasional lunches with her and our relationship really began to improve. However, I was always on guard around her, as I still harbored a lack of trust. I wanted so desperately to have a "normal" relationship with my mom, but knew deep down that that would never happen.

In 1983 I ran my first marathon, a 26.2 mile ordeal that I completed in less than three and a half hours. I made good time, especially since I had not trained specifically for the competition and merely participated on a whim. My brother, who was my coach, just wanted me to run as far as I could. I felt so good that I just kept going and said to myself, "I can do this."

With the culmination of 1983 came the first Christmas day that my mom had spent with us in ages. Ed had not been in my mom's life at that time. A predictable cornerstone of my mother's relationship with him was that when he was in her life, she did not do well at all and became again involved in substance abuse. Christmas 1983 was the first Christmas that I recall her being sober; she was well. But, like always, it did not last.

On New Year's Eve I called my mom; I was excited about having received a new television set for the home as a Christmas gift and wanted to share my jubilation with my mother. I could immediately tell that she was drunk... again. When I inquired about her state of inebriation, she, of course, denied it. Hurt and disgusted, I hung up the telephone.

Around the second week of January 1984, my brother traveled to New York. He had been planning to get married and had journeyed east to visit his fiancé. A week or two later, while my brother was still in New York, I received a call from Gigi saying that my mother had been taken to the hospital by ambulance. I still went to work that day, but since I was expecting further news about my mom, I informed my boss that I might have to leave. Later that morning, I got a call from the intensive care unit doctor who was treating my mother. Apparently, my mom had been passed out for quite a few hours as a consequence of having overdosed on drugs and alcohol. The doctor requested my presence at the hospital to sign some papers. He was of the opinion that my mom would die, and that it was just a matter of time. Having experienced similar episodes with my mom, I suggested that these things had become a pattern with her and that she would soon be up and about. In no uncertain terms, he told me that that would not happen.

Upon entering my mom's room in the hospital, I noticed that she had been placed in some sort of contraption. I was told that its purpose was to try and raise her blood pressure. The hospital being only three miles away, I ran the next morning to the hospital to check on her. I noted that my mother's feet were black and blue, and that they were ice cold. I asked the nurse what was going on, but she was extremely evasive and would only say a surgeon was coming. I then learned that she had gangrene in both feet. Nothing could touch her feet, as it would cause her great pain. I knew the next few days were going to be very hard and emotionally draining.

During occasional bouts of semi-consciousness, my mom kept asking for my brother, but he had decided not to return home from New York sooner than scheduled. She and Rob had always been very close. She had hurt him for the last time; he told me that he was done with her. Even after he had returned home and knew of Mom's requests to see him, my brother persisted in his refusal to see her. In late January 1984, family members began to gather and prepare for the worst. My mother's sister (aunt Mary), whom she had not seen in many years, was contacted. Her husband (uncle Jim) had retired from the military and they had settled in Texas. I had informed Aunt Mary of Mom's condition, but it was her mother (Gigi), an elegant and mannerly lady, who had a flair for the melodramatic, who convinced aunt Mary to make the voyage to Tucson right away.

Toward the end of January, the gangrene had traveled above my mom's knees and she was in excruciating pain. Apparently, when my mother had passed out, she had remained for some twelve hours in a position in which circulation to her lower extremities had been cut off; hence the gangrene was progressing up both legs. The surgeon required a decision on whether or not to amputate my mom's legs. I prayed that God would take her before that happened.

Aunt Mary had to return home on January 29th. She was a teacher and had stayed as long as she could. At that point we did not know how much longer my mom had to live. The rest of us (Gigi, my dad and me) kept vigil at the hospital; my brother never did visit Mom. By January 29th, the pain from the gangrene invasion led to my mom having been placed into a virtual, drug-induced coma and we all agreed that she was dying.

I received a 3:00 am phone call from the hospital the next day, January 30th. My mother had taken a turn for the worse. Gigi, my dad and I rushed to her bedside in the intensive care unit. A pulmonary specialist told us that Mom's right lung had collapsed and that her death was near. I entered my mother's room and was with her when she died. Obviously, it was so very hard to have seen her like that; however, I must admit to having felt as if a huge weight had been lifted off my shoulders. I had been praying every night for God to take her because she was suffering so badly, and it was on that Monday that the terrible decision on whether to amputate my mother's legs had to be made. Even at that stage of infancy in my turning to God (after all, I was within the fruitless confines of Protestantism at that time), I knew that He had, in His grace, rescued us from that devastating decision. Assuredly, my father was incredibly upset; despite all that Mom had put him through, he still loved her.

A month or so prior to my mother's death, she had told me of her wish to be cremated, a determination with which Gigi vehemently disagreed, so I set about making the arrangements. One of the main reasons for the cremation was that my family could not afford a burial. (In hindsight, I now wish she had been buried, given that according to the Orthodox faith all are to be buried.) Thankfully, I used my running as a means of coping with all of my emotions, especially since part of the final arrangements included having to clean out my mom's apartment. Pastor Jeff's wife, Janice, accompanied me on that painful project, which had to be completed quickly so her apartment could be rented out. That meant: prior to her funeral. I found several letters in her apartment from Ed that were very disturbing and upsetting.

For many years, I had felt that my relationship with my mother was one wherein she was the child and I was the parent. It was because of my lack of trust and disapproval of her choice of friends. Most of the time she behaved like a rebellious teenager rather than an adult. When Mom was in the hospital, Ed was not around. I always suspected that he was involved in my mother's January 1984 descent into substance abuse, and perhaps even in her fatal overdose. Thankfully, during that time, the cowardly rodent was nowhere to be found. While I was emptying my mom's apartment, the phone suddenly rang; it was Ed. I began to seethe upon hearing his voice. He actually had the nerve to ask me where and when the service was to be held. I unequivocally informed him that he was not welcome. During the service for my mom I recruited the assistance of two large men at my church; they stood at the chapel doors, armed with a description of Ed and instructions to bar his entry should he dare show up. I never again heard from Ed, thankfully.

My brother had not only never visited my mom while she was hospitalized, but initially did not plan to attend the services. Eventually he relented, and came to what was a quite beautiful ceremony, one during which – and we all thought this was appropriately ironic – one of my mom's friends was in the back of the church... drunk, moaning my mom's name.

A week after my mother died, I was able to return to work, having been too upset throughout the ordeal to have gone in at all. I was grateful to have both work and running as emotional outlets. I must have performed to my bosses' liking, because in June of 1984 I was promoted to warehouse manager. It was a big deal; in addition to functioning in a higher supervisory position, it also made me the only female warehouse manager within the sporting goods company's national chain of outlets. I absolutely loved the work.

The warehouse manager, who was leaving, trained me in the intricacies and duties of overseeing the store's distribution center in the weeks following my elevation to the post. Quite a bit of responsibility was involved, including the unloading of merchandise from delivery trucks. As the store employees were welcoming and very helpful, assisting me in the unloading of merchandise, I made a smooth transition into my new supervisory position. Besides, if there had been any reluctance, I could simply "bribe" them with the delicious baked goods I brought to work. Actually, the guys would often take up collections so that I could purchase the ingredients for their favorite delicacies. They would come to the warehouse on Fridays and hand me the money they had collected, and I would go home and bake.

A couple of months into my term as warehouse manager, an event occurred unlike any other that I had witnessed during twenty-two years in Tucson. There was a report on the September 17th 10:00 pm news about a missing eight-year-old girl. It incited a tremendous flurry of activity over the next few days. I would later learn that within an hour or two the city police, county sheriffs and the Federal Bureau of Investigation (FBI) had set up a command post at a nearby school, where many top law enforcement administrators gathered that evening. To me and to many in the community, it seemed surprising to learn of such an unusually intense reaction to what, at the time, could have been merely a child's visiting, without permission, at a friend's house. It had been immediately decided that the girl, Vicki Lynn Hoskinson, had been kidnapped.

Three days later, on September 20, 1984, Frank Jarvis Atwood was arrested, and like everyone else, I was outraged at him. Atwood's appearance was that of a bedraggled barbarian. He looked like the wild man of Borneo. Furthermore, the news reported that he was a parolee from California who had a record of child molestation. As soon as he was named as the suspect, guilt had been assumed; by me, the public, the media and law enforcement.

From September of 1984, the case was given constant media attention for the next two and a half years. Everywhere I went people talked about the case. Focus on it was inescapable, since store windows had flyers with pictures of the girl and roadways were dotted with billboards depicting Vicki Lynn's image. There had been other horrendous occurrences in Tucson, but nothing had ever received anywhere near as much attention.

Vicki Lynn Hoskinson

As September turned into October, many of Tucson's outlying desert regions were scoured for traces of the little girl. The TV showed volunteers (many who took time off from work), as well as fire and rescue members, search teams, law enforcement, etc. on foot and on horseback, dogs, all-terrain vehicles, even helicopters, all searching for Vicki Lynn. Around the end of October to the beginning of November, the news covered Frank Atwood's return from where he had been arrested in Texas to Tucson. It was the first time that we had a clear, up-close look at him, and the sight was frightening.

Two of the images shown by the news media right after Frank's arrest.

I had been contemplating attendance at college to earn a paralegal degree, and I suppose that the events had stirred my interest in the case – along with being unable to escape its constant coverage in the media. Consequently, I recall several reports in early 1985 about possible infirmities in the investigation. One in particular, a newspaper article of several pages, pointed to initial reports of Vicki Lynn having been seen in a mall on the night she disappeared. The newspaper article pointed to the fact that those reports had been ignored once Atwood's deplorable criminal past had come to light. My interest in paralegal studies stimulated attentiveness to case details, some of which included: the girl having disappeared at around 3:00 to 4:00 pm; Atwood's having been at a downtown park at around the same time; his having been in the company of government witnesses until his arrest three days later, in Texas. The fact that Atwood could not be responsible for Vicki's death if she had been alive in a mall several hours after Atwood had been accounted for, as reported in the newspaper, made the law enforcement's disregard of that sighting in the mall very disturbing.

Then, something else occurred that seemed all too convenient and which raised further questions. In a desert clearing on Tucson's northwest side, a skull and some bones were found; however, it turned out that that particular location was in one of the areas previously searched. How could Frank Jarvis Atwood be accountable for partial remains discovered in April of 1985? The region had been thoroughly inspected in September/October of 1984 and Atwood had been in custody since September of 1984. Something was wrong.

Throughout 1985 and into 1986 I continued my running; I was in really good shape early in 1986. My brother, who still ran and was also a coach, coached me throughout my running career. As 1986 progressed, my training included running seventy-five to eighty miles a week. The intense training continued until that summer, when I hurt my foot and had to take some time off. Whenever I attempted to restart my training regimen, significant pain necessitated yet further down time, and in July I had a walking cast put on for a month to allow my foot to heal. This was very frustrating for me, since I tend to be very intense about things that truly interest me. It didn't help that I was in the best shape of my life when the injury occurred.

I was able to train again in August. Under my brother's tutelage I began serious preparation for the January 1987 Phoenix Marathon; my intent was to qualify for the Boston Marathon. My brother would have me do a 22 mile run we called "the edge". If I could perform that, I could run a marathon. He would do my long training runs with me, always with tremendous encouragement and support. Things were going well at the Phoenix Marathon. I was on pace for a three hour finish, but about halfway through my right leg felt sort of numb and seemed to be dragging. I was able to finish in three hours and seventeen minutes, which did qualify me for the Boston Marathon. The discomfort that lingered after the race turned out to be from a torn hamstring. Some extended convalescence was required, which lasted into the summer of 1987. Since my leg had not gotten better, I went for special treatment in Phoenix twice a week. Thankfully, the regimen was a success and I ran again after about six weeks.

1987 Phoenix Marathon
finish line.

1989
10K road race.

While I was laid up with a torn hamstring I could only go to work and then return home; no running or other activity was on the agenda. As it turned out, the Frank Jarvis Atwood trial began in January of 1987; so after work, I went home and watched the trial. It was the first gavel-to-gavel televised trial in Arizona, and it lasted for over two months; I observed the entire process. Looking back now, I can see how the opportunity to watch the trial unfolded – what, with my leg injury coinciding with the trial's onset – and today, truly believe all of it was God's plan. Had I not been injured, I never would have had the time to watch the trial.

As the proceedings progressed, I kept waiting for some hint of the bombshell evidence that law enforcement and the press had insinuated existed. The hype by the authorities had been pervasive and an aura of overwhelming guilt had been constructed. However, not only was there an absence of evidence against Atwood, but some of the facts seemed to exonerate him. For instance, to believe that Atwood could drive some twenty miles in rush hour traffic, perform indecent sex acts with a child, commit murder and then return, again in rush hour traffic, to the downtown park, within little more than an hour, was a real stretch. Also, the state claimed that he had transported Vicki Lynn in his car; however, law enforcement acknowledged at the trial that Atwood's car had been dismantled and painstakingly examined for traces of the girl. Nothing – no fingerprints, blood, hair, fibers or any other trace of her – was found in the car. As the trial ended, I had some serious doubts about Frank Jarvis Atwood's guilt.

I was at work a few days after the jury had begun their deliberations when the radio announced that there was a verdict... predictably, the jury found him guilty. All I could think

Three different scenes from Frank's trial sessions.

was, "Why?" I had watched the entire trial, and there just was not adequate evidence.

A couple of months later there was the sentencing, and I watched on TV as the sentence of death was pronounced. During the days subsequent to the sentencing, I observed many of the interviews. One was with Atwood himself, and he told the reporter that he was afraid to die. As with the guilty verdict, all I could think of was, "Why?" As a Christian, I immediately thought that there was no need to be afraid. That interview kept haunting me; I wondered whether God was encouraging me to tell Mr. Atwood about salvation, yet I also feared contacting him. Finally, on June 4, 1987, I wrote to Frank Jarvis Atwood about the salvation offered by the Lord Jesus Christ.

Frank, stunned, listening as the judge pronounces
his death sentence.

Chapter Seven

Rock Bottom: The Call

I tremble in horror over how I had ignored God's continuous knocks at my door with such consistency. I now find it simply inconceivable that I had, for so many years, disdained the myriad opportunities God had provided for me to return to Him. Had I done so, I could have dealt with the repeated sexual assaults and the subsequent, rapid descent into perversity. I could have moved toward purification from guilt, anger, pride and other passions. Having done things "my way" had resulted in significant danger to my salvation, as well as in absolute disgrace. There was shame, not only for myself, but also incalculable humiliation for my beloved parents. I had become a social deviant, a sexual pervert, and the suspect in a notorious child murder – not exactly what my father, a West Point graduate and army general, and my mother, born and bred in the upper class, had hoped for.

What's more, as a consequence of my disobedience to my father and to God, my father also lost his faith in the American justice system. With the exception of being a defendant, my father had participated in every aspect of the military's judicial advocate general protocol. He had prosecuted suspected offenders, defended the accused and also functioned as a judge. He knew, intrinsically, how courts, albeit military judicial proceedings, functioned. It was that experience, along with his experiences on several civilian juries, that caused my father to inform the Federal Bureau of Investigation (FBI) of my whereabouts in September of 1984. In short, he was the proximate cause of my arrest in Texas on a federal kidnap charge. He felt that if I had, in fact, committed the crime, then I would require restraint, and if I had not, then the judicial process would function to exonerate me. What a horrendous dilemma into which to have cast my loving father! I had compelled him to wrestle with his conscience at having his own flesh and blood captured by the FBI! Please, forgive me Daddy.

Several months after my September 1984 arrest my father journeyed to Tucson. My cries of innocence compelled him to personally investigate the facts of my case. After having scoured police reports and other evidence my attorney had provided for his examination, my dad understood that I was innocent. Up until that point, his belief in the judicial system's objective fairness had instilled the confidence in him that were I innocent, I would be acquitted. Because the FBI had arrested me in Texas and I had to face federal charges in Arizona, I had to be transferred from Texas to Tucson in what is known as a removal hearing. However, the federal government failed to take that perfunctory step because it was understood that there was no evidence of my involvement. This fact – that the federal government had not even bothered to proceed with the most rudimentary court hearing – is what had served to bolster my father's faith in the system. Unfortunately, the state of Arizona did not have any such sense of prudence. Once I was returned to Tucson, my father watched in abject horror as the Arizona wheels of injustice functioned to ultimately convict his son of kidnap and capital murder, followed by watching me be sentenced to death. Nevertheless, his faith in the American way fostered continued hope in the appeals process, a mechanism that permitted what is called a direct appeal to the State Supreme Court. The final nail in the coffin of my dad's faith in the justice system came when the Arizona Supreme Court, in its initial pages of the Opinion, stated that I had kidnapped, molested and murdered the victim. Molested? I had never been charged, not to mention tried and convicted, for molestation. In fact, the trial court judge had made the specific finding that "this was not a sexual case." Yet, the State Supreme Court ruled that I had sexually assaulted the victim. It was heartbreaking to see my father's belief in the United States of America crumble. The trust he had had in the country, for which he had gone to war and bled, was lost.

It is quite humbling to think back upon all of the blessings the Good Lord had bestowed upon me, especially during those years when I had turned from Him. I can see how some events, such as my embarrassment at having been caught using drugs at military school or the shame I felt at being shunned by neighborhood children and their parents because of my involvement in disreputable endeavors, had instilled a sense of unease in me. Back then, I had only begun to stray from my church and my parents. God was fervently tugging at my conscience, cautioning me; I had wandered into sin. Those early warnings from our Heavenly Father included increasingly severe conflicts with my parents, brushes with the law and an escalating disdain for those in positions of authority. I had refused to obey the danger signs, and what ensued was virtual all-out warfare with my parents, as well as with the law. Having ignored the danger signs and the warnings, which were the very grace of God, I am aware today of having eschewed the purpose of all human life: to pursue a restoration of likeness to God.

During those early stages of my departure from God, a "good Samaritan" always seemed to appear at some vital juncture. Generally, it was someone who was able to secure my attention in order to then teach me about God's love, much in the same way that Jesus' compassion for the adulterous woman is a vastly superior path than that of the strict condemnation made by the Pharisees (cf. Jn. 8:1-11). For example, at fourteen, when I attended a private facility for troubled kids, which was before I had fully immersed myself into drugs and counterculture actions, one of the teachers there took an especial interest in me. Looking a little like the musician Bob Seger in the 1970s, Mr. Bradley had hair that fell to about the middle of his back and a bushy beard. As a consequence of his appearance I felt an initial trust in him. At that time in my life, I found long-haired, bearded men fascinating objects. Since I tended to distrust authority figures, especially teachers, as I was still smarting from my experience with the Commandant at Brentwood Military Academy, my trust in Mr. Bradley was unusual for me. It had grown as a result of how he abstained from the conventional punishments of detention or extra homework for student misdeeds. Instead, he sat with me, in private, and engaged me in non-accusatory conversation about why I had misbehaved. He would first encourage me to explore what I was seeking to accomplish by my misconduct and then, eventually, he focused on the consequences of my actions. Moreover, during our conversations, that godly Christian man concentrated on how I was turning from God, from the gracious Lord who always cared for me.

Another one of my good Samaritans was the reverend from St. Alban's Episcopal Church, Father Norm. That messenger from God never failed to come running whenever he learned that I was in trouble, whether after an especially intense altercation with my parents, or when I was in jail, or simply if I needed a shoulder upon which to cry. Like Mr. Bradley, Father Norm did not invoke conventional propaganda – the "you must listen to me" or "you must do this" scenarios – nor did he try to guilt trip me into obedience. Instead, Father Norm patiently referenced how God always had lovingly provided for me, and then, just as calmly, he would detail where my abandonment of the Lord had taken me. Truly, even as I was turning from God, He always bestowed the sweet grace of good Samaritans upon me.

Tragically, I rarely opted to follow the godly instruction the angelic servants God provided, even when adversities increased. It is crucial that it be understood that I am in no way inferring that God is the author of evils in life; that is not my intent, at all. What I am demonstrating is how, as I turned from God, the recession of His grace ensued and the potential for tribulation became greater. Another way to objectively consider this is to look at how fornication, homosexuality and other abuses of sexuality have become the norm in the United States. These abuses are assuredly a turning away from God and the grace that He once bestowed upon our nation. As we observe the withdrawal of God's grace from our nation, so, too, do we observe rising unemployment, war, economic crises and so on.

My turning away from God facilitated the withdrawal of His grace from me. That, in turn, led to the many disastrous events in my life, for example, the sexual assault that I suffered at age fourteen. The fact remains that once I abandoned God and chose to participate in conduct that made me susceptible to deviants, I placed myself squarely in harm's way. This destructive pattern continued as I persisted in felonious behavior and ended up in jail, where I was promptly sexually violated. Those calamities were engineered solely by me. It was God's perennial grace that allowed for conditions which encouraged a return to Him, almost always via His angelic messengers. In fact, even when I was engaged in evil activities, like persecuting His faithful, God still acted to navigate my return to Him. For instance, while in a California prison in the early 1980s, it had become my practice to sit on some benches along a walkway at a time when I knew that a few Christian kids would pass by. As they walked past me, I hurled insults and taunts at those benevolent youngsters. Interestingly, at about the same time, a friendship developed between Charles "Tex" Watson, one of Charles Manson's compatriots in the late 1960s, and me. His sincere conversion to Christianity intrigued me. We enjoyed many long talks in the prison chapel, where he was the chaplain's assistant, about the hopelessness of self-will and the power of God. At that point in my life I misperceived those interactions with yet another good Samaritan as merely interesting philosophical discourse. Once again, I failed to answer God's knock on the door to my heart.

I also recall the less overt promptings by God to return to Him. There were so many times when I was on lock down in prison and the only available literature happened to be of a Christian nature; movies shown in the prison gym were about ex-gangsters who had converted to Christianity. Many of these stimulants occurred frequently. Truly, despite my continued descent into depravity and my repeated turning aside from any cue toward reconciliation with the Savior Christ Jesus, God never ceased to love me. He faithfully provided constant encouragement for my return to Him. That God never abandoned me is a fact that reminds me of the well-known "Footprints" poem:

> *One night a man had a dream.*
> *He dreamed he was walking along a beach with the Lord.*
> *Across the sky flashed scenes from his life.*
> *In each scene he noted two sets of footprints in the sand.*
> *One belonged to him and the other to the Lord.*
> *When the last scene of his life flashed before him,*
> *he looked back at the footprints in the sand.*
> *He noted that many times along the path of life*
> *there were only one set of footprints.*
> *He also noted that it happened at the very lowest*
> *and saddest times in his life.*
> *This really bothered him and he questioned the Lord*
> *about it:*
> *"Lord, You said that once I decided to follow You,*
> *You'd walk with me all of the way, but I have noted that*
> *during the most troublesome times in my life there is only*
> *one set of footprints.*
> *I don't understand why when I need you most You would*
> *leave me."*
> *The Lord replied:*
> *"My precious, precious child, I love you and I would nev-*

er leave you.

During your times of trial and suffering, when you see only one set of footprints, it was then that I carried you."

I hope, by now, that I have firmly established that my continued disdain of God prompted an ever worsening chain of grievous events. Specifically, not only was I sexually violated on several occasions, but also within the realm of the criminal justice system. From there, I plummeted from minor brushes with the law to a six-month prison sentence, and then on to two four-year terms of incarceration, with yet another six-month stint in prison between those two sentences. Nevertheless, God lovingly bestowed His grace upon me by continually providing for my return to Him. It was my persistent abandonment of Him that had triggered the less than impartial circumstances within the legal arena, which grew more and more dire. It was in exactly this state of affairs that my September 1984 arrest occurred. God knew that I finally had to be clobbered over the head with a hefty two-by-four.

After having been arrested on September 20th, 1984 by the FBI in Texas, I learned that several days earlier, on September 17th (the day that I had left Tucson), eight-year-old Vicki Lynn Hoskinson had disappeared from the very neighborhood in which I had stayed during my weekend in Tucson. On that Monday, during the time that this child vanished, I had been driving around in search of a target to rob so that I could purchase some narcotics before then retrieving my traveling companion from a park and departing from Tucson. Well, the combination of the child's disappearance, my position in the area alone sans any alibi, and my arrest record led to my having been taken into custody several days later. There had been some reports of a girl who very closely matched Vicki Lynn's description, including the same colored dress, with a woman in the Tucson Mall on the evening of Vicki Lynn's disappearance. The woman, Ann Fries, had a history of mental illness and was known to frequent a convenience store in

Vicki Lynn's neighborhood. In fact, at around the same time of Vicki's disappearance, this woman had told the store clerk that she had lost a girl named Vicki via an illegal adoption and that the child attended Homer Davis Elementary School and was eight years old. A check of Homer Davis' class rosters revealed that the only eight-year-old girl enrolled with the name of Vicki was Vicki Lynn Hoskinson. Moreover, when questioned by law enforcement about her movements on the day of Vicki's disappearance, the woman misled sheriff's detectives by contending that she was home all day. A man who dwelt at her residence confirmed her absence during the period when Vicki Lynn vanished from the mall, a locale at which the woman was a frequent visitor.

Despite the clouds of suspicion that swirled around the woman, the police never did follow up on her, a glaring transgression that reveals the government's desire to sensationalize the tragedy by claiming to have captured a madman from California. Thus, once law enforcement came across the information that my vehicle had been in Vicki's neighborhood, my conviction and sentence to death were a done deal. About two days after Vicki's disappearance, law enforcement ran the license plates from my car, and when they came up with my name, all of the prior arrests and imprisonments were revealed. Tucson, a city of several hundred thousand citizens at the time, was up in arms because Vicki was missing. Enormous pressure fell on law enforcement to solve the enigma. Vicki's disappearance also received national as well as international attention in the media. There I was, a felon, on parole for a crime I had committed four years earlier against a child, who had been in the area where Vicki Lynn was last seen without an alibi that could be substantiated. I was the perfect patsy, gift-wrapped and ready to be led to the slaughter.

In fact, subsequent to my arrest, I came under the scrutiny of international media attention after several cable television stations made programs about me that aired repeatedly in Europe, Australia, Africa, the Middle East, and elsewhere. The intense adverse publicity not only misguided law enforcement's investigation of the case, but also resulted in my having become the target of endless vicious insults and threats on my life. The fact remains that when police discovered my presence in the proximity of Vicki Lynn Hoskinson's disappearance, all other leads, even those involving Vicki Lynn having been seen in the mall with a woman, immediately ceased to be of any concern to law enforcement. That woman's home and vehicle were never searched, and falsehoods about her whereabouts when Vicki vanished were never investigated.

Having been arrested by the FBI on a federal charge initially landed me in a federal prison, since being housed in the Behr County Jail in San Antonio was deemed to have been too great of a threat to my safety. Neither, however, did the inmates in the federal penitentiary at Bastrop, Texas take too kindly to my residency. I was placed in administrative segregation and surrounding prisoners, those who lived in nearby cells, immediately began screaming threats and organizing a routine that was intended to constantly keep me awake as they yelled and banged on their walls. Prisoners who were being escorted past my cell by guards also got in on the action, with the enthusiastic encouragement of the officers, as they kicked my door, spat on the small window, and shrieked outrageous insults. There were also some prisoners, who were not on lock down status and were allowed into the administrative segregation area to clean, who wasted no time in making threats while displaying weapons through the window in my cell door. They told me plainly that I would be killed while I was being escorted. On several occasions, they lit something on fire and slid it under my door.

Those menacing conditions lasted for a week or two, after which I was then transferred to a small county jail in Bastrop. Apparently officials believed I would go unnoticed there. As it turned out, despite other prisoners' awareness of my charge, I was to remain unharmed for the nearly one month stay. During this time, the local media attention did not wane, and Bastrop residents campaigned to have me removed from their locale.

The inclusion of imminent bomb threats resulted in the Texas authorities performing what a federal court would later determine to have been an illegal extradition by Arizona officials. Consequently, I was returned to Tucson, an arrival that necessitated my having to be outfitted in a bullet-proof outfit. Moreover, there were SWAT (Special Weapons And Tactics) team members at the airport, along the route to Pima County's detention facility, as well as on the jail's rooftop, strategically positioned in efforts to secure my safety through the frenzy that accompanied my arrival in Tucson. As the caravan reached the jail's parking area, several dozen boisterous members of the press became visible. It was but a mere precursor to the explosive situation I would confront upon initially traversing the jail's interior. The media attention in Tucson was outrageous; before having ever made an appearance in an Arizona courtroom, I had, for all intents and purposes, already been tried and convicted.

Another development, one that would play a key role in my eventual return to God, involved the fact that my prior arrest record in California was well known. As it turned out, prisoners both in the county jail and on death row had seen through the government's subterfuge and understood that it was my record from California, not the trumped-up charges in Arizona, for which I was being ostracized. Thus, there was a radical nature to the frenzy as I entered the Pima County Jail and reached the housing unit where I would be confined for several years. Residents began beating their doors and lighting fires; there was a plethora of death threats as well as myriad other assaultive outbursts.

The pod in which I was housed was two tiered and shaped sort of like a "U". On either side were cells along the top and bottom level and more rooms along the back wall. In front of the cells across the back wall I noticed two staircases that led to the second tier. During my initial months in the county jail I was housed by myself, on one side of the top tier. No one could even use the staircase on the side where I was housed.

I found myself in a very dangerous and isolated predicament, one that was incredibly humiliating. Prior crises, such as having kissed a ten-year old girl or kidnapping a seven-year old boy, had had the potential for public abasement; but I had turned away from such grace, from such compelling prodding to return to the Creator. Now, the Good Lord afforded another optimal opportunity for me to retreat from my debauchery, to deal with all of my lingering emotional trauma, to finally face the results of my past misdeeds, in order to return to Him. I had never acceded to this type of grace from God the Father, yet His eternal love proffered yet one more opportunity. Alas, I had still not reached rock bottom. Instead I continued to misperceive my adverse circumstances as things that incited my intense anger at society. Even in the Pima County Jail, I persisted in abandonment of God.

There were occasions when I toyed with the grace of God. Regular visits, phone calls and letters from my parents in Los Angeles would, at times, induce momentary longing for the protective embrace of God's love that I had once enjoyed. A reading of the Book of Job briefly pointed me in the direction of patiently enduring to the end by abiding in God's grace. However, my common practice was to eschew the very grace of God. For instance, repeated attempts by chaplains at the Pima County Jail to converse with me were met with firm resistance; Christian groups who endeavored to interact with me had their loving advances rebuffed. There were even times when, while Christian visitors were in the pod singing religious hymns, that I either made derogatory comments or engaged in threatening behavior. As a matter of fact, I not only ignored and combatted any grace from the Lord, but I also actively maintained putrid agendas, such as approaching unsuspecting young inmates with homosexual propositions. May God forgive my transgressions.

I now realize my impetus for ignoring God. I had firmly believed that I would be released from jail in the near future. How could it be otherwise, I surmised, when the allegation of having kidnapped someone in my vehicle seemed to be ludicrous on its face? There was no trace evidence to support the assertion that Vicki Lynn Hoskinson had been in my car. Once I was liberated, I intended to make society pay for having put me through such an injustice. My pernicious attitude even persisted when in April of 1985, seven months after Vicki Lynn's disappearance and my arrest, partial remains were located in the desert on the outskirts of Tucson. In May of 1985, a charge of capital murder was added; I was facing the death penalty.

In the month subsequent to Vicki Lynn's disappearance in September of 1984, the same area wherein bones had been discovered in April of 1985 had been the subject of one of law enforcement's most painstaking searches in the history of Pima County. It seemed obvious that someone – besides me, since I had been in jail before the search – had placed the bones in the clearing, a fact that therefore exonerated me of any involvement. However, that was not the case. I was put on trial a couple of years later, in January of 1987, in Phoenix, because the pervasive, circus-like publicity had compelled the change of venue, from Tucson to Phoenix. My trial ended up with my being convicted for kidnap and capital murder. Next on the agenda of seemingly preordained events came the sentencing phase of the proceedings and, of course, I was sentenced to death. On the 11th day of May, 1987, I arrived on death row... a man innocent of the new charges that had been laid against him. I had hit rock bottom.

My arrival on death row in May of 1987, much like with my entry into the Pima County Jail several years earlier, was met with raucous clamor. As I entered Cellblock Six, the administration segregation building where death row and other maximum security prisoners were housed, I glanced into the control room and noticed row upon row of batons, shields, and other riot gear. At about the same time, several hulking officers grabbed me by my arms and hustled me down the corridor to the "squad room." A half dozen or so officers, a few sergeants, a couple of lieutenants, and unit administrators had gathered and were awaiting my arrival. As I entered the squad room, where I was literally thrown into a chair, the administrators took turns impressing upon me that they ran the building with an iron fist and any rebelliousness on my part would be swiftly met with my introduction to their batons and being shown the concrete floor face first. After having been duly threatened with physical harm by the unit's top brass, the burly officers yanked me out of the chair and half carried me down the hallway toward the pod where I was to be housed. Along either side of the hall were large plexiglas plate windows through which prisoners in sixteen man pods could observe my passing. Of course, the housing unit staff had tipped these inmates off about the fact that the notorious and much reviled Frank Jarvis Atwood would be escorted down this passageway. The inmates began to bang and kick their doors, scream and hurl objects (bars of soap, plastic baggies filled with liquids, etc.) at the windows. The guards who were escorting me just laughed and pod officers whispered insults and threats.

After having traversed that gauntlet, I arrived at the doors of the four-man pod to which I had been assigned. The living area was approximately 10' x 25', and within it was a table and shower stall, as well as the doors to four cells; each "house" was about 6' x 9'. The electronically locked door to the pod popped open, and as I entered the area, my cell door rattled open. One of the escort guards shoved me into the cell; as I tumbled to the floor, the officers chuckled. Then the cell door slammed shut and the guards exited the pod... leaving me still handcuffed and absent a mattress, bedding or anything else.

I soon learned that such attempts by the officers to antagonize me was a common practice. At that time, a law had been recently passed that allowed for a minimum twenty-five-year sentence of punishment to be given to any prisoner who drew blood on someone. Since both my record in California prisons and the Pima County Jail were rife with assaultive behavior, especially against guards, and because virtually all Cellblock Six staff knew that I had not committed the kidnap/murder, and believed that I would meet with success on appeal, many guards sought to incite me into assaulting one of them. Then a twenty-five year sentence would be given to me, one that I would be unable to win on appeal.

The diabolical actions of the state employees were quite juvenile at times, something that I realized during my initial journey to the exercise area as I confronted multiple attempts to elicit my violent reaction. In Cellblock Six, whenever we were escorted somewhere we were always handcuffed, with our hands strapped in front of us with a leather belt. On that particular occasion, after I had been secured in an exercise pen, the escorting officer unhandcuffed one of my hands and then started jerking around my still handcuffed hand. It hurt, plenty, but I kept my mouth shut. The guard finally removed the other handcuff, while whispering, "One of these days Atwood." Soon thereafter, another guard came around to each recreation cage to provide water. When he stopped at my pen I held my cup out for some water, but instead of filling up my cup, he poured water all over my hand and arm while loudly exclaiming, "How do ya like that, bitch?" The exercise enclosures, constructed out of chain link fencing, were about 15' x 15'; there was even a chain link roof. In the door was an opening, called a trap, that was about 6" x 24". There were sixteen such pens. They reminded me of dog kennels, and that guard's maltreatment of me was plainly visible to the other prisoners.

It must be said that inmates generally provoke one another into acts of violence, mostly out of boredom and the desire to see some action. If they had been able to goad me into violence, they would have enjoyed treble thrills. Not only would they have witnessed a bit of excitement, but they would also have seen me get brutally beaten, knowing full well that I would have received an additional twenty-five-year sentence. So, once the officer had abused me, prisoners began screaming at me to not let a pig treat me like that. I simply had the temptation to react violently hoisted upon me from all sides. Through what I know now to have been God's grace, I managed to refuse any engagement in retaliatory behavior against the officer, and kept my mouth shut. The resultant reviling nature of hurled insults was so very humiliating; there I stood, in the middle of a cage, being yelled at, spat upon and having water thrown on me.

Prisoners always try to tempt other prisoners to violence. Several weeks after my arrival on death row, a couple of inmates were allowed into the pod to do some painting. One of them was working on the front of my cell and indicated that he was aware of my California reputation. He then went on to suggest that if I wanted to "be right" with Arizona's ringleaders, I merely had to draw blood on one of my pod-mates. Since they had murdered children, they were seen as undesirables. I informed that inmate that neither was I interested in attempting to please Arizona poseurs, nor did I have any desire to attack someone and/or pick up a twenty-five-year sentence. He made it clear that should I refuse the mission I would be targeted for death. I made it apparent that threats by pseudo, wannabe tough guys failed to impress me. I was then offered one thousand dollars to perform an attack; once again I declined.

In addition to the physical and verbal assaults the guards of Cellblock Six directed at me, they also enjoyed requiring me to engage in menial labor for which I was not responsible. Their apparent intent was for me to refuse so that I could then be issued disciplinary reports, a volatile situation that frequently erupts in violent responses by inmates. I was made to clean the filthy shower sans adequate supplies, while my efforts were ridiculed in attempts to provoke a corrosive reaction. Every few days, staff ordered me to scrub walls or the floor, again absent cleaning supplies and with the aim of inciting a physical confrontation. Once these tactics failed to result in their desired outcome, some guards began to allow for conditions wherein other prisoners would be free to attack me. The usual scenario involved my being taken somewhere, like the exercise pens, visitation or the law library, at the same time that another officer was escorting some other inmate. The guard who had control over the other prisoner would ensure that his prisoner's handcuffs were loose. Additionally, the officer would use vitriolic terms to speak of me to the other inmate as a means of inciting that prisoner to slip out of his handcuffs and assault me as we passed each other in a hallway. Truly, God's grace protected me and helped me in resisting all such attempts to engage in physical violence.

Amidst the outrageously dangerous and utterly humiliating circumstances, despised and abused by guards, prisoners and society, God's grace not only protected me, but the Good Lord led me toward a regimen of self-discipline and education via enrollment in rigorous courses of study in the college available to us in prison. Thankfully, that loving grace, once I had at long last begun to grasp it, also functioned to cleanse me of involvement with occult studies. This is not to say that I was not significantly tempted to continue occult practices. For instance, I had met a nurse just prior to having left the Pima County Jail who was a Wiccan. We had struck up quite a friendship based on our mutual interests in tarot, planetary magic and astrology while I was still in Tucson's detention facility, where she was employed. Once I was transferred to the state prison's death row in Florence, a locale that is approximately seventy-five miles northwest of Tucson, Pamela began visiting me. Many of our conversations revolved around New Age precepts. So, despite my increased willingness to embrace God's grace, there was an ongoing presence of occult temptation. Pamela and I were two lost souls who, out of loneliness, desperately attempted to fill the spiritual void in our lives by entering into a relationship. There really wasn't much love between us, nor even much sexual attraction; yet desperation prevailed. We went through the motions of a romantic affair and under pressure to adhere to my lover's religious persuasions, I succumbed, thereby maintaining my ties to the occult.

Admittedly, I labored under many pressures during my initial months on death row. Not only had I been wrongly convicted of child murder, but I had also been branded by society as so depraved that I was unfit to even live in prison. The government intended to put me down like a rabid animal. I was assaulted by guards in their attempts to entice me into physical confrontations; I was abused by other inmates and I continued my involvement in the occult. I now realize that absent those struggles, no purification of passions would have been possible; it was all God's grace. In the middle of it all, God not only did not desert me, he sent me an angel.

Several weeks after my arrival on death row, a Christian woman decided to write me. She had watched the trial on television; my case was the first to have been shown in its entirety on television in Arizona. As a consequence of both her compassion over what she viewed as a wrongly convicted man and her concern for the fate of my soul, Rachel's June 4th 1987 letter was a lifeline. Rachel presented what I would later learn was the common Protestant Evangelical approach for witnessing to unbelievers. In general terms she asked: 1) if I knew where I would go when I die and 2) why. As I had earlier noted, I was no longer enthused with occult study and although I had begun to open myself up to God's grace, it was still on a sporadic basis. (My heart suffered the illnesses of blindness and ignorance of God.) I certainly was not interested in Christianity; however, the simplicity that echoed in Rachel's letter of inquiry and the ambience of friendship intrigued me. Her straightforwardness had secured my focus.

During my more than a decade of intensive occult study, I had given a great deal of thought to the eternal state of my soul. In fact, my concern for my soul was why much of my magical career revolved around theory rather than practice. I feared that I would soil my soul by engaging in rituals that invited malevolent entities into my inner self. Occult studies, including my concentration on Eastern belief systems such as Taoism and Buddhism, involved the concept of reincarnation, a wayward philosophy which I just could never accept. Thus, Rachel's broaching of a realm I had not explored since childhood, the theology of one life on earth followed by the Judgment, encouraged my return to familiar concepts.

As with the good Samaritans that God had previously provided, Rachel's delivery did not encompass trite propaganda. She did not adapt an "accept Christ to be saved or go to Hades" brimstone and hellfire approach. Au contraire, Rachel's presentation stimulated my esteem by engendering a taste of the mystical while also commanding intellectual exercise. God's grace was once again calling me home, and His angel had my attention.

Chapter Eight

Cellblock Six

In debating whether or not to write to the notorious Frank Jarvis Atwood, I wanted to heed what I believed was God's call, but I was very apprehensive. The issue would not go away; there were many nights when I was either unable to sleep or awoke during the night with concern over Frank's eternal state and commiseration for his fear of death. I was really skeptical about whether he would respond; after all, the media had reported that Frank was heavily involved in the occult. Still, given my sole intention to share the Faith, to explain salvation, I wrote Frank and posed the two evangelical questions of: 1) If you were to die today could you be certain that you would go to heaven? and 2) If God asked you why He should let you into His kingdom, what would you say? I also provided some Scripture verses for him to look up. That was it, I intended nothing more. God had a different plan.

Frank responded right away and asked me to write again in a couple of weeks, as he was involved in some legal work and could not respond right away. I wrote him again in two weeks and provided some further information on salvation. Soon thereafter I received Frank's second letter. He let me know that having grown up in the Episcopal Church made him familiar with the beliefs I had shared. Over the next couple of months we discussed the doctrines of Evangelical Christianity in our letters to each other.

Despite my initial intention of having no interest other than a brief explanation of salvation, Frank and I began to develop a friendship, and in September of 1987 we discussed the possibility of my visiting him. Of course I was very hesitant to do so. While I felt more comfortable and at ease after Frank and I had exchanged several letters, the idea of visiting a convicted felon on death row frightened me. Nevertheless, arrangements were made and I was scheduled for an October visit.

I drove about seventy-five miles north of Tucson, to Florence, which is a small town where a multitude of prisons are located. At first I drove to the wrong prison and had to stop for directions. Then I found myself driving through the prison's entry; the ominous nature of the environment was pervasive. The road to the parking lot faces one of the prison's oldest cellblocks, a huge gray monstrosity that had been erected in the earlier part of the twentieth century. As I pulled into the big parking lot I seriously wondered what I had gotten myself into.

I noticed a shack in the middle of the road and walked up to the guard therein for instructions. In order to visit the cellblock that housed death row, a van had to drive visitors to that unit, so I was told where to wait. Eventually a brown, windowless, filthy van pulled up and we (myself and the other visitors) were told to get in. There were no seats, only dirty wooden benches on either side; we were herded like cattle into that dilapidated heap of metal. The van then took off down a half mile of a very rough, bumpy dirt and gravel road; it was quite a chore just to remain seated. Again, I wondered what I had gotten myself into. We arrived at Cellblock Six, and once we climbed out of the van, we had to line up single file and make our way through a metal detector. I was pretty sure we would not be strip-searched; thankfully I was right.

Having cleared the metal detector, we walked up a ramp and entered Cellblock Six. Forms were filled out and then a double door that led to the visitation area rattled open. As I entered, I was struck by the unmistakable institutional smell and the hideous lime green paint on the walls. As my gaze focused forward, I saw that Frank Jarvis Atwood was in the stall that was directly in front of me. He was clad in a blue chambray shirt and Levis, nervously smoking a cigarette. The stall that he was in was more like a cramped cage and I was surprised that he had shaved his head. There was a phone on his side and another phone on my side for us to talk on; a thick plate of glass separated us. After we picked up our respective phones to nervously greet each other, we initially engaged in some general small talk. I questioned him about his daily schedule and living conditions before our dialogue gravitated toward matters of faith. Frank smoked like a chimney during the entire visit. This kind of bothered me since I have an extreme aversion to cigarettes. Then, before I knew it, the two-hour visit was over.

We had decided that I would visit once or twice a month, and continue our written correspondence. Initially, I had Frank send letters to my church's address; it seemed a wiser course instead of having mail sent to my house. After November of 1987 he began sending letters to my home. One particular letter from the fall of 1987 stands out. He wrote that he was soon to marry his

Frank in Cellblock Six, death row (c. 1996).

Wiccan girlfriend. For some reason, I felt devastated and wondered why. I mean, Frank and I were friends who engaged in discussions about theology, but it was at that moment that I realized I had begun to fall in love.

In addition to a sense of real sorrow, the news about his upcoming marriage came as a surprise. Frank had seemed to be moving toward Christianity, yet he intended to become hitched to a pagan. While it wasn't my place to meddle, I still felt uneasy over his involvement with a witchcraft practitioner. Frank had shared some of the details of his relationship with Pamela, including her decision to visit him less frequently despite planning to marry him. He also had told me of her overly dramatic and venomous criticism of my being a Christian. Her utter disdain for Christianity really made me fear for Frank's walk toward Protestantism.

As November blended into December, Frank began to express serious misgivings about his wedding plans. Like me, he knew that to move toward Christianity while romantically entangled with a Wiccan posed an impossible course. He related how his intentions to celebrate the birth of the Savior Christ Jesus had been met with frightening objections from his bride-to be. A week or two before Christmas of 1987, Frank ended it with the Wiccan, Pamela. I was extremely relieved that his journey toward Christianity would not be fettered by involvement with pagan influences. Admittedly, I hoped that perhaps there would evolve an appropriate time wherein I could express my strong personal feelings for him. That Frank was no longer committed to another woman seemed to speak of potential for us. Although I suspected that he was romantically inclined, I was not completely sure; however, I was soon to find out.

It was in January of 1988 when Frank told me that he had fallen in love with me, but he feared that I did not feel the same way. I had refrained from showing my feelings since he had been involved with someone else. Apparently, Frank thought that all I desired was to guide him to the Lord, so he was concerned that I would depart once he accepted Christ. I had my own dilemma; for while I was in love with Frank, he was not a Christian, so I feared being unequally yoked. There was also the very real concern of being involved with someone as detested as Frank Atwood. I was initially afraid for my safety, but had to trust that if this was God's plan, He would protect me. We began talking about our fears and hopes in early January. Neither of us wanted him to become a Christian if it only meant furthering a romantic relationship. On the 20th of January, 1988, Frank accepted Christ as his Lord and Savior and re-dedicated his life to the Lord. The doors were wide open to his pursuit of Christ, as well as to furthering our relationship.

By that point I had begun to visit Frank weekly; our relationship had blossomed. Then came a bombshell; during a visit in April of 1988, Frank Jarvis Atwood proposed to me. I was afraid that his intent was to marry immediately, and I just was not ready to move so quickly. I had to consider my family's reaction, especially my dad's, because the Frank Jarvis Atwood case had created such a media frenzy. I asked Frank to write my father about his intentions; he did by inserting a letter to my dad in one of my letters. I gave the letter to my dad, and after reading it he just sat and cried. I think he wanted something better, or at least different, for his daughter. I believe that his concern was over the implications of my being linked to Frank Jarvis Atwood. Nevertheless, as a consequence of the close relationship between my dad and me, he trusted my judgment. I accepted Frank's proposal, with the understanding that I was not willing to rush into anything. The purpose of an engagement was to affirm the exclusivity of our involvement with only each other and to continue growing in our relationship.

That spring, with annual racing season occurring from fall through spring, I continued to train and compete in 10k races; however, I was constantly plagued with foot problems (specifically plantar fasciitis, an inflammation of the heel). Toward the end of running season, the sporting goods store where I worked was purchased by a corporation back east. The change in ownership included drastic alterations in store policy. I was informed that the warehouse manager position would be discontinued and I was to resume cashier duties. My brother had already quit working there and established a career selling running shoes. After several months as a cashier, I also left the sporting goods business to initiate a cleaning enterprise; in fact, I continued to clean for two of my initial clients more than two decades later.

I met Frank's mother in the fall of 1987. It was an occasion for significant nervousness, since I did not know what she would think of me. I was incredibly relieved to have been most warmly welcomed by both Frank's mother as well as his father, whom I later met in early 1988 when he was visiting Frank here, in Arizona.

As Christmas of 1987 approached, Frank said he was having a present sent to me by UPS. He hoped that his arrangements would result in the gift being delivered to me by Christmas. It was a cold winter; in fact, snow was even in the forecast, something virtually unheard of for Tucson. When I came home from work on the day before Christmas, there was still no package and it had already become dark as I prepared to attend Christmas church services. Then the United Parcel Service (UPS) truck drove up and delivered Frank's Christmas gift. I excitedly opened the package and saw a crystal globe with a red rose; it could be wound up so music would play. It was a most wonderful Christmas; there was even snow on the ground on Christmas day.

As I had mentioned earlier, in January of 1988 Frank told me that he was falling in love and desired an exclusive romantic relationship with me. I then recalled how merely a few weeks previously, around New Year's, a man at church had asked me out on a date. I had turned him down because my thought was, "I can't." I also remembered wondering why I couldn't: I had fallen in love with Frank Jarvis Atwood.

Subsequent to our April 1988 engagement, I continued to visit Frank every week, usually on a Monday. My dad had retired from Osco Drug stores, so as he was not working at the time, he occasionally accompanied me on the seventy-five mile or so drive to Florence. Relations between Frank and me continued to grow, especially when late in the spring of 1988 Frank's mom suggested that my dad and I come to Los Angeles for a visit. By the summer of 1988 I knew that I would marry Frank; I just was not sure when. Frank's mother even purchased my wedding dress. For many years later, we would joke about how the veil cost more than the dress.

In the fall of 1988 I enrolled in paralegal classes at Pima College. I participated in day and night courses and adjusted my work schedule around classes. My routine included getting up at 4:30 am so I could then meet a friend, with whom I would run ten miles. Afterwards, I would rush to get ready for class, and end the day with cleaning houses. I do not know how I kept up that schedule, but I did. Then Christmas arrived and I was able to see Frank in prison during the celebration of Jesus Christ's Nativity. It was nice to be able to bring him Christmas boxes while he was in Cellblock Six. The boxes were limited to three total in the month of December; each box could weigh a maximum of twenty-five pounds. Preparations would begin in mid-November when Frank's dad would send me fifty pounds of canned goods and other goodies. I would then divide those items into three boxes and add perishables – I cooked lasagna, baked goods and other delectables – so that there would be three twenty-five pound packages. I delivered the boxes myself. I would stand in a property room line (sometimes for two or three hours), so that the perishable foods could reach Frank the same day. It was a joy to cook for someone I loved and to know that he, at least temporarily, was well fed.

Frank's parents had implemented the habit of visiting one at a time, a practice that enabled them to avoid leaving their home unattended and having to put their dog in a kennel. My dad would make the drive with me to the prison on a Sunday, so I could visit Frank and then enjoy some time with his mom or dad. This continued for many years, until Frank's parents became too old to travel.

Frank's mother also arranged to have an Episcopal priest

visit Frank. As it turned out, there was an Episcopal Church in Coolidge, a town a little larger than Florence and about ten or fifteen miles away. Father John happily agreed to visit Frank. That was around September of 1988. At first the good Father was allowed contact visits and could easily serve Holy Communion. As the years went by, Father John was installed in a larger parish in Tucson and visiting conditions in Cellblock Six became more restrictive, with the cessation of contact visits and less leeway on visitation days. However, he still made the journey every month or so to see Frank and provide the Eucharist.

While Father John was in Coolidge, my dad and I would see him along with Frank's parents. Of course, once he relocated to Tucson I saw him with increased frequency and I added his church in Tucson to the roster of my cleaning business. All of us – Frank, his parents, my dad, and myself – enjoyed a wonderful relationship with Father John. In fact, Frank's dad (an organ aficionado) even assisted Father John in the design, installation and maintenance of the church organ that graces St. Michael's Church. Father John, may God bless his kind soul, continued to see Frank about once a month. (He has since moved.)

Growing up, we had always had pets, but in the fall of 1988, we did not have any pets; so I decided to get a cat, specifically, a Persian cat. Frank sent me two hundred and fifty dollars and I responded to an ad in the newspaper that had been placed by a much respected Persian cat breeder. Thus, I became the owner of a beautiful female Persian that I named Litzie, a name intended to honor Frank's parents, as his dad had always called his mother, Litzel.

I quickly became good friends with Roxanne, the Persian cat breeder, and our friendship led to the opportunity to breed Litzie with a grand champion named Ryder. Roxanne tirelessly taught me the ins and outs of the Persian cat business, details such as the correct standards for Persians and fundamentals like proper maintenance (Persians are a very high maintenance breed). Over the next ten years, much of my life involved the breeding and showing of Persian cats.

In 1989 my running became more and more difficult, as for much of that year the plantar fascia problems in both feet had grown progressively worse. In fact, many times after training sessions I returned home only to soak my feet in ice. I also went to a chiropractor who did weekly treatments on my feet. The problem really began to affect my training and racing.

Then, in the latter part of 1989, I learned of a podiatrist in Long Beach, California who had an excellent reputation among world-class runners. I arranged to see him several times in late 1989 to 1990; the prognosis involved the need for surgery, so I began to plan for that unpleasant eventuality. Since a close relationship had developed between Frank's parents and me, I stayed with them when seeing the podiatrist in Long Beach. Arrangements were made for me to undergo surgery and then recuperate at my future in-laws' estate in Brentwood.

The surgery was performed on both feet at the end of June 1990; it was a "fascia release." The process involved cutting tendons on the soles of my feet in order to loosen them. After that ordeal I spent a month at Frank's parents' house. It was quite an experience; in the car on the way home I thought I might never walk again. My feet still hurt so badly and were in casts. The doctor's instructions were to not walk other than to the bathroom and to wait a couple of months before trying to run. Well, I attempted to run after a few months, but had developed a cyst on one of my feet, making it impossible to run. I returned to the doctor in Long Beach to have the cyst on my right foot surgically removed. That landed me back in a cast for another three weeks.

I was never able to get back into racing shape after all of the foot traumas; I simply could not put in the requisite training and workout sessions. Thus, my running had been reduced to basically a few miles here and there. That took place in the fall of 1990. I was grateful to be involved with Persian cats in order to replace the huge void of not running competitively.

My friendship with Roxanne developed, and with her help

I continued to get better quality cats to breed and show. Her aid was indispensable; with such a solid foundation in place, my breeding and showing involvement flourished. I even had several champion Persians and one grand champion. Truly, a love for this interest had developed and I was successful.

Rachel at a cat show with one of her Persian Champions.

... and with one of her kittens.

Rachel's Grand Champion Persian (Buster).

Late in the fall of 1990, I received a telephone call from Frank's counselor, who informed me that Frank had been beaten up by some guards. Understandably, I was distraught, but the counselor assured me that Frank was not badly hurt and would be able to call me shortly. As I anxiously awaited Frank's call, all sorts of scenarios ran through my mind. I was so relieved to receive his call later that day and to know that he had suffered only a few bumps and bruises. Then again, the harm from both his disciplinary proceedings and spiritual welfare detriment was significant. On subsequent visits I was to learn in greater detail what had transpired, details such as Frank having refused direct orders and ultimately assaulting an officer. Yes, to discover how prison staff had abused rules and beat up my fiancé was troubling, but Frank's part in the incident disappointed me. While, perhaps, some punishment may have been warranted, I was in no way prepared for what was to come.

Having become familiar with visits at Cellblock Six, which, after all, was a maximum security building, had given me the impression that I knew about the worst that the Arizona Department of Corrections had to offer. I was not even close! As I was to find out, there was SMU I (Special Management Unit One), or Cellblock Eight (CB-8), a hulking gray monstrosity that seemed to have been dropped out of the sky into the middle of nowhere. CB-8 was about a handful of miles from CB-6 and surrounded only by barren desert. As I approached that beastly dungeon I wanted to cry, to think that my Frankie J. was being housed in such an awful place... the difference from Cellblock Six was that drastic. Aside from the imposing physical appearance, an evil feeling was palpable, one that was quickly reinforced by much tighter regulations and the almost nasty treatment by rude guards. It was horrible.

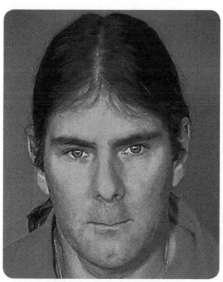

Frank in SMU-I (Cellblock 8).

Chapter Nine

Thirsting for God

Having arrived on death row, and enduring tremendous amounts of hideous abuse, along with an absence of any semblance of decency, was quite a lot to confront. I desperately dived into reviewing legal documents in an effort to figure out what had gone wrong. My sole frame of reference dwelt in the legal arena. There simply did not seem to be the requisite evidence to have sustained a conviction, a fact that more than one news reporter had acknowledged to me (off the record, of course). At that time, I still did not recognize that my dire circumstances and flawed conviction were yet another prompting toward purification. Even when God's angel decided to write me, I initially responded with only a cordial note. Thankfully, in the months following the onset of our correspondence, our focus on Christian topics heightened so that, despite the severity and discomforts of my situation dawning on me, I felt somewhat encouraged. Looking back is a truly humbling experience for me. I recognize that God's grace was at work, and can now easily observe how even a modicum of cooperation with Him promoted hope, even in my increasingly darkened circumstances.

I still went to the exercise pens on a regular basis. In those days a weight machine was in each cage and I endeavored to maintain at least a little fitness. In Cellblock Six outdoor recreation encompassed three two hour periods a week, during which time other inmates persisted with their routine of abuse. I could always count on the barrage of verbal assaults, whether they were extraordinarily vile comments about me and my family, or threats, or other attempts to frighten me, such as theorizing that courts would never grant a scumbag like me any relief and that I would soon suffer an awful death. There was also the occasional water throwing or spitting. I felt extremely conflicted about that abuse. On the one hand, it was incredibly painful, especially for someone like me who had commanded respect on some of the toughest prison yards and who had always been the one to inflict fear and intimidation. The tables were turned; I had become the helpless victim. On the other hand, somewhere in the back of my mind I began to see an opportunity, a chance to escape the downward spiral that had previously foreclosed any pursuit of God. The demon of pride had been my all-too-constant companion for far too long. As the seeds of cooperation with God's grace began to be sowed, I still, even at that early stage of cooperating with God, relied on human power and ingenuity. For example, rather than to permit pride to blindly control me by throwing water on or spitting at others, I harnessed self-effort toward the business of being cooperative and friendly when suffering abuse. One way in which this manifested was the time when I was working out on a weight machine as other prisoners kept up a steady diatribe of verbal assaults, expressing abominable homosexual desires or intentions to physically harm me. I happened to hear inmates in adjoining pens complaining about how wet the morning dew had made the weight machine benches. I figured that, since I would remain shirtless for the next hour or two, it would be considerate to offer my t-shirt to one of them and passed it through the chain link fencing. Of course, my act of kindness was perceived as weakness; the verbal tirades increased in intensity, and my t-shirt was soon being used as a rag to soak up grease from a weight machine. Despite the temptation to react with sinful outbursts, I gathered inner strength to rebuke the temptation. The point is that all too often, I piloted along on human willpower, which frequently cast me into another form of pride – the evil of seeking human praise, even as insipid anger governed my thoughts.

Coming to grips with my status as the frequent victim was made even more difficult because I continued to invoke self-will instead of humility from God's grace. I still sought to carry the day rather than relinquish it to God. I also tried to avoid being involving in evil activities. I sought, instead, to become responsible for my behavior, and one way I did that was to cease my involvement with drugs. I was frequently and considerably tempted to either use some of the rampantly available narcotics or to engage in a little payback, as inmates solicited my assistance in transporting dope between exercise pens. I was usually offered a portion for my cooperation, which I always politely declined. Not once did I handle someone else's parcel of contraband to only then keep or destroy it out of spite. Nevertheless, adapting an amicable demeanor, undertaking college courses and ceasing intoxicants, while all noble enterprises, still kept me shackled to the realm of human effort.

Thankfully, God had made one of his loyal and devoted servants available for me to lean on. As I discussed some of the abuse that I experienced and the resultant feelings with Rachel, she always led me to reliance on God's grace. It was her patient guidance that enabled me to begin understanding how difficulties in life function as medicine from God to purify our passions. Believe me, at times it took the patience of Job for Rachel to marshal my focus toward God. For instance, during one visit, after she had related some of the horrendous conditions Apostle Paul endured in jail, my response was to opine that as a magician or sorcerer, he could have probably accomplished many wondrous feats. Much of my attention had previously centered on establishing a formidable posture (the passion of vainglory, wherein

I sought recognition from others [human glory]). I began to understand as Rachel explained that by patiently enduring public humiliation, I would be cultivating the antithesis of esteem from others. I gradually learned that the Good Lord was lovingly providing the remedy for my passions through the difficult circumstances I was confronting. His angel was leading me by the hand into the fires of purification.

In the midst of what I took to be tremendous public humiliation, God's grace did not cease to manifest itself. As I contemplated a return to God, I began to encounter sorrow over past misdeeds, especially my mistreatment of my parents. Their sacrifices in hopes of my promising future when I was a child had turned into despair as I became a teen. Not only had I disappointed them, but I had confronted them, time and time again. I found it hard to cope with the memories of my many transgressions. I recall a time in my mid-teens when I had taken off to Hollywood and run across a group of performance artists and decided to hang out with them for a couple of days. I actually dared to call my mother for a few hundred dollars. To my surprise, she agreed to meet me at the corner of Highland and Hollywood Boulevard with the requested money, and I excitedly told my new friends of the good fortune. We reached the corner and about fifteen to twenty minutes later my mom showed up, with my dad; "uh-oh," I muttered. Of course my father read me the riot act. He properly castigated me for having upset my mother so terribly, missing school, hanging out with derelicts and having had the nerve to seek funding for my misdeeds. As I turned to walk off down the street, my dad reached for my shoulder, at which point I flailed my arms and bumped his eyeglasses. I still recall, with shame and disgrace, seeing my loving father standing on Hollywood Boulevard, with a mixture of love, shock and intense sadness in his eyes, his glasses askew and a touch of blood on his face. Oh dear God, help and forgive me; I am so very unworthy!

The recognition of the evils I had perpetrated had begun in the fall of 1987, before my return to a life in Christ. As I shared some of my pain with Rachel, she was able to employ my disclosures as motivation for an acceptance of the Lord Jesus Christ as my Savior. That is, she sympathized with the intense hardships that I was suffering at the hands of both other inmates and Cellblock Six staff, as well as for the emerging guilt I had begun to experience. One attribute that really led me to fall in love with her was the way she always pointed to the necessity for my salvation. For example, there was one day that I had endured an especially spirited bout of verbal abuse in the recreation cages prior to going to the visitation area to see Rachel. It had become my practice to usually ignore the depraved rantings of others in the exercise area. That had the unintended effect of infuriating them, since their evilly crafted verbal darts did not result in stimulating a tangible response. On that particular occasion, several inmates had been proffering homosexual propositions. As I simply continued to work out on a weight machine, they became enraged and their insults began to take the shape of musings about sodomizing my mother, an obviously very upsetting set of events.

Soon after the visit with Rachel had started, it became apparent to her that something was wrong and she asked what the matter was. As I reiterated a few highlights (or rather, the "lowlights") of what had bothered me so much, I could see that she was becoming disturbed, so I changed the topic to discussing how difficult it was for me to refrain from retaliating with my own barrage of profane insults. Thus, rather than to continue dwelling on prior sorrows, we were able to consider cooperation with God's grace. Rachel knew that I was acquainted with Sacred Scripture as a consequence of having eagerly participated in the Episcopal Church as a child. She felt comfortable in steering the conversation to a description about one of Apostle Paul's imprisonments, during his second missionary journey: "Then the multitude rose up together against them; and the magistrates tore off their clothes and commanded them to be beaten with rods. And when they had laid many stripes on them, they threw them into prison, commanding the jailer to keep them securely. Having received such a charge, he put them into the inner prison and fastened their feet in the stocks. But at midnight Paul and Silas were praying and singing hymns to God, and the prisoners were listening to them." (Acts 16:22-25)

Rachel's intent was to guide me from self-pity to hope as she detailed how Apostle Paul, a faithful servant of God, had been unjustly cast into jail and beaten, yet did not permit worldly conditions or the attitudes of others to define how he felt or behaved. Instead, the Apostle kept his focus firmly fixed on God; thus, rather than feeling bitter over having been beaten and imprisoned, St. Paul was found singing joyful hymns to the Lord. At that early stage of seriously contemplating a return to Christianity, I did not know what to say about such an amazing account of faith in God. I responded by uttering something completely ridiculous. How Rachel so patiently endured my nonsensical irreverence, I'll never know. God bless her.

Although I intended to return to God, I fell victim to another interior conflict. While I had witnessed within Rachel the love and grace of God, actualities that had attracted me to the Lord, I also had a significant romantic attraction to Rachel. With the dawn of 1988, my desire to return to Protestantism grew more intense and surpassed, by far, the station of merely some passing fancy. Included within that development was a profound deliberation of all the damage that had resulted under the auspices of self-will. I had fully recognized the need to undertake an allegiance to Christianity as a way of life. A dedication that had to encompass complete obedience to the Lord had become a crystal clear necessity for me. Concurrent with my internal crisis, I desired to explore more than a casual involvement with Rachel; however, I was afraid that Rachel's interest in me was merely platonic. I thought that she was only intent upon inducing my conversion to Christianity and then either moving on or, at best, simply wishing to remain friends. Thus, over the initial weeks of 1988 I wrestled with whether my return to God would void any potential for romantic engagements. Perhaps, I ruminated,

Rachel may even misperceive my intention to pursue God as a misguided attempt to seek amorous relations with her. I eventually had several candid discussions with Rachel about my desire to re-approach relations with God, and about my feelings for her. Of course, none of those discussions were easy, and a recent debacle on my part significantly complicated things.

I had nearly made a terrible and tragic mistake in the fall of 1987, when I had begun to plan for my marriage to the nurse, Pamela, who was of Wiccan leanings. It was not that the relationship with her was going particularly well. Actually, I felt an undercurrent of unease that I now realize was God's small still voice instructing me to abort that unholy alliance. Speaking of God's influence and ungodly affairs, it must be said that one of the many factors of life on death row is the sense of abysmal rejection. It is pervasive – from society having discarded a person to the trash heap of irrelevancy by proclaiming that he is even unfit for its prisons; from the concomitant overwhelming sense of loneliness, which makes residents of death row highly susceptible to entering upon any relationship possible in a desperate attempt to feel needed. I'm not sure if that was the case with me and the witchcraft practitioner, but the liaison had the potential for confounding any romance between Rachel and myself. I had concerns about whether I seemed all too willing to leap from one relationship to another and about how solid of a candidate I appeared to have been for my darling Rachel. Thankfully, our focus on God saved us from a potential trap as we realized that it was the mad dash away from further involvement with the occult that had led to my severance of relations with Pamela; it was not merely some impulsive lark. Glory to God that engagements between the witch and myself began to chill and then ultimately vanished entirely. God's grace averted absolute disaster... and opened wide the portal for my true mate, Rachel.

After the near catastrophe with Pamela had been averted and the relationship between Rachel and me had taken a decidedly romantic turn, Rachel expressed her sense of disappointment when I had informed her of my marital intentions with the Wiccan. She told me of the sadness that had surprised her and which had compelled her to realize her desires for more than platonic interactions with me. She had kept silent about those inclinations until our early 1988 discussions, when she revealed her fear that perhaps I was contemplating Christianity only because of my longing for amorous involvements. Thus, it was a multitude of issues with which we were concerned – my growing inclination for a Christian walk; the fear of my hopes for romantic relations with Rachel remaining unfulfilled; Rachel's wishes for romantic developments between us; as well as her concern that my desires might be the animate force behind my pursuit of Christianity.

Having acknowledged our mutual hope for a romantic relationship left us with still having to abolish concerns that my return to God was not the result of romantic interests. After many profound dialogues, we firmly accepted that my becoming a Christian arose from a sincere aim for salvation, and we gladly embraced our having become equally yoked. Thus, putting God first when contemplating decisions is what has permitted us to navigate the myriad obstacles that my being on death row has inflicted. It was on the twentieth day of January 1988 that I accepted the Lord Jesus Christ as my Savior; I swore to learn about, follow and obey Christ Jesus.

Rachel had attended a Bible church in Tucson for about ten years and had labored faithfully toward God under the tutelage of that church's pastor. Much of what that entailed was her attending every Sunday service and at least one weekday service, along with having involved herself in church functions and reading a variety of Protestant publications. Since I was permitted several appliances, including a combination radio/cassette stereo, Rachel would sit in the front row of her church and record the services on a portable recorder. She would then send me the cassettes on a weekly basis so I could also listen to the teachings and study companion Scriptures. On our visits we would discuss the various doctrines that we had been taught and explore how to apply those principles in our lives. I was content with this pursuit of the life after Christ in that my commitment truly encompassed the active application of the Lord's commands, even though it remained very much an intellectual enterprise at that point.

It was all that Rachel and I would know of Christianity for more than a decade. Unfortunately, Orthodox Christianity is relatively unknown in the United States. In fact, as the collapse of the Soviet Union unfolded, I remember Protestants' discussions about the purported need for them to "Christianize" Russia. It seemed to be at the forefront of their concerns. They were simply not aware that Russia had become Orthodox in the tenth century. Nor did they have any knowledge of its seminal role in Christian history during the fifteenth century to nineteenth century Turkish rule of what had been the Byzantine Empire. In fact, Protestants did not recognize any presence of Christianity in Turkey since the first century churches of Asia Minor. Of course Asia Minor, or modern day Turkey, has been the seat of the Ecumenical Patriarch since the fourth century.

It was in the months subsequent to my re-acceptance of a life after Christ that romantic affiliations between Rachel and me took off, so much so that by mid-spring of 1988 we determined to be an exclusive item. It culminated in my asking Rachel to marry me in April of 1988. I must say that my proposal definitely frightened Rachel. It was, obviously, a most understandable response. For her to not only have contemplated marrying someone who was in prison, but who had also been condemned to death for a crime that had inflamed the community in which she had spent her entire life was a big deal. After all, I was still seen as public enemy number one; what an unexpected development for God's little angel. I felt extraordinarily guilty about not having considered my proposal of marriage from the perspective of someone who had to endure being in love with a man who was utterly reviled by the metropolis in which she resided. However, Rachel did decide to become engaged to me... with the understanding that a marriage might never occur. In other words, the purpose of our having become engaged was based on continuing to develop our relations within the romantic arena, while also continuing our joint pursuit of God.

Although 1988 went fairly well, during that summer threats against my life became what security staff described as "imminent" and I was moved into protective segregation. While I & I (Intelligence and Investigation Unit of the Arizona Department of Corrections) believed that the immediate danger to my life had been defused by my transfer to another part of Cellblock Six, my new environment placed other strains upon me. Protective segregation is a strange locale. Most of the inmates housed there had been placed in this setting as a consequence of endangerment from others. Therefore, their fervent desire to not be stigmatized by protective custody housing frequently resulted in their attempt to play "tough guy". The combination of my being the "rookie" in my new residence and still being seen as notorious placed a huge bull's eye on my back. I was not at an extremely high degree of risk from life-threatening attacks, but there was still significant danger to my safety, as well as the likelihood of insidious, obnoxious assaults.

The area into which I had been placed looked like a flattened out "V" shape, with eight cells on the lower tiers and eight more cells on the upper tier. It housed a total of sixteen inmates, inmates who thought that throwing substances on each other made them manly. Thus, I had rotten milk, watered-down feces, urine and other foul liquids thrown into my cell and on me whenever those miscreants sought to puff up their self-image. Their reprobate actions usually occurred when an inmate was being let out of his cell for a shower (we were permitted to go to and from the shower stalls sans handcuffs). The offender would then sneak up on my cell and toss his putrid cocktail at me while I was unsuspectingly listening to church tapes (and making notes) or listening to music (while doing university work or writing Rachel). The danger came when someone decided to heat some water and then try to hit me with boiling liquids. Unfortunately, I often retaliated by hurling colorful insults or proffering verbal threats of violence. Thanks to the Good Lord's grace, there was no way I could have physically confronted my attackers and utilized my martial fighting skills. If I had done so, then it would have been because I wanted, not merely to discourage them from any further assaults on me, but also because my pride goaded me to try and save face.

In the midst of that diabolical setting, yet another of God's good Samaritans appeared. My parents were thrilled by my return to the Lord and had arranged for a local Episcopal priest to begin visiting me. Father John was the priest at the Episcopal Church in Coolidge. From about the fall of 1988, our initial visits took place at the front of my cell, and were then changed to an attorney's visiting room, before being exiled to the non-contact visitation area. Unfortunately, our interactions were rather perfunctory as I spent most of our allotted time merely railing against my conditions and neglected to take advantage of Father John's breadth of knowledge. Still, he kindly instituted a monthly visiting schedule, one that continued for several decades, even after his having been re-assigned to St. Michael's in Tucson. Again, I stand in awe of God's grace.

Troubles of another sort found me in late 1988. There was a prisoner who had been a huge thorn in the prison's side for years; however, an accident that took the sight from one of his eyes culminated in an infection that traveled to his other eye, so that "Stoney" ended up totally blind. In an attempt to be rid of him, Stoney was transferred out of state, but was eventually returned to Arizona. Because of his blindness, he was brought straight to the protective segregation unit where I was housed. During my nearly ten years in the California prison system, I was known as a somewhat successful "jailhouse lawyer" – a prisoner who files lawsuits and/or other pleadings for convicts. My prowess in legal arenas continued after I had arrived in Arizona: there was the successful litigation that flowed from the illegal extradition in Texas; a variety of civil and criminal pleadings filed in Arizona courts on behalf of other prisoners while in the county jail, and so forth. Therefore, Cellblock Six's administrators decided to grant me a job as an inmate legal representative; the blind prisoner was assigned to my caseload.

At the time, I had been on death row for nearly a year and a half. Endeavors to obey Christ had been generally successful; relations with Rachel had progressed; I was proficient in pursuing my education at college; I had not received any disciplinary reports (tickets or write-ups). In California prisons, I had always very aggressively litigated all of the court actions that I had filed; however, that did not turn out to be a wise choice in Arizona. Within weeks after beginning to represent "Stoney" a number of guards began to harass and threaten me. They did not take kindly to a prisoner with charges like mine assisting another inmate with actions against the prison. I had re-animated two previously filed lawsuits against Cellblock Six staff, both involving "Stoney" having been assaulted by Cellblock Six personnel. My having breathed life back into both suits upset prison officials since they had thought the cases to have been abandoned. Satan is a persistent beast, always tempting us in areas where we are weakest. I was ensnared by the appeal to my pride and sense of fairness. I wondered why they had assigned me, a successful jailhouse lawyer, to represent "Stoney" if they did not intend a vigorous pursuit of previously filed suits. Furthermore, officers' threats, after all of the abuse suffered by inmates, infuriated me even more. Of course, I knew that to continue representing prisoners, especially the blind inmate, would not be in my best interests, yet to cave in to the intimidation of guards seemed so offensive to my pride. In discussing the predicament with Rachel, she again directed my attention to the Apostle Paul. (As Protestants, we had no knowledge of the rich examples left by saints and Church Fathers.) Rather than gripe about prison injustices, Apostle Paul transfixed all focus on God. If only I had heeded my angel's advice.

For the next year and a half I engaged in fierce battles with guards and the prison system in general; in other words, I was guided by the passion of pride. How did this work out for me? Well, not very well at all! I litigated many actions on behalf of inmates, including attacks in the courts on criminal convictions and/or sentences, civil lawsuits on medical neglect or conditions of confinement issues, and representations before disciplinary committees that frequently resulted in not guilty findings or the dismissal of charges. I recall several slip and fall lawsuits, an action that I would file after a prisoner had fallen on a wet floor, that resulted in successful settlements. And I had successfully deliberated quite a few cases of indifference to serious medical needs litigations, such as the one over an inmate not being taken for an x-ray, despite having broken his ankle in a freak accident. Plus, I achieved favorable results in a few criminal court cases, such as when pursuing parole for "Stoney" from his fifteen-to-life sentence, as well as when seeking to have his four twenty-five-to-life sentences run concurrently. (These sentences were imposed after "Stoney" managed to obtain a handgun in Central Unit, which he then used to shoot and kill four gang members). At any rate, the end result was tireless harassment by Cellblock Six staff. During this time, I was found guilty of more than a dozen disciplinary infractions and incurred the rabid wrath of many staff members. And I did all of it in a misguided attempt to invoke a sense of respect from other prisoners by not backing down, even under the insanely intense pressure.

All of that conflict culminated in two actions that cemented my eventual transfer from Cellblock Six to the control unit at Special Management Unit One. The first was a massive conditions of confinement lawsuit, filed on behalf of myself against over sixty staff members, including guards, supervisors, administrators, personnel in the Phoenix central office, medical persons and others. I ultimately settled this lawsuit in exchange for a contact marriage and an ensuant two hour contact visit. Obviously, my "declaration of war" only served to exacerbate tensions and retaliation. Then, I poured fuel onto the fire. The devil certainly had his claws in me because I opted to significantly participate in a class action lawsuit that had been filed by the American Civil Liberties Union. (A class action involves litigation on behalf of many prisoners, who are all similarly situated, and this one involved inmates from institutions across the state.) Since I was only one of two plaintiffs from Cellblock Six, the resultant abuse by guards was immediate and immense. On one instance, I had been preparing for a visit with Rachel and was unable to attend to my assigned duty for that day, so I secured permission from the officer to continue shaving. When I returned from the visit, the same guard informed me that he had reported me for having refused to work. Then he launched into a series of verbal taunts, such as, "How do ya like that Atwood?" and "Come on! Do something about it!" When he failed to solicit the desired reaction, he actually began to shove me while informing me that if I continued my involvement with the ACLU, my safety could not be ensured. I was handcuffed in a hallway, alone with that brute as all of this transpired. Finally, I calmly asked to see his supervisor. For my audacity, I was given two additional disciplinary reports, one for supposedly refusing to return to my cell and the other one for having attempted to start a riot. On other occasions, guards threw ice at me, or would search my cell and seize all of my university textbooks. Still, I refused to relent. Instead I stubbornly acted, once again, from merely a worldly and passionate perspective.

I suppose that my blindness to God was, in part, derived from the small peek I had had at the supposedly good deeds in which I was then participating. At the time I was listening to two to three weekly church service tapes. I had also earned an associate of arts degree from Central Arizona College and was pursuing a second one from Ohio University. With my eyes fixed firmly on worldly achievements, it was no wonder that I persisted in seeing court actions against the prison as the correct path upon which to tread. The results were devastating. They wreaked spiritual and worldly havoc on me, and also infected my precious Rachel. In the worldly realm, things came to a head in the fall of 1990 when

I was accused of having taken part in a violation in which I had played absolutely no role. Admittedly, I had listened to music at a loud volume innumerable times and during all hours. This time, however, a prisoner downstairs began to play his stereo full blast in the middle of the night and because of my history of this same pattern of misconduct, the guards presumed that it was my stereo. Within minutes two officers and a sergeant rushed up the stairs and appeared in front of my cell where they breathlessly informed me that I was to receive a write-up. Several officers had remained in the hallway from where they had a clear view of my cell. They could see that my stereo was on the table while I had continuously remained on my bed. There was no way for me to have turned off the music, but I guess it just was not in their best interests to countermand a supervisor. Given my innocence in the matter and the adverse turn of events, I unfortunately bowed to the temptation to belligerently protest. My protests fell on deaf ears; they ordered me to be handcuffed so that they could re-move my television set and stereo from the cell. Interestingly, they were not permitted to seize my items, as the es-tablished procedure was for them to issue a disciplinary report and then allow that process to unfold; or, if they believed that a disturbance would continue, then de-partment protocol allowed them to turn off the electric-ity. Undoubtedly, I was be-ing unfairly treated, but to refuse direct orders to place my hands out through the food trap and allow officers to handcuff me was certain-ly not the appropriate and

A food tray attached to the door of one of the cells of Cell Block 6.

godly way to address injustice... as I was soon to find out.

The sergeant threatened to have his officers "suit up". (This means to get dressed in riot gear so that they could then rush into my cell and perform a forced extraction.) This took place during the graveyard shift, and since I'd never heard of a nighttime cell extraction, I did not believe their threat to suit up. (I later learned that there was some sort of bounty on who could instigate an incident with me that would result in the administration's ability to transfer me to Cellblock Eight, the control unit at SMU I, and that the graveyard shift intended to collect on that bounty.)

Upon my refusal to comply with any of their instructions, the gaggle of officers retreated out of the pod, only to return in about a half hour... in full riot gear. I was lying on my bed, having completely ignored further commands to be handcuffed. Then, to my utter surprise, the cell door opened and about half a dozen guards rushed in behind a riot shield. I continued to remain lying on my bed, offering absolutely no resistance. Nevertheless, I was lifted off of the bed and slammed, face down, on the concrete floor. Several officers began to viciously strike me in the ribs and kidneys with their knees, while another guard grabbed a handful of my hair and smashed my forehead against the concrete over and over again. While that brutal assault continued, other officers handcuffed my hands behind my back and shackled my feet. Eventually I was yanked into a standing position, and then rushed down the stairs and out of the pod. En route to an isolation cell, guards on either side of me attempted to inflict further pain by squeezing pressure points in my neck area while uttering threats and obscenities. Again, I offered no opposition. When we reached the isolation cell, I was thrown onto the bed with such force that my head crashed into the wall. Then, of course, I had to endure another brutal attack on my kidneys as the restraints were being removed. Unfortunately, my patience expired and I leapt off of the bed and struck a guard in the head with enough force to have sent him to the hospital.

Obviously, I received a write-up for having assaulted a

correctional officer, as well as one for having refused to be handcuffed. A search of my property the next day uncovered an abundance of postage stamps. A third ticket was therefore issued for the possession of contraband. Seeing that I had only one recent minor write-up, the disciplinary officer counted my disobeying a direct order and possession of contraband as minor infractions, and sentenced me to a loss of privileges term. By noting the major assault on staff in his disciplinary report, he figured that it was more than enough to accomplish my transfer to SMU I.

Circumstances became more intense subsequent to my having assaulted the officer. I had incited the understandable anger of the guards by attacking one of their own. Their desire to exact retribution permeated their treatment of me. For instance, there was an incident while I was being escorted from the law library back to my cell; a guard did his utmost to compel a physical confrontation. As we exited the law library the officer spoke to one of his colleagues about an upcoming deer hunting trip, expressing his wish that I could accompany him on the excursion, because it would mean that I would never come back. When I kept silent, the officer continued his verbal offensive by focusing on my fiancé. Rachel is a bit on the skinny side, so he suggested that she had contracted AIDS by having permitted all of the Black boys in Tucson to have their turn with her. I then made a few comments about well-known rumors surrounding his sexual perversions, but immediately noticed a handful of guards at the top of the stairs near my pod door. I made it back into my cell without further incident. A couple of days later a friendly guard told me that the episode had been a set-up. The officers involved had intended to provoke a conflict wherein they could assault me without the presence of a camera. (When staff suits up to rush a prisoner's cell, a camera must record the scene, whereas a spontaneous confrontation permits the use of force sans a camcorder.) The aim had been for them to have beaten me severely without any repercussions on them. Moreover, the "friendly" further informed me about the day shift's displeasure that I had not been badly injured during the graveyard cell extraction. He warned me to exercise great care, since they intended to continue their endeavors to incite a disturbance.

The disciplinary report I had incurred for having assaulted staff was dismissed on a technicality. Because the disciplinary officer had taken too long to hold a hearing, the case had to be tossed. Of course, not only was he furious over that development, but it increased pressure on him to have me sent to the SMU I control unit. The plan had always been my move to Cellblock Eight and a prime opportunity had vanished. Thus, the disciplinary officer embarked upon a series of shenanigans that would lead to my transfer. Despite his having already known of my three minor disciplinary reports within a ninety-day period, he lied by feigning ignorance about it. The prison must issue a ticket within twenty-four hours of becoming aware that a violation has occurred and the hearing officer had known of my three minors within ninety days for a month or two. He issued me a ticket and then pursued the violation as a major infraction. That would allow the raising of my institutional risk score from a four to a five and trigger my transfer to the Special Management Unit. In order to also ensure a finding of guilt he formed a disciplinary hearing committee that was made up of his friends from another unit. Consequently, a finding of guilt was preordained, as was my relocation to CB-8 in early February of 1991.

Up until 1997 death row had been housed in the administrative segregation unit (ad seg) known as Cellblock Six (CB-6) and there was also the Special Management Unit (SMU I) that was several miles down the road. SMU I had opened late in the 1980s; believe me, it was a nightmare. Then again, once in SMU I, and separated from the CB-6 turmoil, I began to realize God's grace. Even while I had begun to resume old characteristics such as pride, anger and disdain for authority while in Cellblock Six, I had maintained a steadfast dedication toward consistent Bible study, doctrinal examinations from various Protestant fundamentalist ministries and church service tapes sent by Rachel. Unfortunately, much of what I learned subsisted as merely intellectual or theoretical fodder. My anger and pride blinded me such that the putting into practice of the teachings that I so carefully studied was elusive. With time in SMU I to refocus on Christ's commands, I had a real opportunity to renew my efforts at applying scriptural mandates. However, my endeavors were mostly absent the grace of God, as they were propelled by meager human willpower.

My stay at SMU I spanned about six months, from February of 1991 until July of 1991, during which time I was labeled a model prisoner by the unit's major. I took anger management courses and endeavored to not merely learn Christ's commands, but to implement them in my daily life.

There was one development that became a significant challenge. The degenerative back disease that had begun to plague me prior to my departure from Cellblock Six became so bad that I collapsed several times and required injections for relief. In fact, eventually I had to be transported to the Maricopa Medical Center in Phoenix on three occasions for treatment. Since 1991, I have had to use a lower back support apparatus, a transcutaneous electrical nerve stimulator, as well as various medications, such as pain pills and anti-inflammatories on a continuous basis.

Upon my return to Cellblock Six I noticed that the majority of officers with whom I had experienced difficulties no longer worked in CB-6. I had an opportunity for a fresh start. Once again God's grace had blessed me, and with a re-energized sense of purpose, I renewed my pursuit of God.

About a month after my return, I was taken off of protective segregation status and placed in a sixteen-man pod with a much better class of inmates. The drawback was that severe abuse continued in the recreation pens. One alarming development was the onset of rock throwing. Prisoners in adjacent pens would gather marble-sized rocks or pieces of concrete and hurl them at me through the openings in the chain link fencing. It seemed that staff encouraged the behavior; after all, it occurred right in front of them. Thankfully I escaped those assaults with only occasional minor injuries. I was also subjected to one particular form of abuse by staff, perhaps a remnant strand of retaliation or maybe as a consequence of my charges. During searches of my cell, guards would frequently engage in what they jokingly referred to as "seek and destroy missions." They would dump boxes of paperwork all over my cell and then seize all of my schoolbooks. We were permitted seven books, but the Cellblock Six deputy warden had provided me with a waiver that authorized all required university textbooks in addition to the seven book limit. The guards knew this, yet they still made off with the textbooks because they knew it would be a several week process to secure their return. Nevertheless, I worked diligently on my studies and was able to earn a second associate arts degree. I subsequently continued at Ohio University and worked toward a Bachelor of Arts degree as a pre-law English major.

As Rachel and I continued our pursuit of God, and with my determination to no longer be distracted by prisoner or staff antics, our discussions of marriage also became more concentrated. I'll never forget the exquisite autumn day in 1991 when, after having been engaged for three and a half years, Rachel told me she was ready to be married! I nearly fell off of my chair. I had difficulty breathing, because my heart was pounding so hard. Prior to having landed on death row I had never wished to be married. It seemed unfair to enter into marital commitments to then only travel around the country alone or to maintain the practice of going in and out of prison. Then, once I was on death row, and for all of the wrong reasons, I had intended to marry a heathen – the Wiccan – simply to feel included. Rachel and I had discussed our views of marriage; we believed it was so much more than some contractual obligation. We understood it as the literal joining of souls. Certainly, there were legal advantages to marriage, aside from those that are routinely enjoyed by connubial couples outside of prison. For us, it would mean legal rights for Rachel to visit, inquire about my welfare and so on. However, given the circumstances of our physical separation, the focus of our relationship had centered on spiritual concerns. So, to unite my soul to Rachel's was truly an incredibly wonderful manifestation of God's grace; "And the two shall become one" (Gen. 2:24).

On the 17th of December 1991, with my mother and Rachel's father in attendance, we were married by our Bible church pastor. As part of an arrangement that included my having agreed to drop the huge lawsuit that I had lodged in 1989 against dozens of state employees, Rachel and I were granted a contact wedding. It was the first time we touched, and I was in heaven.

Visiting in Cellblock Six and SMUs was between glass – except for a brief period in Cellblock Six, from 1994 to 1997, when an incentive program of varying levels, some of which gave death row inmates contact visits, had been implemented. In both the Arizona Department of Corrections' administrative segregation building (CB-6) and control units (SMU I and SMU II), visitors are brought to a common room, averaging approximately 40' x 40', while each prisoner is lodged into a separate minuscule 4' x 5' cage. Inmates in the supermax setting have only a stool, affixed to a post bolted to the floor, upon which to sit and there is an 18" wide counter between the stool and the window. Visitors have a similar counter in front of the window and use plastic chairs as seating. The window that separates prisoners from visitors is very thick and measures about 5' x 5'. In CB-6 visitors and prisoners communicate over a telephone, while in the SMU conversation occurs through what are called "acoustic strips" (little strips of metal on each side of the window with dozens of small holes, constructed in such a way that they prevent any possibility of passing anything through them.

Following the wedding, again as part of having settled the lawsuit, Rachel and I were allowed a two-hour contact visit. We entered a 10' x 10' or so room, and were able to hug and kiss and sit at a table, which seemed as if it would have been more at home in a park as a picnic table. We had to sit on opposite sides of the table, but could hold hands. Of course I also took the opportunity to again hug and kiss God's angel at the conclusion of our visit.

Subsequent to our marriage, Rachel and I continued thirsting for God. There were all too frequent times over the next handful of years (from 1992 until my 1997 departure from Cellblock Six) when the destructive serpent of pride would overtake me, mostly when I became blind to the grace of God's medicine. This would commonly entail: my confronting some perceived affront or unfair situation, such as inmates viciously abusing me or staff ignoring policies; failing to recognize the adversity at issue in order to uproot deeply buried passions; and reacting sinfully. A prime example of my blindness transpired in the summer of 1995, when Rachel required a very serious operation.

At that time Cellblock Six death row prisoners had been classified to one of three different program stages. As a level one inmate I was able to enjoy occasional contact visits with immediate family members. Rachel was to undergo surgery. Shortly thereafter her father planned to see me so that he could offer me comfort and explain in detail how my wife was faring. Apparently, there was some confusion regarding the scheduling of visits in the sole contact visitation room. The visitation officer had inadvertently slated two at the same time (both my father-in-law and another prisoner's wife). Instead of providing each with an hour in the contact visitation room (visits were two hours), my contact visit with Rachel's dad was cancelled. I knew that disappointments happen in life, and that as a pursuer of a Christian walk I was to put faith into action during times of difficulty. I had learned that when unfairness or other adversities arose, I was to draw upon the Lord's promise that "all things work together for the good for those who love God" (Ro. 8:28). Unfortunately, when I was informed that my contact visit had been cancelled, my watchfulness suffered a lapse. Rather than accept my spiritual medicine, I permitted the demons of anger, pride and despondency to enter the gate of my heart. My reaction to the disappointment of losing a contact visit had not one iota of humiliation as I erupted in a vile display of distemper. I not only screamed profane insults at the visitation officer, but also fell so far as to have threatened his life. The severe discipline that ensued was the obvious outcome of my fall, but it fails to reveal the entire plethora of damage I had done. My precious wife had to endure recuperating from major surgery under the duress of concern for her husband and sorrow over my lapse. My father-in-law suffered shame and disappointment; he had no idea of my antics as he, along with other visitors, was being escorted toward the visiting area and only observed my being dragged down a hallway by half a dozen officers. The infection I had inflicted upon my soul was incalculable – nor did I realize that the infection would extend to the soul of my wife.

At that point in our pursuit of God, Rachel and I had absolutely no accurate understanding of suffering. While we had some comprehension of the need to ever increase our faith and to flee from sin, our type of wholly rudimentary apprehension utterly failed to illumine sacred Scripture. Our affiliation with non-denominational Protestantism, an offshoot or strain of Fundamentalism and Evangelism, required an understanding and acceptance of that unsupportable philosophy of eternal salvation that occurs at the moment of belief in the Lord Jesus Christ, otherwise known as: "eternal security". Once it is attained, it can never be lost. Looking back upon that fallacy now, it is so readily apparent that its origins are so far from godly that it may be termed demonic. Eternal security precepts add to our blindness to our need to struggle toward salvation. In other words, when we pilot along under the "once saved, always saved" delusion there is no concept of why the Christian undergoes or needs to undergo suffering. With no salvation to lose, the need to endure to the end in order to have a hope of heaven cannot even be imagined. Still, Rachel and I did our best to endure suffering unto the Lord; or rather, she did her best and guided me along.

There were times when I confronted disappointment and was able to abide patiently until I could speak with my faithful wife. One such all too rare occurrence transpired in the summer of 1993, when I was transferred from one sixteen-man pod to another. Despite having been moved into a better class of inmates in 1991, tension continued between other prisoners and myself. I was not always humble about having embarked upon the pursuit of God or having engaged in higher education; plus the benefit of being supported by a loyal and loving wife stimulated jealousy from others. Saddled as I was, albeit unjustly, with a notorious high profile case, was yet one more reason for other prisoners' hostility toward me. Thus, in the summer of 1993, my pod-mates initiated a concerted effort to have me moved. Their undertaking had its roots in the long standing and common practice of inmates sending kites (forms that a prisoner fills out and then sends to staff). My pod-mates had submitted kites that warned of danger to my safety, their pretext being that it would be wise to move me. They achieved their intention by circulating a petition which suggested my endangerment and urged my removal. All but a couple of prisoners had signed it. I was moved all right, smack dab in the middle of the same inmates who had been throwing rocks at me and spitting on me in the exercise pens. I did my best to seek God's grace in helping me refrain from reacting until I was able to discuss it with Rachel. We both saw it as such a ridiculously irresponsible and dangerous course of action, in that those who were charged with ensuring my well-being had placed me in proximity to those who had been routinely attacking me. Rachel and I could only conclude that God had a purpose beyond our meager human understanding, so we placed our faith more fully in Him.

Predictably, things rapidly worsened. What began as the relatively constant yelling of insults and threats, along with the occasional throwing of items when I was locked in the shower, soon turned into much more emboldened attacks as the other prisoners noticed the absence of any staff response toward the abuse. I endured for several months until the assaults could really no longer be ignored – not with inmates breaking out of the locked shower to then hurl boiling water into my cell or throw batteries, feces and urine at my cell. Every incident I experienced is an extraordinary example of how God protects His servants from harm, for I was never seriously injured, and of how He lovingly guides us toward purification via seemingly disastrous circumstances.

Amidst such pressures, I continued to pursue a bachelor's degree from Ohio University. However, my intent to be awarded an undergraduate diploma in English and to then attend law school was derailed. Then President Clinton had signed into law a decree that effectively did away with Pell grants for prisoners. It eroded a good portion of my funding for law school tuition fees. Moreover, there was intense pressure, from both private sector and government entities, to cease the admittance of prisoners to law school. The likely motivation for that campaign was that, upon finishing law school, an inmate could not take the bar exam and practice law, so an incarcerated person's presence at law school was considered to be the waste of a position that a potential attorney should have. I also suspect, since it was the government against which inmates nearly always brought suit, that it was the state and federal agencies which lobbied for our preclusion from law school. I saw it as a way for them to make it more difficult for prisoners – to further tilt the already extremely lopsided field upon which prisoners were forced to litigate. Fortunately, I realized that it would be counterproductive to pursue legal action in court for perceived inequities. It would be akin to suing God for having provided His loving grace. I did receive a bachelor's degree in the mid-1990s; but instead of applying to law schools, I was accepted to the graduate program at the California State University at Dominguez Hills (CSUDH) as a candidate for a Master's degree in literature.

The terrible fallout from the visitation fiasco that had occurred in the summer of 1995 forced us to sense that attendance at some self-proclaimed Bible church left us ill-equipped in our thirst for God. Unfortunately, it took another misstep by me to cement that realization.

Late in 1995 our Bible church pastor recruited me to intervene in his young teenage daughter's drug abuse. At the time I thought it would be a wise strategy to develop a rapport and aura of trust with his daughter by establishing my credentials in the drug trade. Thus, I spent time with her reminiscing about my prior adventures in the world of contraband substances. It seems to me now that I had once again succumbed to the sin of pride by acceding to the temptation to appear cool or hip. Having faced such intense hatred and abuse on death row, I sought the rehabilitation of my tarnished image via impressing a naive kid by disclosing past misdeeds. It was not long before the pastor learned of our discussions. He wasted no time in making my errors public by telling one congregation member after another that I was satan incarnate, and that I was in no way shape or form a fledgling Christian. He even went so far as to express his view that it was a waste of tax payer money to keep me alive and furthermore, he would gladly volunteer to be my executioner. Rachel and I were terribly hurt by his remarks, especially since they issued from our longtime pastor. Nevertheless, we strove to see my portion of responsibility for his anger and soldiered onward. It was at about the same time that the pastor began lessons on 1 John about the love of God. Under a shroud of embarrassment, Rachel would attend church, sit through and record those sermons, send me the cassettes so I could listen, and then discuss the teachings on visits with me. Admittedly, it was extremely difficult for us to listen to those sermons on the indispensable need for love while remembering the nasty attitude of that man toward us. In addition to his continued campaign against me, he also besmirched Rachel for having stayed with me. As the strain began to wear on us, we wondered whether God was prompting us to embark upon a new direction. After significant deliberation, we left that establishment in 1996; unfortunately, we still knew nothing about the Holy Apostolic Orthodox Church.

We initially affiliated ourselves with an evangelical church in Tucson. We continued with the same arrangement of Rachel recording services to then send me the tapes so we could study what had been taught. Neither of us were very excited. I'm not sure whether we really knew why our enthusiasm had waned, but in hindsight we now definitely realize that God was speaking to us, urging us to come home to the one true Church. For my part, I felt there was something missing – not only from that particular evangelical church, but from Protestantism in general. It seemed to me that Protestantism, or Western Christianity, was some mere intellectual pursuit. I perceived that what was being offered from Protestant pulpits were attempts to hijack the Lord's teachings as vehicles by which to achieve success in worldly endeavors. If that was indeed the case, I reasoned, then Western Christianity made claims in direct contrast to Christ Jesus' proclamations about why the world will hate and abuse His children. I searched for something more, for a system wherein the aim was to depart the world, to transform my own inner world. In my quest, I even delved into monastic Buddhism, Taoism and other Eastern philosophies.

At that time, my post-conviction lawyer uncovered what was thought to have been categorical evidence of my innocence. (In post-conviction court proceedings any new evidence can be presented to the trial court in an attempt to obtain a re-trial by jury or some other form of relief. Such proceedings occur after trial, sentencing and direct appeal to the state supreme court.) I will never forget my forty-first birthday in January of 1997. My attorney had learned that Vicki Lynn Hoskinson had to have been buried for at least a couple of months. The bomb shell fact of her burial meant that I could not have kidnapped and murdered Vicki Lynn due to the amount of time it would have taken for me to have dug a grave. Further evidence of my innocence could be seen in the fact that someone had to have exhumed partial remains while I was in jail and then placed them in the desert where they had been found... in a locale that had previously been searched, again, subsequent to my arrest. Thus, as Christmas of 1996 approached, my lawyer filed the final post-conviction relief pleadings in court. We had real hope that after the required evidentiary hearing (a sort of mini-trial where evidence that supported how the victim had to have been buried could be presented) I would be exonerated and released. Just days prior to my forty-first birthday the judge dismissed the entire claim, in contravention of the overwhelming evidence of innocence and absent the mandatory evidentiary hearing.

When what is called a "colorable" claim has been alleged, state and federal law requires that a post-conviction relief court hold an evidentiary hearing. In general terms, a colorable claim is one that if taken as true would probably have changed the verdict at trial. My attorney had secured the assistance of a nationally renowned forensics expert who concluded that Vicki Lynn undoubtedly had to have been buried; the presence of adipocere, or grave wax, on her bones was amongst the determining factors. The state could not come up with a single expert to rebut the fact of burial and merely proffered some inane lay person opinions in opposition. Of course, the judge sided with the government. Even though the law required him to construe the claim of burial as true and to hold an evidentiary hearing, these measures did not occur.

Rachel and I were crushed. To this day we are still unsure of God's purpose in having opened the door to my release, via incontrovertible proof of absolute innocence, to only allow the door to be slammed shut. We continue to trust in Him and to pray for enlightenment, since that is His will.

As the year of 1997 continued to unfold, I finally began to release my inner anger. I had always felt a sort of dark presence lingering somewhere just beyond the bounds of consciousness. I knew of its existence and, therefore, always felt a sense of nervousness, as if I was ever on the verge of confrontation. In the summer of 1997 the ominous presence momentarily departed and I began to relax. As I let God's grace fill me, the demon of anger had no choice but to flee; glory be to God.

Then, in the middle of summer, there was a disaster on the death row chain gang. In the mid-1990s condemned row inmates were required to go on a chain gang, an activity that involved ten prisoners at a time being escorted to a field that was near Cellblock Six to work in a vegetable garden. Having suffered with degenerative back disease since 1990, along with never having been permitted to work around other prisoners (I couldn't have a job in the kitchen, on any of the cleaning crews, in the law library or elsewhere.), precluded me from chain gang duty.

One chain gang inmate had convinced his wife to show up on the other side of the fence with an automatic rifle so that, under the cover of her fire, he could make a run for it. Well, the guards were also well-armed; predictably, both the prisoner and his wife were shot and killed. What was not as expected was how the Arizona Department of Corrections used this tragic incident to transfer all hundred-plus death row inmates from CB-6 to the far worse dungeon that is Special Management Unit II (SMU II). Rachel and I had to progress in our thirst for God under very different circumstances. I felt the dark presence of anger return.

An Arizona State Prison Complex SMU-II entrance.

10-man pod on death row in SMU II.

Chapter Ten

Coming Home

S pecial Management Unit II. One would think that one lockdown unit, wherein prisoners are confined in a cell for twenty-three and a half hours a day, would be about the same as any other, but the difference between SMU II and Cellblock Six nears the distinction between being at home and residing in a local jail. Some of the more dire changes from CB-6 to SMU-II included:

- no windows
- a cell light on 24 hours a day
- loss of my word processing typewriter
- other property item losses (the stereo system with home components [separate 80 watt receiver, dual cassette deck, and compact disc player], hair dryer, hot pot, etc.)
- no hobby craft (beadery, painting, etc.)
- termination of all contact visitation
- inability to ambulate back and forth to the shower absent handcuffs and a police escort
- no more hot lunches (only a bagged meal)
- cessation of any work activities

115   **114**

SMU II death row cell (outside view)

SMU II death row cell interior (facing outside)

SMU II death row cell interior.

Since most death row inmates presented no disciplinary problem whatsoever, draconian reductions were simply unnecessary, given that the sole prisoner responsible for the chain gang fiasco had been killed. The September 1997 transfer to the Arizona Department of Corrections' control unit brought about a time of abject sorrow for me.

Interestingly, upon having been informed that condemned row was being transferred to Special Management Unit II, I had surmised that I knew all that was necessary to know about it, given my previous 1991 stint in SMU I. (Other than there being eight cells per pod in SMU I and ten cells per pod in SMU II, SMU I and SMU II are exactly alike.) I could not have been more wrong. SMU I had been run with military precision, so there was the comfort of knowing what to expect on a day-to-day basis. At SMU II the emphasis fell upon the creation of uncertainty. By the mid-1990s prisons had honed their skills in ensuring prisoner compliance and keeping prisoners off balance. In other words, by focusing prisoner concerns on what the institution can control (such as mail delivery, property policies, store purchases, visit or phone call schedules, etc.) and then never consistently holding to a set pattern of implementation, the prisoners were kept in a constant state of uncertainty. In fact, rules violated by staff to accomplish this objective furthered their ability to reshape the mental construct of control unit residents.[5]

Another interesting development, as a result of the move to SMU II, was one that also came as a surprise. Given the inherent deprivations behind prison walls, it only makes sense that an attachment to the material world diminishes for those who are incarcerated. However, during my initial weeks in SMU II I learned that things were different. Within a day or two of my arrival I was provided with my television set, but the receipt of the rest of my property took a few weeks. The delay caused a significant feeling of unease that I attributed to having been pirated

---

5   See: *Control Unit Prisons* at www.churchfathertheology.com.

Los Angeles Times Magazine

October 19, 2003

The Cruelest Prison

With Utterly Stark Cellblocks, Pelican Bay
Has Perfected the Science of Isolation.
But Is It a Breeding Ground for Insanity?

By Vince Beiser

11´ X 22´ recreation room in SMU II

away to SMU II so suddenly. However, once my several small boxes of property were delivered, I was stunned at my reaction. I had set up my house (The way prisoners arrange their belongings in a cell offers the sole opportunity to exert a sense of individuality.) and then been escorted to the SMU recreation area, a room that is approximately 11' x 22' with twenty-foot high walls and a wire mesh ceiling, to do a little running. For the first time, since having been transferred to the supermax unit, I had the benefit of my personal items. Obviously, staff went through our meager belongings with a fine tooth comb, and a tremendous amount of it was deemed to have been contraband and seized. As I jogged around the exercise pen I had feelings of satisfaction and fulfillment. The exaggerated sense of well-being, as a result of the minuscule gathering of my trinkets, truly opened my eyes to the human propensity for attachment to material possessions.

The restrictions on property items in SMU II even impacted medically prescribed appliances. Since 1991 I had benefitted from the use of the TENS unit and a back brace. After I was placed in SMU II, the effort to have these medically necessary apparatuses for my degenerative back provided to me proved to be a long and especially arduous undertaking. Additionally, I was never allowed the prescribed heat treatment. Instead of a heating pad, or even a rubber hot water bottle, the SMU medical staff handed me a towel and instructed me to soak it in lukewarm water from my sink and then apply it to my back. Instead of my back brace, after nearly a year, I was given an ace bandage wrap as back support. It was many months until I finally received the TENS unit. In fact, it even took nearly a month to obtain any pain medication.

At the same time that I was desperately endeavoring to receive any treatment for my degenerative back, I was given a piece of devastating medical news: I had been infected by the Hepatitis C virus. While outside of prison in 1984, I had shared hypodermic syringes with my traveling companion, who had subsequently passed away c. 1993 from liver failure due to Hepatitis C. By the time I was diagnosed, I had been infected for over a dozen years. The SMU's health care provider informed me of the positive Hepatitis C result and then went on to inform me that there was no treatment for the virus. It was a blatant prevarication that eventually, along with the denial of medical appliances and pain medication, became the topic of federal court attention. Once I had been informed of the positive Hepatitis C test, my wife, Rachel, scoured the internet, contacted Arizona's state health department and located several other sources in attempts to obtain information on Hepatitis C. Rachel learned that the initial Hepatitis C screening test occasionally gave false positive results and a confirmatory test was required. The Arizona Department of Corrections feigned ignorance about the requirement of the follow-up procedure. Moreover, Rachel came across information about a fairly successful combination therapy treatment, involving interferon injections and rebetron capsules over a six month to a year period. The Department of Corrections denied the treatment regimen. To have been sick with a potentially deadly disease for thirteen years and to then be misinformed about the availability of treatment, plus to also languish in excruciating pain from a degenerative back as a consequence of the prison's unexplainable refusal of prescribed care, were extremely bitter pills to swallow... especially on top of the aforementioned frustrations from the transfer to SMU II.

Corrupter that satan is, I, of course, once again began to misperceive the unjust developments in my lack of medical care as personal affronts. Satan is such an insidious beast, ever employing the medicines that the Good Lord intends for our purification as the seeds of temptation toward pride. Without a second thought, the rebellious attitude that I had had toward authority that had plagued me for most of my Cellblock Six years raised its ugly head. In hindsight, I can now observe how, in Protestantism, a lack of knowledge about the necessity of struggles for salvation hamstrings all hope for a return to the likeness of God. Consequently, most of 1998 found me in preparation for yet another lawsuit against the state of Arizona and the Department of Corrections.

Rachel and I did strive for some awareness of benefit in the SMU, but the endeavor was truly difficult. For example, we had lost contact visitation, an assuredly devastating condition for us. To search for some advantage in the midst of such severe disappointment took much effort, but, with great persistence and the grace of God, we achieved a modicum of success as Rachel and I began to appreciate our increased privacy. In Cellblock Six the cramped visitation stalls were separated from one another by metal grating. Conversations were easily overheard between cages and prisoners were visible to each other. In SMU II there are solid concrete walls between the cubicles, so there is far greater privacy. Those walls enabled Rachel and me to enjoy an enhanced quality of doctrinal study and personal conversation.

In regard to our examinations of evangelist teachings, the months subsequent to the SMU II transfer saw me experience further disenchantment with Protestantism, while the church that Rachel had frequented weekly since 1996 had become unsatisfactory for her by 1998. We both retained an intense hunger for God, but did not feel that it was being fed. We began to participate more and more in independent Bible and doctrinal study courses from various organizations, and eventually Rachel migrated to another evangelical type church, wherein we both labored after God for several years. Nevertheless, my restlessness with Protestantism began to manifest in several ways. I had an increased interest in Eastern belief systems; in fact, my master's degree thesis, completed in 1998, concentrated on comparisons and contrasts between Christianity and Taoism.

As I now look back at those significant adversities: the transfer to SMU II; learning that I had Hepatitis C; the denial of care for Hepatitis C and for degenerative back disease and the increased embitterment with Protestantism, God's love is apparent. It is clear that He lovingly permits pressures to befall His children in order to prompt our return to Him and our movement toward purification. It is, quite simply, God's grace. Unfortunately, my response to those afflictions reveals the vacant nature of Protestantism.

Another indication of the vacancy of Western Christianity is complacency. Rachel and I placed such great reliance on positive court developments, a domain of worldly concern that virtually never produces any authentic benefit, even if success is achieved. In March of 1998 my death penalty case entered federal court, that realm of jurisprudence wherein the vast majority of relief in capital punishment litigation dwells. Consequently, admission into the federal arena seemed to offer a degree of chance at a favorable outcome that had never existed in the state justice system. The state justice system had been less than impartial: the state court conviction at my trial and the subsequent sentence of death had been a foregone conclusion; the state supreme court had avowed that I had molested the victim when mine was not a sexual case; the state post-conviction relief court had dismissed the fact of burial absent the required evidentiary hearing and so forth. On the other hand, advance in the progress of my case was also a bit alarming, given that it indicated a progression in the process that could ultimately culminate in my execution. At any rate, hope for appellate relief as an accomplishment of worldly good fortune was intensified a few months later when one of the best attorneys in the state of Arizona was assigned to represent me in federal court. That was followed by the unusual development of a federal judge from the state of Washington having been chosen to preside over the habeas corpus proceedings. ("Habeas corpus" is the technical term for asking a federal tribunal to find that one's detention is constitutionally infirm.) As veteran Protestants, Rachel and I perceived my chance for success in court in merely material ways, as a sort of ultimate destination. Although our joy over some apparent positive result in worldly justice did indeed stimulate our thankfulness to God for His blessing, we failed to place that result within the context of movement toward purification. We persisted in the hope of salvation.

I am not inferring that there were not moments when, as Protestants, we recognized God's hand at work within the justice system process for the purpose of increasing our faith in Him, as the very fact of my incarceration reveals. Had worldly justice initially occurred, I would have been found not guilty after the 1987 jury trial, and then released from a California prison subsequent to having served a twelve to eighteen-month parole violation. Had that transpired, there is a good chance that I would be dead and in Hades today. Rachel and I were aware of this, and we also understood that my unjust conviction for a child murder functioned as God's grace in that it propelled me into His waiting arms. In short, we had a rudimentary understanding of how my residency on death row as a man innocent of the crime for which he had been convicted acted as an impetus toward accepting Christ as my Savior. As Protestants our understanding was merely intellectual at best. We wholly failed to grasp that such suffering is the reason why we must continuously struggle and endure to the end as a means by which to work out our salvation.

The church tapes Rachel sent from the evangelical church we were frequenting became less fulfilling as the spring of 1998 progressed. Furthermore, a development with one of the pastors gave rise to significant concern. Pastor Pete, who had recently lost his wife to a terminal illness, began a romantic involvement with one of his congregants who happened to be divorced. As the relationship proceeded, a discussion of marriage arose. We were troubled because of Christ Jesus' commandment against marrying someone who has been divorced: "whoever marries a woman who is divorced commits adultery" (Mt. 5:32). The combination of dissatisfaction with the doctrine taught at that church and the grave sin of adultery by one of its pastors (Pastor Pete did marry the divorced woman.) pushed Rachel and me away. I was reminded of how we felt when we had been subjected to constant slander by our Bible church pastor, especially when he was teaching about love from 1 John. There were times when I felt that God was strongly guiding Rachel and me in a specific direction – first, with the Bible church and then, with the developments at our new church. In both instances, we were prompted to flee.

At around this time I had increased my exploration of Eastern philosophies when, while going through a catalog, I noticed a listing about a book that was described as Christian mysticism. One of my greatest complaints about Western Christianity has always been its superficial nature and failure to address one's inner condition. This book professed discourse on both one's inner state and Christianity; it fascinated me and I ordered it at once. Admittedly, the term "Christian mysticism" seemed oxymoronic to me at the time, given that I considered the mystical as that which belonged to the occult and some Eastern belief systems. However, as I perused the pages of Riding the Lion I was, to state it succinctly, blown away.

Riding the Lion was about the author's (Kyriacos C. Markides) journey to Cyprus where he interacted with two Cypriot monks. I had always been delighted to read of monastic lifestyles, such as those of the cliff-side Buddhist monks in Tibetan monasteries, wherein the sole concern in life was a spiritual pursuit. I had never imagined that such monasticism existed in Christianity. That one simple book opened my eyes to the fact that a hermit-like pursuit of God was a rich tradition throughout Eastern Christianity! Rachel had never approved of my Eastern belief system exploration; she ascribed our inner emptiness to our shortcomings in the Christian walk rather than to the vacancy of Protestantism. Nonetheless, she indulged my request to obtain Kyriacos' contact information and I sent him a letter. Kyriacos, as it turned out, was a professor of sociology at the University of Maine. In response to my inquiries about the monks in his book, he kindly provided me with one of their addresses. It was that one tiny detail that led me to the doors of the one Church established by Christ Jesus in the first century.

Soon after having written to the monk, a Father Athanasios, I received his return letter. (At around that time, he had been elevated to the Office of Metropolitan, so I greatly appreciated

the precious time that he so graciously provided.) Having had previous experience
with innumerable adepts in so-called spiritual realms, from swamis and gurus to Zen
masters and occultists, worlds in which the
slaying of the ego and a pursuit of meek-
ness are supposed objectives, I was completely flabbergasted to be the recipient of
Father Athanasios' humility and wisdom.
In subsequent correspondence he taught
me about the Holy Mountain. Mount
Athos, or Agion Oros, is in the easternmost

Father Athanasios,
Metropolitan of Limassol,
Cyprus.

reaches of Greece, on the Chalkidiki Peninsula. This peninsula
looks like three fingers that extend into the Aegean Sea and the
Sea of Thrace; the Holy Mountain is the third, or eastern, prom-
ontory. It is thirty-five miles long, six miles wide (encompassing
some two hundred and sixty-four square miles), and comprised
of elevations that range from sea level to over sixty-five hundred
feet. Large-scale monasteries began to develop in the tenth century and while at one time there were upwards of forty thousand
monks on the Mountain, that number has tragically dwindled to
only several thousand. Currently, there are twenty monasteries
sprinkled across the landscape. Mt. Athos is where men go to
find prayer and is often referred to as the "Garden of the Mother
of God". Bishop Athanasios familiarized me with Church history
by sending book after book on the lives of Church Fathers and
the saints. I learned about masters like St. Gregory Palamas, St.
John Climacus (St. John of the Ladder), St. Seraphim of Sarov
and many others. He sent me many works on Greek Orthodox
Christian spirituality, including those by Archimandrite Soph-
rony and Metropolitan Hierotheos Vlachos. Bishop Athanasios
also trained me in monasticism, his counsels underscoring the
need for absolute obedience to a spiritual father.

These recollections of my introduction to Eastern Christianity are not intended to infer my smooth transition into a more

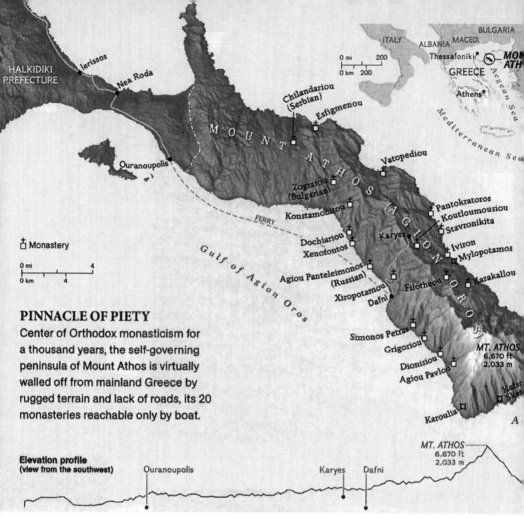

Mount Athos, third "finger" on Chalkidiki peninsula, Greece, with its monasteries.

complete obedience to Christ's commands. Sadly, I retained one foot rather solidly in worldly affairs. One of my writings, the treatise entitled Control Unit Prisons, is the culmination of my investigation into the sordid history of isolation unit prisons in the USA. Its publication resulted in making me something of a hit in anti-prison anarchist circles, a development that both played to my ego and reinforced my remnant disdain for authority as I began to write for and edit the material of the Anarchist Black Cross. This confederation began in the early 1900's in Czarist Russia under the epithet of the Anarchist Red Cross. The name was soon changed to the Anarchist Black Cross in order to put an end to its confusion with the well-known international Red

Cross. It was a means by which Russians could band together to help those who had been beaten and imprisoned by the Cossacks and Bolsheviks at the onset of the Bolshevik Revolution. The Anarchist Black Cross has continued to support prisoners, and in the 1980s it made its way to the USA. Most of my involvement was with several European factions and some US chapters of the Anarchist Black Cross, especially with the Black Block arm. The Black Block is the more radical segment that carries out clandestine direct action engagements, but when visible to the public can be seen wearing black bandanas over much of their faces. My participation in underground anti-establishment activities was an unfortunate misstep that I found all too easy to gravitate toward. It inflicted not only grave consequences for me in SMU II, but also severely stained my soul as I, once again, began to resist the medicine that God was providing for my salvation.

The manner in which satan engineers temptations in seemingly disparate domains to then meld them together in order to distract us from our pursuit of God is frightening to behold. Such was the case with the serpent's appeal to my pride via recognition from innumerable anarchists, especially after the years of constant abuse from guards and prisoners. The appeal to my pride was then combined with the ongoing assault on my pride through the SMU II health unit's refusal to provide necessary medical care. Even as I persisted in succumbing to the passion of pride, the Good Lord continued to bestow His loving grace on me through the steady hand of Rachel and the continuation of relations with Bishop Athanasios. However, having been catechized (taught the fundamental basics of Orthodoxy) long distance by mail, there came a time when more immediate and direct training was required. After all, a bishop in Cyprus could not perform the intimate functions of a spiritual father, such as baptism, confession, serving Holy Communion, assigning daily prayer rules and other obediences. As it turned out, there is a Greek Orthodox monastery just a dozen or so miles from SMU II. In 1999 Bishop Athanasios contacted Father Paisios, the Abbot of St. An-

Father Paisios, Abbot of St. Anthony's Greek Orthodox Monastery, Florence, AZ.

thony's Monastery. St. Anthony's is on the outskirts of Florence; the Florence prison complex, where Cellblock Six is located, and the Eyman prison complex, where SMU II is located, are both right next to Florence. Soon thereafter, Father Paisios and I met in the SMU II visitation area. Bishop Athanasios had asked me to come home to the Apostolic Church established by Christ Jesus, and with that first visit of Father Paisios, I was absolutely home.

I was pleasantly surprised by Father Paisios' appearance. This shy and extraordinarily humble middle-aged monk entered the visitation area and took a seat in front of the stall where I had been nervously waiting. While it is the general rule for Greek Orthodox priests to wear beards, I did not know that monks never cut their beards or their hair. Father Paisios had a thick beard that fell to his chest and his long hair was tied up under his monastic cap. He wore the usual monastic habit, a sort of robe that was ankle-length, and had a beautiful smile that could easily melt the heart of even the most hardened heathen. After the initial nervousness faded we found ourselves deeply engaged in comfortable discussion about a host of theological concepts. Before we knew it, our two hours had elapsed. While departing, Father Paisios let me know that he would set up a visitation schedule with the senior chaplain for the Eyman prison complex so that my precious abbot could continue to teach me on a regular basis. Therefore, as the millennium came to a close I had, at long last, begun to journey toward a correct perception of Christianity. As I recognized the Church as our spiritual hospital, wherein the treatment of passions occurs and the struggle toward salvation is shepherded, I knew that I had also begun a journey toward purification.

It has been quite enlightening to reconstruct the road home in my mind. I had been arrested, convicted and sentenced to death for capital murder. Rachel's loving guidance then took me to the pursuit of God in January of 1988, followed by Rachel and me laboring under the tutelage of a Bible church pastor for eight or nine years. Then came the first push toward an exit from Protestantism as the hypocritical and mean-spirited maneuvers of that preacher made our continuation there untenable. Knowing only Protestantism, Rachel and I stumbled through a couple of other Fundamentalist, or Evangelical, houses of worship, enterprises that eventually ended up with our attendance at a church where one of the pastors openly engaged in adulterous relations. Hence, God's grace had allowed for a second unmistakable push away from Western Christianity, a propulsion that ultimately led to the doors of the authentic Church established in the first century by Jesus Christ. As our excursions into different Protestant denominations demonstrate, there are literally tens of millions of well-intentioned Christians in the USA who have no awareness whatsoever of the One True Apostolic Church. This is quite upsetting since, as I had previously detailed, Protestantism has failed to even comprehend the very nature of salvation. It mistakes an initial belief in Christ as the Messiah for a salvation that cannot be lost. Consider the ramifications of this implausible postulate, not the least of which is a stripping away of any apprehension of the purpose of suffering. The misperception of already being saved precludes the awareness of adversity as the medicine for purification. Thus, it is evident that Protestantism strips away the core of our return to likeness of God.

Another manifestation of how Protestantism has tragically abandoned God's grace can be observed within the context of the sacraments. As a Protestant I had no idea that baptism is a literal washing away of sin; baptism is a real death, burial and resurrection with the Lord Jesus Christ (cf. Rom. 6:3-5). Instead, I viewed it as merely some public acknowledgment of a symbolic belief in Christ. Moreover, I was unaware of the necessity for three complete submersions in the name of the Father and of the Son and of the Holy Spirit (cf. Mat. 28:19). I was completely stunned when I realized that Fundamentalists in Western Christianity not only condemn baptism as some empty ritual laden with mere symbolism, but also dismiss Holy Communion as a barren ceremony that only serves as a reminder of what Christ had accomplished on the Cross. They have done away with the actuality of the bread and the wine literally being the Body and Blood of the Lord Jesus Christ, of which we must partake for eternal life (cf. Jn. 6:53-56). Even the sacrament of holy confession has been virtually abolished by Protestantism, since the confession of one's sins to a priest is said to be blasphemous. Of course, this wholly ignores the many times Sacred Scripture refers to the priests' ability to forgive the sins that we confess to them (cf, Mat.16:19; Mat. 18:18; Jn. 20:23; 1 Jn. 1:9). Tragically, Fundamental Western Christianity has ripped the heart out of God's grace. It is frightening to consider that the one who profits from the dismissal of God's grace in the sacraments is the devil himself.

Under the careful guidance of Father Paisios, the grace of God enabled me to come to an understanding of Eastern Christianity. From there, I was able to perceive a glimmer of comprehension regarding the indispensable role of suffering in the working out of our salvation. At the same time, those precious seedlings of illumination still did not wholly deter me from pursuing an agenda of distraction, as I continued to entertain the demon of pride. The refusal of SMU II to provide necessary health care unfortunately culminated in my lodging a civil lawsuit in federal court in the summer of 1999. Predictably, it ended abysmally. As I now look back at how events unfolded, it is easy to observe how satan slowly spread his insidious web. He began by playing upon my aversion to the injustice of having been purposefully denied treatment, knowing that my failure to cut the provocation off at the very moment of its inception would draw me further and further into his clutches.

I had spent nearly a year as a catechumen under Father Paisios when arrangements were made for my baptism. Rachel had maintained her attendance at an Evangelical church. Her internal struggle with the vast difference between the Eastern Orthodox Church and what she had known for more than two decades in Protestantism presented such a tremendous contrast that she continued to faithfully soldier on in what she had known and was comfortable with since the 1970s. The spring of 2000 found my precious wife seeking a more profound relationship with God in the form of an evangelic baptism. Despite my concerns about it being an empty ritual, a symbolic acknowledgment in a public forum of belief in Christ, with only one submersion, I lovingly supported my godly wife with great happiness over her desire to pursue the likeness of God.

My own baptism, which was my participation in the death, burial, and resurrection of Jesus Christ, occurred at SMU II in the summer of 2000. With it, I also entered the One Apostolic Church that Christ Himself had established in the first century. I was home.

Frank in SMU II death row (May 24, 2007).
This photo was taken around the time of his baptism. Frank's overall facial expression, compared to all of his previous photos in this book, profoundly reveals Christ's joy and Frank's deep repentance, all at the same time. Glory to all-merciful Christ our God!

-187-

Chapter Eleven

And the Two Are Becoming One

In the summer of 1991 I again journeyed to Los Angeles to visit Frank's folks. While there, I discussed my fears about marrying Frank and my concerns over the intense adverse publicity that had surrounded his case in court with Frank's mother. The potential of harassment or harm to me and/or my family was frightening, but God had provided the grace of faith that my family and I would be protected and safe. Frank's mom helped me determine that since I was in love with Frank, I should marry him. The grace of God gave me the strength and faith to know I was making the correct decision for my life. I was at peace, and could not wait to return to Tucson to tell Frank that I was ready to marry him. The next visit we had, I told Frank the news, and he was very surprised and extraordinarily happy.

Soon thereafter I began to make the wedding arrangements, including the prerequisite meeting with the prison chaplain. I was not prepared for the nightmare that would happen next. In the tiny, cramped office on the Florence Complex prison grounds, an employee of the prison interrogated me on why I would want to marry a convicted murderer. The more I reiterated my intent to marry Frank, the more that "chaplain" attempted to discourage me. At one point, he venomously referred to Frank as nothing but a brutal child killer. I had not expected such ferocity. Although he worked for the state, I had presumed that as a chaplain he would have exercised at least some courtesy. I guess he simply viewed his responsibilities from the perspective of a state agent whose job it was to discourage death row marriages. The meeting ended with me in tears and humiliated, but not wavering in my decision to marry Frank. Other marital arrangements included working with Frank on having the wedding approved, obtaining the marriage license, arranging for an officiator, setting a December date with the prison and other details.

In the weeks leading up to the wedding there were several upsetting events that involved my pastor. I had met with Jeff to advise him of my intention to marry Frank in December of 1991. Upset, he tried to dissuade me, to no avail. He said he needed a few days to give the matter further consideration. I later learned from Jeff's wife, Janice, that he was very upset over my decision to marry Frank. Jeff had always seen me as a daughter, and did not approve of my marriage to a prisoner. He was concerned that our unconventional marriage would not permit Frank and me to live together, and he did not want that kind of life for me. Still, a week or two later Jeff reluctantly agreed to perform the marriage – after I had informed him that if he refused I'd find someone else to marry Frank and me. In hindsight, I sometimes feel it would have been best to have found someone else, especially when considering how our relationship with him ended.

I had some fears about telling Roxanne of my plans to marry Frank. She and I had become good friends, but I had not told her about Frank. She and her husband had two small children, and because of Frank's conviction, I wanted to be sensitive. I decided, a few weeks prior to the wedding, to take Roxanne to lunch and tell her about Frank and our upcoming wedding. I started by telling her I had something important to share with her. After I told her the news, she laughed and said she had thought I was going to tell her I was a lesbian since I had never mentioned a boyfriend. She was very touched by the story of how Frank and I had met, and started to cry when I asked her to be with me on my wedding day.

As the big day neared, I looked back at all of the events that had led Frank and me to this point, and I was truly amazed at God's grace. I was ready to become Mrs. Frank Atwood and face the challenges that would come, knowing God was with us through it all.

On the morning of 17 December, 1991, I awoke early; it was the big day... my wedding day.

I excitedly began to prepare for the seventy mile journey to Florence, packed the car and awaited Roxanne's arrival; my father, Roxanne, and I were going to drive together and meet Frank's mother at her hotel, where final preparations would occur. The trip was pleasant; a nervous excitement prevailed. Once we got to the hotel room, Roxanne completed my hair and make-up. It was finally time to put on my wedding dress and veil. What a thrilling occasion!

Roxanne would not be able to attend the wedding, so she waited at the hotel. My dad, Frank's mom and I hopped into the car for the short jaunt to the prison parking area, where we met my pastor, Jeff. It had begun to rain, so all of us were huddled under the minuscule excuse for a pavilion which the Department of Corrections had erected for visitors to Cellblock Six. We must have been quite a sight, as everyone was crouched around me in an earnest effort to preserve the integrity of my hair, make-up and dress. Passing guards were chuckling with amusement.

The van arrived shortly and we all piled in for the trek down the very bumpy gravel road to the administration segregation unit. Although that was always quite an excursion, we reached the unit none the worse for wear and were ushered into the visitation room. Within a few minutes Frank came in. He had never been on the visitor's side; visits were always non-contact, with visitors and prisoners separated by thick glass.

I was nervous, but nowhere near as nervous as Frank. He looked like, well, like a deer caught in headlights. As the ceremony began, I noticed a few officers and Frank's counselor in the room. Frank J. also reminded me about how happy he was to be getting married in Levis. The service was very nice; afterwards, we were escorted to a small room for a two hour contact visit. That visit was wonderful; I was able to kiss and hug my husband and hold hands. Still, prisons have exceedingly rude ways of reminding one of their surroundings. It so happened that another prisoner, who was being escorted back to his cell from a Bible study, observed Frank and me on our contact visit and screamed "baby killer" along with other profanities. It was very upsetting to have been treated like that on my wedding day, but I did not allow it to steal the joy that I was feeling. It was very hard to leave Frank after our visit, but I had tried to prepare myself for that, too.

Before our all too short visit ended, I was able to again hug and kiss my husband. I had heard that the wedding was to be the lead story on that evening's television news, and of course, I wanted to see it. Roxanne and I made the trip back to Tucson in her vehicle, while my dad and Frank's mom traveled in the vehicle she had rented. We all arrived home just as the story had begun to air. That evening was the onset of several days in which television and print media reported on the wedding; it was the lead story on newscasts and ran on the front pages of daily news-

Rachel, a blushing bride.

papers. My father was quite concerned about the pervasive publicity, so he instructed me to remain home for the next few days. However, that evening, prior to Frank's mother returning to the family estate in Los Angeles the next day, we were able to safely enjoy a celebratory supper at a local restaurant.

The following few years elapsed without incident and were fairly normal. I began to show Persian cats with greater success and had a steady clientele for my cleaning business. I did attempt once more to begin running again; however, the foot injuries had taken their toll and so I unfortunately had to abandon that endeavor. I continued to attend church several times a week, always recording and sending the services to Frank so that we could do our level best to be guided in life by Gospel commandments.

It was in 1995 when Frank and my pastor's daughter began corresponding, a development that, in retrospect, was a bad decision. The intent was for Frank to function as a drug abuse counselor, since Pastor Jeff's daughter had become more and more involved in the use of many substances. Over the summer a few letters were exchanged, and then I took her with me for a visit with Frank. She seemed to have been doing better; her school attendance and participation improved and their correspondence increased toward the conclusion of 1995.

Early on in January of 1996 my brother got married. While it was a momentous occasion, it had been slightly marred by the death of my favorite Persian. The day after my brother's wedding, I had gone to visit Frank, and upon arriving home, Ali climbed up on my bed and expired from kidney failure. It was as if he had waited for me to come home so I could comfort him as he died. While I was extremely upset by Ali's death, I had already determined to cook dinner for the family the next night as a celebration for my brother's marriage. Since I had been busy with the meal preparations, I was rather taken aback when my pastor and his wife showed up unannounced the next afternoon.

Apparently, my pastor's daughter had mailed a correspondence (voice) tape to Frank on which she candidly discussed her current drug use. That led Jeff to accuse Frank of somehow dragging his little girl into the realm of contraband chemicals. It was a surprising turn of events, as it was obvious that the girl had been very involved with drugs for several years – a fact that everyone, other than Jeff, seemed to know. Jeff simply was in denial about his daughter being a druggie, so he had convinced himself of Frank's responsibility for her substance abuse. He made some very derogatory comments about my husband before I asked him to leave.

That development created significant strains on relations between the pastor's family and me. Even though several people sought to smooth things over, the tension in personal interactions spilled over into our association with the church. After a few months Frank and I decided to move on. For me, it was really a difficult and painful juncture; after all, Jeff's establishment had been my church home for some twenty years, and Frank had been a member for about a decade. I had been considered part of Jeff and Janice's family and had cared for the children like they were my own. It was the first of many instances where I faced rejection because of whom I had married.

Consequently, the latter half of 1996 found me attending another non-denominational Protestant place of worship in Tucson. After about a year I remained dissatisfied and unfulfilled, and so I continued to search for a new church. There was such an aura of judgment by congregants over my marriage to a death row prisoner.

I had already felt uncomfortable at the new non-denominational church, so when renewed publicity in my husband's case developed in late 1996 to early 1997, Sunday church services grew even more stressful for me. I was aware of a very large non-denominational church nearby, and was even familiar with several parishioners. Even though we were not in the habit of "church hopping", Frank and I decided a re-location to that new center of worship would fulfill our spiritual void. I began attending services there in the spring of 1997 and immediately felt as if I fit in nicely.

Chapter Twelve

Working Out Our Salvation

Federal court has never been a friendly arena for prisoners who file suit against government officials, especially when the litigant proceeds pro per (without the representation of counsel). I found myself in that exact situation – present in hostile territory and absent any assistance from legal professionals. As the lawsuit wound its way through the judicial system, more and more of my time was required. I was also frustrated by my treatment at the hands of federal judges in Arizona. For instance, in pre-trial proceedings each side must list all of the evidence they plan to present during the jury trial and provide the opposition with copies of all documentary evidence as well. State attorneys for the Arizona Department of Corrections had listed my medical records as evidence that they intended to use and initially refused to provide me with a copy. Their refusal led to my having filed a motion to compel (a pleading in which the judge is asked to force the other side to provide a copy of their evidence). The judge refused to order the state to give me a copy of my medical records. I was dumbfounded. There was no way I could try my case before a jury without my medical records; to me, the judge had an acrimonious and indifferent attitude. While the state ultimately relented and provided me with the copies, this example demonstrates the frustrations that were routine throughout the history of that lawsuit.

Rachel had continuously pleaded with me to dismiss the lawsuit. She saw that the case was requiring more of my time and souring my focus on pursuing salvation as a result. Blinded by pride, I refused to back down. As the case neared trial in late 2001, the judge made yet another unheard of decision: I would not be permitted in the courtroom for trial. Even the state attorney was shocked by the judge's outlandish abuse of judicial discretion. Requiring a prisoner plaintiff to appear by video while handcuffed and shackled, with the shackles chained to the floor, had never even been contemplated by a court of law. Still, rather than see the continuous, ridiculous rulings by a rogue tribunal officer as God informing me that I was straying down the wrong path, I redoubled my efforts. In so doing, I sabotaged obedience to my spiritual father.

Father Paisios had assigned me a daily prayer rule, a prescribed regimen of prayer every day. Included in my obedience is the reciting of the Jesus Prayer for an hour a day. The specific wording of this Prayer is "Lord Jesus Christ, Son of God, have mercy on me, a sinner." It is frequently shortened to "Lord Jesus Christ have mercy on me." The Jesus Prayer has its roots in both the Old Testament and the New Testament. In Gen. 4:26 we find that in the time of Seth, Adam's son, "men began to call on the name of the Lord," and petitioning the Lord for mercy occurs repeatedly in the Psalms (e.g. Ps.4:1; 9:13; 30:10; 51:1; 70:1). In the New Testament, many faithful called out to the Lord Jesus Christ for mercy in the Gospels (Mt. 9:27, Mt. 15:22, Mt. 17:15, Mk. 10:47-48, Lk. 17:13, Lk. 18:13). With the scriptural foundation of praying to the Savior for mercy, along with the biblical mandate "to pray without ceasing" (1 Thess. 5:17), early Egyptian desert fathers initiated a rudimentary form of the Jesus Prayer, a practice that soon spread into Sinai and the Middle East.

Eventually, it reached Greece and Russia and assumed the specific form known today.

There is also some important background information on the Jesus Prayer. The initial half of the Prayer ("Lord Jesus Christ") acknowledges Jesus Christ as the Son of God. "Lord" verifies the Lordship of the Son of God and us as His servants; "Jesus" awakens our memories to His earthly life, and "Christ" confesses our belief that He is God. The second part of the Prayer, "have mercy on me, a sinner" avows our fallen state and need for the Savior's aid. Knowing that the Jesus Prayer both confirms Christ as the Son of God and affirms our inability to do anything without Him, we can simply bow our heads and continually recite the Jesus Prayer.

Along with an hour of the Jesus Prayer daily, Father Paisios had prescribed one hundred prostrations. During prostrations, one crosses oneself – by touching, in succession, the forehead, below the belly button, the right shoulder and the left shoulder with the balls of the middle finger, index finger, and thumb pressed together as an indication of the Father, Son and Holy Spirit. The ring and little fingers are folded into the palm to affirm the two natures of Christ, divine and human. Thus, during a prostration, one crosses oneself and utters, " Lord Jesus Christ," then drops to both knees and bends forward, until the forehead and both palms touch the ground, with both forearms flat on the ground. He then recites, "have mercy on me," before he finally returns to a standing position. Father Paisios also assigned one hundred "Hail Marys," which is the repetition of "Holy Virgin Mary, Mother of God, save me." To my assigned daily prayer rule I added the reading of daily Sacred Scripture, meditations from Dynamis (a publication issued by St. George's Cathedral in Wichita, Kansas) and the reading of a chapter from the New Testament every morning. I also attempted to pray the hours, which are seven in number, and encompass:

- The midnight office, usually performed at sunrise
- Matins (in the Orthodox Church this is known as orthros),

read at 6:00 am
- First hour (psalms 5, 89 & 100), prayers generally said right after matins (orthros)
- Third hour (psalms 16, 24 & 50), read at 9:00 am
- Sixth hour (psalms 53, 54 & 90), read at noon
- Ninth hour (psalms 83, 84 & 85), afternoon prayers read at 3:00 pm
- Vespers, evening prayers performed at sunset
- Compline, prayers recited at bedtime

When praying the hours, set prayers are chanted from what is called an Horologion. I also set aside time for my own daily prayers to God, as well as time to study and write.

Unfortunately, as the winter of 2001-2002 dawned I experienced more and more evaporation of my daily prayer rule. I had actually begun to spend eight to ten hours a day in trial preparation. Jury selection had been originally scheduled for February of 2002, but a continuance requested by the government had re-set the trial for May of 2002. As the countdown progressed, I grew more concerned. I was already handicapped just by being a state prisoner who was complaining about denied medical apparatuses. Why would citizens who were uninsured or who had experienced difficulty in receiving health care be concerned about me, someone on death row, having been refused free treatment? I was also troubled by the added obstacle of not being present in the courtroom for trial. It was a great disadvantage to have the jury realize that the judge believed I was too dangerous to be transported to court and into their presence. Once the jury observed me on a TV monitor in a faraway prison, where I was clad in a bright orange jumpsuit, shackled to the floor, with both hands chained to my waist, and wearing a visible shock device on my forearm, then, for all intents and purposes, the trial was over. How could it be otherwise?

In the days before trial I had at long last begun to hear God's small still voice. I faced the extant problems, described above, which invoked the likelihood of losing the jury trial. I was also facing the potentiality of several more years in court as I pursued appeals on the trial judge's outrageous directives. The amount of time I had lent to trial preparation had resulted in the decline in the practice of my daily prayer rule. I justified that decline via my expectation that all judicial involvements would end with the trial and that I could then resume the prescribed prayer rule. However, when the very real possibility of much more entanglement in court proceedings loomed, I certainly had to re -think my posture. Consequently, I concluded that a stand had to be made; so, I swallowed my pride and dismissed the case on the eve of trial.

"I swallowed my pride." Well, actually that turned out to not be entirely true. I had geared up for a courtroom battle against the government that never did occur, and so I was left, so to speak, "all dressed up with nowhere to go." I had put in eight to ten hour days of intense trial preparation, which were followed by the sudden cessation of all judicial pursuits, sans the much anticipated climactic trial by jury. Thus, within a matter of weeks, in late May of 2002, I began to explode.

It is illuminating to observe how satan eternally attempts to befoul our efforts to engage in our search for God. Sadly, in the spring of 2002, I fell prey to temptation. For several years, security staff had permitted me to take a makeshift prayer rope out to the recreation area so that I could pray the Jesus Prayer while outside. An Eastern Orthodox wool prayer rope, constructed of thirty-three, fifty or a hundred knots, is commonly used to count Jesus Prayer repetitions. The prison would only authorize me to use a makeshift, which was a Catholic rosary with fifty-five small plastic beads. Without warning, around the end of May, an officer decided to disallow the practice. When he refused to summon a supervisor, I lost my temper and yelled at him; clearly I lacked humility. Thankfully, a few days later, as he was working in my housing area, I was able to apologize. However, the story that I could be antagonized by interference with religious practices had been circulated amongst the guards; the damage had been done. It was not long before there was another successful attack by staff that was intended to agitate me through the refusal to let me carry a rosary to the exercise room. I again asked if a supervisor could be contacted, and while he indicated a willingness to do so and exited the pod, I could see him standing just outside of the door and not speaking to anyone. It's not that religious artifacts are prohibited in recreation rooms; quite the contrary. For instance, there is no smoking in the SMUs, but American Indians were given a lighter and tobacco, or some other combustible plant material, to burn while outside, as apparently, the smoke cleared the area of evil spirits in a ritual known as "smudging". I am not trying to excuse my loss of control. I have no justification for my actions once the officer returned and falsely claimed to have discussed the matter with his sergeant, because it was I who acceded to temptation. I was being escorted in handcuffs to the exercise room, while the demons of pride and anger not only accompanied me but had also captured my heart. I simply would not let it go and began to verbally abuse the officer. Under verbal fire, the guard returned me to my cell. He cancelled my recreation period and then radioed for a lieutenant and back-up squad. Upon their arrival, I screamed further insults while the lieutenant kept ordering me to the front of the cell to be handcuffed. I continued to yell at him that I was already in handcuffs, because the escort guard had never removed them. Then, regrettably, I spat in the lieutenant's face. My actions resulted in being sprayed with gas and enduring other harsh recourse: I was taken to the health unit on a gurney; moved downstairs; had Plexiglas bolted to the front of my new cell; given no property or bedding for nearly five days and disciplined for an assault on staff. However, the most devastating consequences were the shame that fell on my wife and the Holy Orthodox Church.

Rachel had developed congenial relations with prison staff, interactions wherein most had truly taken a liking to her over the years. She not only had to suffer the heartache that my outburst inflicted on her, but whenever she thereafter entered the prison to visit me, there were some officers who were decidedly distant toward her.

Insofar as the Orthodox Church... the shame that I brought on the Church was severe. It also reveals another distinction between the Apostolic Orthodox Church and Protestantism. Since the Eastern Orthodox Church has continually existed as one wholly united Church and one body for two thousand years, whatever happens with one congregant, impacts the entire flock. As applied to me, my assault on a correctional lieutenant infected the entire Church, may God forgive me. In contrast, given its mere several hundred year existence, Protestantism has divided itself into thousands of divergent sects, which means it is not possible to envision Protestantism as one body. I learned this and so much more under the tutelage of Father Paisios.

After Father Paisios began visiting in 1999, a practice that he has mercifully maintained ever since on an every other week basis, I underwent a period of catechism which culminated in my baptism in the summer of 2000. I was christened with the name Anthony, after the fourth century pioneer of Egyptian desert monasticism, St. Anthony the Great. From that point on, Father Paisios agreed to be my spiritual father.

Since my horrible affront against Holy Orthodoxy, I have endeavored to sincerely refrain from embarrassing the Church again. For the next dozen years I suffered only one minor write-up (for hanging a towel on the front of my cell) and actively sought salvation, despite attempt after attempt by prisoners as well as staff to dissuade my efforts to lead an Orthodox life. One such effort by prison personnel involved what many people construed as an attempt on my life. In the middle of a 110°F scalding hot Arizona summer afternoon, I found myself locked outside in the recreation room. I had been in SMU II for five years, during which time there had never been a case of a prisoner being placed in the exercise area during shift change, so I was ill prepared for my sojourn to the recreation room. The problem occurred because all staff, even the tower control officer, had vacated the housing area; there was no one to hear my cries for help. Suffering from heat stroke, I collapsed in the shower, which is where staff found me once they finally did a security check. Through the grace of God I was taken to the health unit on a stretcher and survived the incident. It was a real challenge to humbly endure an attack by those responsible for my welfare. Again, the grace of God saved me by enabling me to maintain the working out of my salvation.

Principally, I feared that my transgressions would deter Rachel from accepting Orthodoxy. Yes, she had noticed many significant changes in me; however, there were also many lapses which, I felt, caused our conversations about Eastern Christianity to become somewhat strained. I know it was much easier for me to become Orthodox, since I had sought an inward approach to God. Furthermore, due to my incarceration I was separated from and did not have to concern myself with worldly affairs; consequently, the monastic dispositions of Bishop Athanasios and Father Paisios were exceedingly attractive to me. Graced with the benefit of instruction by Bishop Athanasios and Father Paisios and edification from the many books they had provided, the scales of Protestant deception had been thoroughly cleansed from my eyes. All Rachel knew of Christianity was Fundamental and/or Evangelical Protestantism. For her, to contemplate something as alien as Eastern Orthodoxy was a frightening prospect.

Complicating our discussions on Orthodox Christianity was the fact that Rachel had to acknowledge her trepidation that if Orthodox Christianity is the sole pillar and ground of truth, then it meant that everything she had believed for several decades was – and is – incorrect. Consider the following: Rachel and I had been fervent adherents of the eternal security ideology of Protestantism. Once I became Eastern Orthodox, I had to struggle with the realization that what I had professed, even in published pamphlets, was an outright heretical philosophy. Similarly, when Rachel and I discussed the eternal security ideology subsequent to my Eastern Orthodox conversion, it was an extremely scary prospect for her to contemplate that her belief in a foundational doctrine of Christianity (salvation solely by belief in the Lord Jesus Christ) was defective. Furthermore, my all too frequent lapses did not create a comforting environment for my precious wife's fears; nor were they conducive to teaching her about Orthodox theology. All Rachel had was me, a husband whom she had often observed in transgression. I did my utmost to scour various texts for details on theology, such as those on salvation requiring endurance to the end. And I took notes that I subsequently transcribed onto little scraps of paper and smuggled to the visitation area, so that Rachel and I could carefully study them.

During that time, from around 2003-2006, I found it a little difficult to not only explain the fundamentals of original Christianity (the first century Orthodox Church) to Rachel, but it was also an exacting exercise to elucidate Orthodoxy to my parents. My mother and father still resided in Los Angeles and I was imprisoned in SMU II, way out in Arizona; so most of our communication had to occur via the U.S. mail. They had consistently visited, one at a time, during my imprisonment, every month or two so that someone could remain home to maintain the residence and care for the pets. Somewhere between 2002 and 2003 they became too aged to comfortably travel and visits became a rarity. We did not have the optimum format for profound discourse on theology. My father was Episcopalian and my mother, even though she attended St. Alban's Episcopal Church with my dad, had continued her Catholic faith. Neither of them had ever heard a word about the Eastern Orthodox Church. In fact, when I first began to describe Orthodoxy to them and to explain that a monk in Cyprus and another monk in a nearby monastery were my teachers, they feared that I had been seduced by a cult. With patience I was able to demonstrate, both by discussions in our letters and through my evolving attitude of obedience, the nature of Orthodoxy – that it has existed since the time of Christ with an unbroken line of apostolic succession. Unlike virtually all of

Protestantism, the Episcopal Church understands the concept of current-day bishops being able to be traced back to Apostles, as does Catholicism; so it is a reality that my parents knew about. I further related that Orthodoxy has centers in places such as Jerusalem (where Christ had visited) and Antioch (where believers in the Lord Jesus Christ were first called Christians), that it has some three hundred million congregants across the world, and so on. Not only were my parents eventually able to apprehend Orthodox precepts as original Christianity, but they also observed how the concept of obedience to the commands of Christ had begun to manifest in my sincere endeavor to follow Him by striving to live in accord with scriptural principles. They saw my effort to obey Father Paisios as well as my attitude toward them having really become one of respect and deference. Thus, my mother and father came to realize the authenticity of Orthodox Christianity as a means by which to effect one's inner change and to seek salvation in God.

It has been a difficult struggle to maintain the Orthodox path. Hardly anyone had heard of the Greek Orthodox Church. In fact, since Father Paisios began visiting in 1999 there have only been four Orthodox prisoners in the several thousand inmates of the Eyman prison complex. Currently I am the only one. When I respond to inquiries about my religious persuasion, most of the time people simply attempt to fit Orthodoxy into a familiar brand of Christianity. Often, the reaction to my explanation that the Eastern Orthodox Church was established in the first century and that there has been a continuous line of succession to this very day of bishops who have descended from the Apostles, is an inquiry into which Protestant denomination Orthodoxy ascribes. When they finally realize that Orthodoxy is not a denomination, most people endeavor to dismiss Orthodoxy as some offshoot of Catholicism. Some people even misconstrue the Orthodox Church as a derivative of Jewish Orthodoxy. At some point, they come to an understanding that the Orthodox Church cannot be compartmentalized as either Protestant or Catholic. Confused, many thereafter proclaim that my belief is a delusional adherence to some sort of cult. At any rate, I have been able to engage in opportunities for a profound examination of the history of Christianity with fellow prisoners. These examinations have indisputably revealed that the Protestantism espoused by Martin Luther in the sixteenth century absolutely precluded it from being the Church established by Christ Jesus in the first century. To then meet such resistance to this truth has been extremely disappointing and serves to demonstrate the deep roots satan has cultivated in Western civilization. The Apostolic Orthodox Church established by the Lord Jesus Christ has become all but invisible throughout the world![6]

In addition to my discouragement at the blindness of fellow prisoners to authentic Christianity, I felt disheartened by the conflict that my efforts in obedience to Christ engendered in others. In penitentiaries across the USA, there is a phenomenon known as a "jailhouse conversion." This derogatory term implies a pseudo or superficial assertion of Christianity by prisoners. In my decades of experience behind bars I can acknowledge that this is a very common occurrence because jailhouse conversions lack the very essence of a life after Christ, which is the sincere effort of obedience to Christ. In other words, rather than a prisoner strive to conform to Christ's commands, he attempts to maintain his own will and to fit Sacred Scripture into his preconceived notions. This particular anomaly allows inmates to lay claim to the status of "model prisoner" because of their involvement in Christian programs, while all the while preserving the underlying noxious patterns of thinking that made them slaves to sin in the first place.

Having previously detailed my many lapses, I have no

---

6   The sad lack of knowledge in the USA about Eastern Orthodox Christianity led to Frank writing a book on Church history entitled *The Gates of Hades Prevaileth Not* (Anthony of the Desert; iUniverse, 2012). For more information on this book and other companion works, please visit www.churchfathertheology.com.

intent to toot my own horn. I will only say that I have genuinely endeavored to become more receptive to the Holy Spirit and more animated by the commands of the Lord. This undertaking often puts me at extreme odds with other prisoners... even those who assert a Christian allegiance. For example, during the rare occasions when I realized that disappointments or abuses from others were the medicine for my salvation, my efforts to recruit Protestant prisoners into a like enterprise fell by the wayside virtually every time. In the end, I was accused of having an attitude that was overly supportive of staff.

I recall one occasion when an inmate, whom I perceived as the "most Christian" of Protestant prisoners, endured his television having been broken during a cell search by guards, who then condemned the TV to contraband status and seized it. The prisoner turned to me as a sounding board for his complaints, but instead of reinforcing his anger I gently directed his attention to the injustices and far harsher conditions Apostle Peter and Apostle Paul suffered for merely being "guilty" of preaching Christ Jesus. Unfortunately, my effort was belittled and perceived as justifying or excusing staff misconduct. All I had hoped to accomplish was to engage in a moment of Christian fellowship and to perhaps enable an environment wherein mutual encouragement would develop. There were other times when I observed self-professed Christian inmates engage in outright satanic discussions about the fineries of women who were featured in pornography magazines or waxing poetic about rather un-Christian shows such as Buffy the Vampire Slayer. My attempts to point out the serpentine nature of those topics were generally met with ridicule and other forms of verbal abuse. Under what I later learned were false pretenses, the above mentioned inmate eventually began to speak with me about various religious programming on television, because he hoped I would then help him purchase a new TV. I did facilitate the procurement and, as it turned out, on the evening when the television was delivered some movies about several Apostles were scheduled. I excitedly informed him of the good news and he expressed enthusiasm; however, the next day found him talking with other prisoners about how much he had enjoyed a Buffy the Vampire Slayer mini-marathon. Of course, he had not viewed any religious programming.

Some of my most disappointing and frustrating encounters involved those who had been commissioned with the task of providing for my religious needs. After my lamentable assault on a corrections lieutenant, I made reference to the denial of an Orthodox prayer rope for me, a denial that spanned nine years. Soon after Father Paisios began to visit in 1999, I submitted a request to the SMU II chaplain for the prayer rope, but the application for an essential religious item was refused. Apparently, because the religious division of the Arizona Department of Corrections had never heard of an Eastern Orthodox prayer rope, a blanket prohibition went into effect. For six years (from 1999-2005) I had to engage in an illegal transaction by paying a Catholic prisoner for the use of his rosary beads.(Inmates are strictly forbidden to barter with one another or to exchange any items.) In 2005 a new senior chaplain was convinced to permit me my own rosary beads, but it was not until 2008 that Father Paisios was allowed to send me an authentic Orthodox prayer rope. Any Orthodox Christian on the outside can obtain a prayer rope in a matter of minutes. However, what would seem to also be a most simple task – even in a prison – of approving possession of a fundamental religious artifact required a nine year ordeal. It is precisely such frustrations that have outraged and discouraged me during my incarceration.

It must be said that bitter medicine is required for the purification of passions, even if we fail to recognize the medicine while it is being poured out for us. It is only afterwards that we can perceive that medicine as grace. This is certainly the case with me. It often seems that the knowledge that God provides everything for salvation resides only in my intellect, where it manifests as a desire for some Christian fellowship in my daily life here at SMU II. Frankly, I have found it most difficult to continue working out my salvation while being so isolated from the Church, unable to converse with anyone on a daily basis. However, despite the pervasive feeling of isolation (or abandonment) over the years as an Orthodox Christian, there have been times when I have been blessed to transcend that loneliness by contemplating the grace so lovingly provided by God. The lack of fellowship and the inability to query my spiritual father about pressing theological questions become far less significant when I focus on God. During those moments, I realize that my isolation in a supermax prison has something in common with the life of a desert hermit: it can become a workshop in which to chip away at distractions and transform the inner man. Those are the moments in which the grace of God is so apparent that it is overwhelming. Assuredly, God is merciful and provides absolutely for our purification and salvation. I only wish that the grace I perceive would journey from my mind to my heart, and from there, exert an influence over the inner man, such that it would lead toward dominion over all my thoughts and behavior.

Patience (epomone, ee-po-mo-nee, accent on the last syllable in Greek) is quite a word. Not so long ago, it was common for devout Christians to embark upon a pilgrimage that covered hundreds of miles to see a venerable elder and ask him for a word. One day I looked at Father Paisios and asked, "Geronda [a Greek term for one gifted with deep reverence for the gifts of the Holy Spirit, discernment and love to provide spiritual direction], give me a word." With a glance at me, as if he had been expecting the solicitation for some time, he lovingly responded: "Patience." Up to that point, much of what I had understood about Sacred Scripture was merely conceptual knowledge; it was not experiential knowledge like that which one has about the mundane, or day-to-day details of his life. To struggle in attaining the virtue of patience under the instruction of Father Paisios was to begin experiencing the commands of Christ – not in my head, but in my heart. It was quite a revelatory encounter with God's grace, as I finally understood what it means to perceive events from a salvific rather than a worldly perspective. For instance, the daily rancor I felt due to: the absence of daily support from fellow members of the Body of Christ (Orthodox Christians); intense struggles to obtain even the most rudimentary necessities (such as a prayer rope); the inability to secure timely responses to theological inquiries; the isolation in a control unit prison; and so forth had all led to a predominant feeling of abandonment. As I started to obey the counsels of Father Paisios, especially his command to struggle to attain patience, I began to see that what I had viewed as senseless adversity were the very circumstances that were required for my salvation. How ironic it is for this one-time anti-establishment radical to come to this understanding. God knows exactly what we require for the working out of our salvation, even if it means to be on death row. Consequently, the antidote to sorrow over what I had identified as an intolerable situation is patience.

Even as I have prayed for patience there have been stressful events that demand humility and suffering as circumstances continue to place me at crossroads. I must choose between self-imposed anger over supposed abuses or the patience required to endure to the end. Having previously misperceived abuses and injustices as nothing more than exercises in frustration, Rachel and I came to recognize the necessity of a continuous struggle for salvation as the purpose of life. Protestantism has no such understanding of salvation. Slowly, Rachel and I were being prepared to truly journey together toward eternal life.

While my understanding of the need to struggle for salvation had occurred prior to Rachel's conversion to Orthodoxy, she benefitted from our discussions on Orthodox theology. The little scraps of paper we had studied on visits were eventually turned into a book written under my Baptismal name (Anthony), entitled West of Jesus (Regina Orthodox Press, 2006; reprinted by Xlibris, 2012). The concept of struggling to the end for salvation had entered her precious heart. That is not to say that she had already embraced the entirety of Orthodox theology, for there were times I felt so helpless as I encouraged her toward the Orthodox Church. My beloved wife would often pose a question to which I had no answer. Unable to immediately contact my spiritual father or to otherwise research her query, I felt of no use to her. At the same time it was God's grace, especially during those moments of discouragement and frustration, that really directed Rachel toward the Orthodox Church. The visible development within me of patience, a virtue that had been utterly absent while I was a Protestant, provided tangible evidence for her. I am not inferring that I was always patient – far from it – since even on a daily basis I have often distanced myself from this virtue. The fact remains that my patience had developed enough to encourage Rachel toward Orthodoxy.

It was on an afternoon visit in December of 2006, that my darling wife provided me with a gift that equaled the joy bestowed upon me on another December day many years earlier – that exceedingly exquisite moment when Rachel and I were married in December of 1991. Rachel asked me to hold onto my seat, and then with love in her eyes, she informed me that she had decided to become Orthodox!

Rachel is not at all the kind of person that enters into a commitment rashly, nor does she make promises to merely please someone else. That much is clearly evident from the care and consideration she exercised in contemplating marriage. When Rachel expressed her intent to become Orthodox, I knew that inherent in her decision was her desire to commit herself to the Orthodox Church. I was in Heaven; truly, we two were becoming one.

Chapter Thirteen

Eastern Orthodox Paradise

During the time I was a member at Christ Community Church (CCC) I became involved in several of its activities, regularly participating in the women's Bible study group. I felt very comfortable at that church, and had my husband not introduced me to Orthodox Christianity, I would most likely have still been there. It was in 1999 that Frank informed me of his intention to become Orthodox. Out of ignorance, my immediate reaction was one of anger. I could see that my response had really hurt my husband, yet I remained confused. I had no idea about where, when, or why he had made such a tremendously huge and seemingly rash decision. I was not aware of his intense studies of Orthodox Christianity until later.

My husband was baptized into the Greek Orthodox Church in July of 2000. Over the next year or two, whenever he tried to discuss Orthodox Christianity with me I put up obstacles to each and every discussion. My experience, up until then, had been solely with Protestant denominations. The Christianity that I understood was only that which they had filtered through their lenses. I had been involved in so-called non-denominational churches, which have ties to Fundamentalist and Evangelical leanings, but was also aware of other strains, such as Baptists, Lutherans and Pentecostals. There are other groups professing Christianity, including Mormons and Jehovah Witnesses, but mainstream Protestantism views these as cults. The sheer size of Catholicism tends to preclude it being seen as a cult; however, many Protestants still consider the Catholic Church, like cults, to have severely distorted the apostolic faith. Initially, after my husband had proclaimed allegiance to Eastern Christianity, I remembered that Catholics rely on priests and the Pope, so I attributed a similar dependence to the Orthodox Church. It remains a sad fact that the only thing I knew about Eastern Orthodox Christianity was that a local Greek Orthodox Church held some sort of annual festival. These are some of the issues that motivated my obstruction to and frustration with my husband's Orthodox faith.

The greatest issue I had was a sense of loss, for my husband and I had listened to sermons together and then read and searched for interpretations on our own. We had always piloted along under the banner of solo scriptura (The Bible Alone). That I would have to contemplate working with others for an understanding of Sacred Scripture was disconcerting to me.

Interestingly, once I began to study Church history I learned when, where and how our misguided concept of using reason to understand God had arisen. The West (Catholicism and Protestantism) has been terribly infected by Augustine of Hippo (354-430), especially through his having advanced the notion that rational thought (human reason) can enable knowledge of God. This exercise in pride increased in the West during the eleventh to fifteenth century Scholastic period. Anselm of Canterbury (1033-1109) taught that we must first accept God in order to then "prove" His existence by logical arguments. Thus, instruction in the West centered on the elevated mind being able to know the Holy Trinity, a heresy that intentionally placed Scholastic thinkers over Church Father theology. Included here is my own error in seeing a progression (in the Christian life) from faith, to knowledge, to understanding and, as such, seeing spiritual gain as an advancement of human reason. The folly in this concept rests precisely in the thinking that I was my own judge of true scriptural interpretation. I had done nothing less than placed my own ideas, and therefore stationed myself, above Prophets, Saints and Apostles. Clearly, such a use of reason in attempting to know God can only result in concocting an imaginary and non-existent god. The sense of loss I suffered was vast. First, I could no longer listen to my church sermons with Frank. I felt that I was losing the grounding of the faith which I had understood so well for so many years. Then I began feeling troubled by the drastic differences between how Protestantism and Eastern Orthodox Christianity understand God. Eastern Christianity was so foreign to me, that I found it upsetting to deal with my husband's conversion to the Orthodox Christian Church.

At last, Frank asked me to visit Father Paisios – this faithful servant of God is Frank's spiritual father and the Abbot of St. Anthony's Greek Orthodox Monastery in Florence, Arizona. I visited Father Paisios a few times. He counseled me to pray for guidance and to then wait for God and to follow in His time. It was a difficult period for me. I felt that my husband and I were no longer of the same faith, because it seemed that he was questioning all that I thought we had believed. It was as if only I believed in the faith we had heretofore pursued together. I experienced great turmoil over our no longer being on the same path, so much so that it was at that time that I realized I was suffering from depression.

I had experienced on and off bouts of depression for most of my life, and I began to feel more upset over the concerns I faced involving the vastly different faith paths my husband and I were taking. My friend, Margaret, told me of a couple at CCC and suggested that I see the wife. Flo was a psychiatric nurse who counseled some of CCC's parishioners. I first went to see Flo in the fall of 2003 at her home office. After a lengthy introductory session, she suggested that I speak to her husband. Floyd was a psychiatrist, and after having interviewed me, he diagnosed chemical depression and put me on some medication. I began the prescribed regimen and began to feel a little better over the next few weeks. I was no longer experiencing so much anxiety and felt far less overwhelmed. I saw Flo for a while. She was very helpful in assisting me with a variety of issues, many of which stemmed from childhood and had inflicted problems involving rejection, which included a tendency to become easily overwhelmed and feelings of inadequacy. The first several months of counseling were extremely painful as we began delving into the issues from my childhood. I had never faced those feelings head on and it was extremely difficult to do so. Many times, after a session, I would go home and have to go to bed from the exhaustion. We soon moved on to discussing my dissatisfaction over my husband having converted to Orthodox Christianity. Interestingly, Flo also had a divinity degree, so she had some knowledge of Orthodoxy. She also purchased several books on the Orthodox Faith for me to study.

During one particular session, I discussed my feelings about others' rejection to my marriage to Frank, an especially sensitive subject for me. Flo suggested that perhaps others felt awkward as a result of not being sure of what to do with me – that is, the highly unusual circumstance of my marriage to a death row prisoner was hard for most people to handle. We explored how rather than people being judgmental over my marital decision, some sense of discomfort may have flowed from not knowing how to react or how to lend their support. Others may even have been afraid to become close to me and Frank, lest in the end my husband was executed, which was a possibility they could not handle.

As the months went by I began to experience more emotional stability, and became confident enough to avoid hypersensitivity. I no longer needed to see Flo as often. I felt less inadequate and had fewer feelings of rejection. I was, however, developing an increasing sense of discomfort at CCC. During both weekly church services and the women's Bible study, I felt more disenfranchised with mainstream Protestantism. When I expressed those feelings to my husband, he advised me to seek out a local Orthodox priest to air my questions and concerns. It was then that I made precious Father Philip's acquaintance.

I contacted Father Philip, the priest at the Holy Resurrection Antiochian Orthodox Church in Tucson, Arizona, and we set up a meeting. Our first talk lasted about two hours. I was comforted by his patience and sincere effort to be helpful. Father Philip suggested that I read the book, Becoming Orthodox by Father Gilquist. Although this outstanding work answered many of my questions, I found that once I had perused Becoming Orthodox and other books, I had other questions. My husband thought that some of my questions could be answered if I attended an Orthodox Christian service; I determined to do so at the very next instance.

My first visit to a Holy Resurrection service was a bit surprising. Everything – the icons, use of incense, absence of musical instruments, solemnity of the service, etc. – was very foreign and unfamiliar, not at all like the Protestant services to which I was accustomed. As I look back at my initial brush with the Orthodox Church, I simply have to smile. Everything that I had found so alien, everything of which I had been so critical, everything is what I have come to deeply love. As a Protestant I had been led to believe that praying to saints was a form of necromancy, an occult communication with spirits of the dead. I had thought that the act of signing myself with the cross was a superstition and that venerating (honoring, not

Father Philip.

worshipping) icons was idolatry. As I continued to study Church history, in part by reading about the lives of the saints, Bible verses I hadn't previously considered sprang to life. I realized that the prayers of the faithful, and those of the prophets and saints in particular, are extremely powerful. "The prayer of a righteous man has great power..." (Jas. 5:16). I also understood that the faithfully departed remain alive in Paradise; that is, God is the God of the living (cf. Mt. 22:32). Based on this understanding, it became natural to see that saints continue to pray for us, even after their physical death. Therefore, it is as common to seek their prayers as it is to request the prayers of those with whom we attend services. Similarly, Scripture that instructs us to "put on the [ ] armor" and use weaponry against demons (cf, 2 Cor. 6:7; 2 Cor. 10:4; Eph. 6:10-17) took on far greater significance as I read about the power of the Cross in passages by St. John Chrysostom and St. Athanasios.[7] Moreover, verses that speak of the use of icons made of "carved likenesses" (cf, Ex. 25:18-19; 1 Ki. 6:23; Ezk. 41:17-18, 25; Heb. 9:5) became real to me as I gazed at the icons in Holy Resurrection Church. Through reading Church history I learned that icons were fully endorsed after the defeat of anti-icon proponents (iconoclasts) in the eighth century by the Seventh Ecumenical Council.

I was struck by one Scripture verse in particular which clearly points to the unification of Scripture verses and Holy Tradition: "Stand fast and hold the traditions which you were taught, whether by word or our epistle," (2 Thess. 2:15). That verse reveals the greatest Protestant deviation from truth: the eternal security ideology. That false ideology is based on certain verses in

---

7   "When therefore you sign yourself, think of the purpose of the cross, and quench any anger and all other passions. Consider the price that has been paid for you." (St. John Chrysostom, *Commentary on Matthew*) "... by the sign of the cross... all magic is stayed, all sorcery confounded, all idols are abandoned and deserted, and all senseless pleasure ceases, as the eye of faith looks up to heaven from the earth." (St. Athanasios, *On the Incarnation*)

isolated usage, as in "Whoever believes in Him should not perish but have everlasting life" (Jn. 3:16), in order to come to a fundamental misunderstanding of the "we were, are, and will be saved" aspect of their brand of Christianity. Protestantism lacks essential teachings, like "we must work out our salvation to the end" (Phil. 2:12); "faith without works is dead" (Jas. 2:17, 20), and the dozens of verses affirming that we must endure to the end in order to be saved (e.g., Mt. 10:22; Mt. 24:13; Mk. 13:13; Lk. 21:19; Heb. 3:14; etc.). By neglecting to promote a holistic understanding of sacred Scripture, thousands of horrible departures from the Truth have taken root. I had even subscribed to the Protestant proclamation that the Most Holy Mother of God had given birth to other children, even though the Second Ecumenical Council at Constantinople (in 553) and the Bible state otherwise: "Then the man brought me back to the outer gate of the sanctuary, the one facing east, and it was shut. The Lord said to me, 'This gate is to remain shut. It must not be opened; no one may enter through it. It is to remain shut because the Lord, the God of Israel, has entered through it'" (Ezk. 44:1-2). It became abundantly clear to me that Protestantism has ripped the very heart out of the First Century Church established by the Lord Jesus Christ.

Looking back, I can see that the prior ignorance on my part came from the lack of theology in Protestantism. I recall false premises, such as man having been created perfect in the Garden (man as immortal by nature) and that his fall had been from that perfected state – one has to wonder how perfect man could fall! As a Protestant I had no understanding of humanity having been created as capable of becoming perfect, "Therefore you shall be perfect, just as your Father in heaven is perfect" (Mt. 5:48). With this verse firmly in hand, I understood that rather than having been made perfect, Adam was instructed to not eat of the tree because in his unperfected state he could not have assimilated its knowledge. In other words, we are made immortal by grace and not by nature. The Western understanding – that of perfect man unable to comprehend all knowledge – is obviously ridiculous. Speaking of immortality, the fact of man's death discredits the West's delusional stand that man was created perfect.

My growing love for Eastern Orthodox Christianity continued to flourish. I learned that the Western church doctrine, which asserts that all humans have guilt which creates a debt that demands God's justice, is false. The "original" sin concept states that God's wrath is due to Adam's disobedience; thus, all mankind has to be punished. The absurdity of that concept became clear; for according to Western belief, death was created by God, and evil (satan) is a tool of God's punishment. "If any man does not confess that the first man, Adam, through his transgression suffered the wrath and indignation of God and, because of this, death, let him be anathema [reviled, shunned]" (Catholic 1546 Council of Trent; Fifth Session, First Canon). This concept was also supported by the teaching of Aquinas that there is "satisfaction of divine justice," because captivity to the devil is considered to be punishment by God. Protestantism had led me very far from a true understanding. Church history, however, led me to the truth, because the Third Ecumenical Council (in 431) verifies that we were not condemned together with Adam. Adam's sin is "ancestral"; it is what caused passions to enter and make human nature sick. In this reality it is demons (not God) that influence us toward evil; they are the cause of temptations. Therefore, Aquinas was wrong; redemption is actually liberation from the devil, and it is salvation from corruption and death, as well as the healing of human nature. I was not aware of Eastern Orthodox theology because I had been so enmeshed in Protestantism. I had even accepted the West's blasphemous claim that God's grace (His energies) had been created, because I had understood grace to be the elevation of human reason. Clearly, if God's energies had been created, then God could not be uncreated. My studies of the teachings of the Church Fathers rescued me from the devil's playground that is Protestantism, and I continue to fall further and further in love with the One Holy Apostolic Orthodox Church.

I met regularly with Father Philip and also began to read catechetical books (including the multi-volume set by Father Thomas Hopko of St. Vladimir's Seminary). At the same time, I began to attend more services at Holy Resurrection; so my attendance at the Protestant Christ Community Church decreased. As I continued to move toward Orthodoxy, I asked Father Philip how I would know when it was time for me to become an Orthodox Christian. Given that every catechumen, at some point, receives in his/her heart inner information or advice from God on when it is time to undergo baptism, he explained that I would become Orthodox Christian during a Divine Liturgy (what Protestants wrongly refer to as Holy Communion) service. And so it was shortly afterward that I simply felt that the time had come for me to leave Christ Community Church.

In late 2006, I became a catechumen. In the Orthodox Church converts must undergo a process of instruction. In ancient times this spanned up to three years, but now it generally lasts for less than a year (from Christmas/Nativity until Easter/Pascha). During the catechetical process I read as much as I could on the lives of the saints and Church history. Thankfully, Frank had a few dozen books on these topics and I was able to make use of some of them. The catechetical process was exciting and fulfilling, especially the beautiful Nativity service (my first), that began at 11:00 p.m. and went into the early morning hours. Protestantism, and its willy-nilly each-church-make-it-up-on-their-own-standard, was never like that. I felt such an attachment to the first century ancient Church.

I continued as a catechumen until April 7th 2007, which was Pascha (Easter) eve and my dad's birthday. I must say, the baptismal event on that day was a very unique experience. Jeff's Bible church did not stress the necessity for baptism, and my "baptism" at Christ Community Church was understood as little more than a public confession of belief in Christ. There was no such thing as chrismation, either. In the Orthodox Church we are baptized and chrismated (anointed with chrism, which is consecrated holy oil, during the sacrament of chrismation). Baptism is our cleansing and the onset of life in Christ: "Arise and be baptized and wash away your sins" (Ac. 22:16) and "For as many of you as were baptized in Christ have put on Christ" (Gal. 3:27). Chrismation, which immediately follows baptism, is our reception of the Holy Spirit by being anointed with chrism, which is oil mixed with numerous aromatic spices that has been consecrated: "You were sealed [anointed] with the Holy Spirit" (Eph. 1:13) and "You have an anointing from the Holy One" (1 Jn. 2:20). When baptized, we wear white garments and undergo three full immersions, in accord with Sacred Scripture, to "[baptize] in the name of the Father, and of the Son, and of the Holy Spirit" (Mt.28:19). Baptism is a literal death, burial and resurrection with the Lord Jesus Christ (cf. Col. 2:12 and Ro. 6:3-4). The priest also gives us a godparent who is with you during the entire baptismal event. My godparent is Elizabeth, and she has been such a blessing to me.

After having been baptized by three full immersions in water, in the name of the Father, Son, and Holy Spirit, I was anointed with the oil of chrismation. Father Philip applied the oil on my eyes (to see the life in Christ), ears (to correctly hear instruction), mouth (to protect my speech), heart (to guard my heart), hands (to watch over acts/work) and feet (to guide my walk in Christ). After I was chrismated, I was tonsured, an act wherein a lock of hair is cut off as a means by which to affirm my rejection of the world, love of body, the old man (my old self or attachments to particular thoughts) and passions. Then I was given the baptismal name of Sarah. Prior to attending my first Divine Liturgy, I changed into more white garments; in fact, I wore white to Divine Liturgy for the next four weeks in order to be set apart as a new convert. At the end of that first Divine Liturgy Father Philip tossed a basket of rose petals on the congregation; then a meal was held for new converts and family. That night, which was Pascha eve, we also received a gift basket that had a candle, potted flower, icon and prayer book before returning home until it was time for

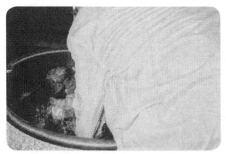

Rachel, during her 3 immersions in the baptismal water.

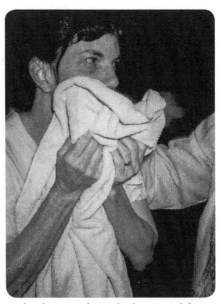

After her exit from the baptismal font.

Pascha services. My conversion and continued attendance at Divine Liturgy make it clear that I have left behind the empty usage Protestantism makes of crackers and grape juice to infer remembrance of Christ. The Divine Liturgy makes it possible to wholly embrace the first century teaching of Jesus, "Take, eat; this is My body... this is My blood" (Mt. 26:26, 28). The "this" that is being eaten at every Divine Liturgy is the Lord's literal flesh and the drinking of His literal blood (cf. Jn. 6:53-55), and we do so for our purification (cf. Heb. 4:12).

I was back in church at 10:00 p.m. for the Pascha service, which went until about 2 a.m. Elizabeth explained as the service proceeded, as I did not understand some things. At its onset there was a sense of so-

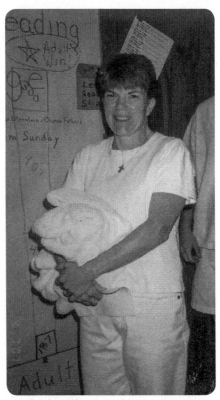

Orthodox Christian, like her husband.

lemnity; the church was very dark and lit only with candles held by parishioners. (The solemn nature of this service is intentional and signifies that Christ Jesus is still in the grave.) At midnight, everyone went outside and walked around the church. Having walked around the church once, while holding candles and singing, we went back inside, where I noticed that the lights had been turned on to represent Jesus Christ having risen. At that point the Divine Liturgy began; after it concluded we all enjoyed a wonderful feast. As the Great Lent fast had ended with the resurrection of Christ, the food for breaking the fast (meats, dairy, etc.) had been placed in baskets that were at the base of the cross at the front of the church. It was my first Divine Liturgy and Pascha feast as an Orthodox Christian. I truly felt complete, both individually and in my marriage.

A few weeks after Pascha of 2007, some visitors who were disciples of Bishop Athanasios in Cyprus came to see Father Paisios at St. Anthony's Monastery, here in Arizona. Bishop Athanasios had told them about my husband and myself and they wanted to meet us. Abbot Epiphanios, Abbot Nicholas (both became bishops just a couple of months after their return from the USA) and Father Theoklitos went to see Frank at the prison the day before I was to travel up to the monastery to see them. They told me that to visit someone on death row was a truly overwhelming experience. On the day of my arrival at the monastery, I initially spent about an hour with just Father Theoklitos. He was relatively fluent in English, while the abbots were able to speak very broken English, at best. Eventually, Abbot Epiphanios and Abbot Nicholas joined Father Theoklitos and me. They wanted to hear about how I had met Frank and how I became Orthodox. With Father Theoklitos as the interpreter, I related to Abbot Epiphanios how Frank had told me of his intention to convert to the Orthodox faith in 1999. I also mentioned that when he had expressed this to me, I thought he had gone crazy. In broken English, Abbot Epiphanios said, "And now you are crazy, too!"

I also shared with these three faithful servants of Christ

a few details on my baptism. They had indicated that when they had visited Frank the day before, he had showed them photographs of my baptism. Father Theoklitos informed me of Abbot Epiphanios' instruction to us regarding writing our autobiography. It was then that Frank and I embarked upon this work (may God forgive our delay).

About five months after having seen the Cypriot monks, Bishop Athanasios visited St. Anthony's Monastery. Even though he was the Cypriot bishop who had led Frank to Orthodoxy, we had never met him; so it was a great honor to have the opportunity to do so. He went with Father Paisios to see Frank at the prison. As with Abbot Epiphanios, Abbot Nicholas and Father Theoklitos, Bishop Athanasios found it a very overwhelming ex-

Right: Abbot Epiphanios, Bishop of Ledra, Machairas Monastery, Cyprus, during his 2007 visit in St. Anthony's Monastery. **Left**: Elder Ephraim, ex-abbot of Philotheou Monastery, Mount Athos, Greece, founder and spiritual father of St. Anthony's Monastery, AZ and 20 more Christian Orthodox Monasteries in the USA and Canada.

This photograph of Rachel was taken in the beautiful gardens of St. Anthony's Monastery, AZ, on the 40th day after her baptism, during her meeting with the fathers from Cyprus, who had visited the Monastery and also, Frank in prison in 2007.

perience to visit someone on death row. He met with me several days later at the monastery. Having met with all of these obedient disciples of Christ really encouraged me at the onset of my life in the Savior.

Unfortunately, the reaction to my conversion to Orthodoxy by most of my Protestant acquaintances was quite adverse. Seeing their negative attitudes through the window of my residual low self-esteem made their rejection very hurtful at first, especially when those who had been my friends turned their back on me. However, by the grace of God, in the Orthodox Church I have begun to learn that it is not positive self-esteem that ought to be developed, but humility. That is not to say that I am never susceptible to what others think of me. The road to humility is truly a long road and requires much patience. For instance, patience was required when many friends from my Protestant days believed that I had only become Orthodox because my husband was Orthodox. Again, God's grace comforted me as I realized that it was from an ignorance of God that others failed to under-stand my conversion to Orthodoxy.

Near the end of 2007, a friend of mine, who had no church experience, was very supportive of my having become Orthodox. Ruth had moved to Tucson from New England in 2006, and was the daughter of a friend of mine. As soon as she arrived in Tucson she began cleaning houses with me. In so many ways, Ruth was a real blessing in my life. She and her husband have two chil-dren, and all of them became a part of my family (Ruth's son and daughter were the grandkids that my dad never had). While she has difficulty in understanding why I wanted to marry someone who was on death row, she has always supported my decision; she is truly a good friend.

By mid-year of 2008, my life totally changed. I had just returned that May from a two-week vacation with my aunt in San Antonio when I was summoned to Los Angeles by my husband's parents. I received a call from their housekeeper, who, in very broken English, told me that my father-in-law had been taken to the hospital after having fallen and suffering a compression frac-ture in his back. My mother-in-law needed me to arrive as soon as possible. I called the University of California at Los Angeles (UCLA) Medical Center in order to talk with my father-in-law's doctor and see exactly what was going on, arranged for a plane reservation and made an appointment to see my husband at the prison before leaving for Los Angeles.

I saw Frank that Saturday, on May 24th 2008, and he gave me a letter to deliver to his dad. Of course he did not realize that it would be the last letter that he would ever write his dad. I was to leave for Los Angeles on Sunday and return on Tuesday. Little did I know that I would remain in Los Angeles for a month.

Upon my arrival at LAX (Los Angeles International Air-port), I was met by my cousin and we immediately went to St. John's Hospital, where my father-in-law had been transferred. I gave him Frank's letter, and he seemed very touched by its con-tents. I was able to spend some quality time with him; however, he was very weak and in much pain. In fact, he was unable to walk and had been told that once released from the hospital, he would have to spend several weeks in a rehabilitation center. Upon hearing that, I knew that it would be far more than a couple of days before I would go back home to Tucson.

From the hospital my cousin took me to the family home on Saltair. My mother-in-law wanted to immediately be taken to the hospital to see her husband of nearly sixty years. I had not seen the folks in a few years, but quickly knew they were deteriorating as soon as I saw my mother-in-law who had bruises on her face from having fallen in the yard. As we were preparing to leave I told her that her husband was unable to walk and would have to spend time in rehab. She was not willing to accept that news and repeatedly declared so to me, as if to confirm that she had correctly heard the tragic development. She seemed to be trying to process the meaning of the tragedy that had befallen them. At the hospital she disbelievingly cited the news to her husband and stated that he could return home and have a nurse care for him. Dad tried so patiently to explain the impossibility of that scenario.

I recall an occasion that had taken place several years earlier, when I was in Los Angeles and my father-in-law had to be taken to the hospital. At the time, I was struck by how my mother-in-law had become, in effect, like a child; that is, she was so fearful and helpless. I was watching the exact same thing unfold. I believe she was very scared, which made reality even more difficult to comprehend.

As my mother-in-law and I left the hospital, neither of us had a clue that we would never again see Brigadier General John Warmington Atwood alive. We both believed that his hospitalization was not a life-threatening condition. While a compression fracture in an eighty-eight year old man's back is indeed serious, even the doctor had spoken of some form of recovery. That night I spoke with my father-in-law on the telephone. He was in a good mood and was very happy that I was in Los Angeles to care for his beloved wife. I had no idea that I would never talk to him again.

The phone rang the next day at about 6:15 in the morning. The hospital was on the line and I was being told that my father-in-law had aspirated. Then, while I was still talking to the doctor, a nurse told him that dad had suffered a heart attack. He was dead!

I got off of the phone, my head spinning, as I had to quickly figure out how to tell my mother-in-law about her husband's death. She was still asleep. I called my dad and told him the news, and then asked his advice on what to tell Mom. He suggested that I simply wake her up and tell her what had happened. Over the course of the following weeks, my father continued to be a great source of support and help, even from all the way out in Tucson. Since my mother-in-law was totally deaf, I had to always write everything down for her. In this instance, I gently woke her so she could read my note about her beloved husband's passing. She read the note, then stared at me for a minute. Then she said that it was probably his heart. I wrote down how the doctor had told me that he had aspirated and then had a heart attack. While she understood, throughout the day she continued to ask how her husband had died. I was amazed to notice that she did not seem that upset; she simply got out of bed and began her daily routine. She was obviously in shock, and performing her daily tasks was probably the best thing she could do at the time.

Later on that morning I told her that we needed to go to the hospital to take care of arrangements. She began to stall and I saw that she dreaded the eventuality. Throughout it all, I thought of my husband and wondered how on earth to tell him of his daddy's death. I called his priest, Father Paisios, to see if he was available and to inquire about how he could arrange to see Frank. As it turned out, he was not at the monastery, but stated that he could be at the prison by 11:00 a.m.; that was a usual visitation for a Monday. So I called the visitation office and asked if, given the circumstances, Frank's priest could see him. Normally visits had to be scheduled at least twenty-four hours in advance. They permitted the exception; I was extremely relieved since I wanted Frank's spiritual father to be the one to tell Frank that his dad had died. I did not want the news to be delivered by prison personnel and asked visitation to be sure that no leakage of information occurred. It was the beginning of many blessings that occurred during the next month. I truly saw God leading and guiding me every step of the way through the very painful journey I had to go through.

For some reason, rather than my simply driving my mother-in-law to the hospital, she instructed me to call the housekeeper to drive us to the hospital. Upon arriving at St. John's Hospital, Mom was very hesitant to enter her deceased husband's room. After we had spoken with the doctor, she decided not to go in to see dad. Immediately after I had been to see dad, Mom asked if he was really dead. I wrote the note that told her he had passed away. She was very upset that there was so much paperwork to deal with before we could leave the hospital, and it was very difficult to help her understand the protocol when someone has deceased.

At that point I could tell that my mother-in-law was exhausted and we returned home. Upon arriving at the family estate I began making calls; there were mortuary arrangements, telephoning my father-in-law's sister, other notifications, and so on. I was able to set up an appointment for the next day with the funeral director, who was very kind and extremely perceptive. My father-in-law's sister desired a large military funeral, whereas my mother-in-law intended a simple service; a conflict was clearly a potential. I had great difficulty in explaining to dad's sister that her brother would not be buried at Arlington National Cemetery, the main military burial site in Virginia, and that the plans for a funeral at Arlington had long since been changed. Finally, I told my father-in-law's sister to please not make an issue of the burial arrangements because it was very upsetting to my mother-in-law; at last she agreed to the military burial plans in Riverside, California.

After we had arrived home, my mother-in-law's behavior became extremely irrational, an anomaly that would continue for several months. She had waves of intense sorrow that were followed by bouts of frightening rage. For example, despite the obvious need to take the time to call to make arrangements and notifications, my mother-in-law kept asking me why I was on the telephone all of the time. When I explained the need to provide notifications, she immediately became irate and said that no one had to know. Occasionally, I would find her trying to go through heavy containers, an alarmingly dangerous venture for a frail ninety-two year old woman. When I suggested she cease her activity, my mother-in-law would angrily declare that she would do as she wished and that no one was going to control her.

I was very frustrated over the sudden responsibility of having to handle things that I had never imagined or done before. In addition to my mother-in-law's irrational swings, part of my frustration included the need to explain everything via the arduous process of writing notes to her. Complex topics, such as death benefits, business affairs, etc, all had to be discussed only in writing. It was a great blessing to have been able to talk daily with my husband on the telephone during the first few weeks after his dad's death. The standard procedure was for prisoners to receive only two calls weekly, but for some reason we were getting two calls daily. That was also a blessing from God, since this never had happened before. I felt a sense of satisfaction in knowing that my dear husband was obtaining news of daily developments, and it was a real source of encouragement. It was also good to be able to vent, instead of banging my head against the wall!

It was difficult to journey to the mortuary and make funeral arrangements. The funeral director was a very kind man who understood immediately what I was dealing with. He was very patient with Mom and tried to explain everything to her in a way that she would understand. I believe that Mr. Baker was also a blessing from God. He said he would help me in any way that he could to make for a smooth transition. When we returned from the funeral home, Mom asked me for the mail. I gave her the bills and she sat at dad's desk and looked at them. I knew there was a bank statement in the pile, and wondered what she was thinking as she looked at it. I had some idea of the state of the finances, but she had none. I was lying on my bed when she came into the room holding the bank statement, and said that she wanted me to call the realtor, Mr. Kennedy. I flew off the bed, knowing that this, too, was an answer to prayer. In the past several years, dad had attempted to help Mom see the necessity of moving from their home. The cost to maintain it had become a real burden and source of stress for dad. He and I had had many discussions on the topic. She had dug her feet in on the issue and refused to listen whenever he broached the subject. So I contacted the family's realtor to inform him of dad's death and Mom's desire to sell. Mr. Kennedy indicated a desire to attend the funeral and to then arrange the sale of the Saltair estate.

The funeral service was held in the chapel of the mortuary. Dad's sister and her husband flew in from Texas, as did his niece and nephew; that was all the family that remained on dad's side. I had some concerns over the estranged relations between Mom and her husband's relatives and also felt an edge due to dad's sister's displeasure at there not having been a burial at Arlington National Cemetery. Thankfully, tensions thawed and events flowed smoothly.

On the day of the service the family housekeeper was to transport Mom and me to the funeral home; at the last minute Mom insisted that her boxer dog accompany her. When we arrived at the mortuary, the funeral director saw the dog and did not hesitate to grant permission for the attendance of dad's beloved pet at the service. It was yet another example of Mr. Baker's kindness and perception. Everyone except Mom viewed the body; she had remained steadfast in her refusal to observe dad after he had passed away. The service itself was very short. Dad was Episcopalian, but estranged from the ultra-liberal Episcopal Church he had attended for all of his life. Father John, who had been visiting my husband monthly for twenty years, arranged for an Episcopal priest he knew to conduct the funeral service, since he was unable to; but not many attendees arrived. I found that so very sad. For a man of dad's stature, an army general and president of Los Angeles' main television cable company, to have not had even a dozen people at his funeral was tragic. My cousin, who lives in Los Angeles and attended the funeral, made the same comment.

After the service Mom wanted to return home; so the housekeeper took her and the dog back to the family home while I traveled with the funeral director to the Riverside National Cemetery. We drove in the same hearse that had carried President Reagan; Mr. Baker told me that he had thought, given dad's status, that I'd like to know that detail. Dad's relatives journeyed in a separate vehicle. It was a long drive, some two hours. As we drove, the funeral director inquired about family relations; he was intrigued by the relationship between my husband and me.

Arriving at the cemetery, we noted that everything had been already set up, including the canopy, military personnel to play taps and perform the gun salute, etc. The burial was difficult for me and receiving the folded up flag that had covered the casket along with the spent bullet casings was a very emotional experience. Moreover, my husband had tearfully pleaded that his precious father not be buried alone, so I was present at the burial site as they lowered his casket into the ground.

The drive home was a long one and I was totally exhausted when I walked into the house. Mom posed many questions; I patiently relayed all the details to her and then presented her with the flag. She seemed really touched. I also explained that arrangements had been made for her to be buried on top of dad, one casket on top of the other, in the same excavation.

Dad's sister and her family had expressed a desire to visit Mom; so I suggested that dad would be pleased if she permitted it. Mom approved the request, which was another blessing from God, given the very estranged relations between Mom and dad's sister. They came over the next day and stayed for a short visit. Mom gave one adult child some of dad's personal belongings and bestowed upon the other one a beautiful portrait of dad's sister. As Mom was very tired and wanted to rest, they took me to lunch. I was quite pleased that familial relations had been restored, at least for dad's funeral.

Frank J.'s mom and dad.

Father Philip, my priest, had been in constant contact with me since dad's passing. He knew I was in L.A., virtually alone, to handle all the affairs. I told him that Mom was being very stubborn about allowing me into the file cabinet, where dad kept important papers. It was necessary that I go through the papers in there, and soon. He told me that he was coming to L.A. with his brother to help me. I was stunned by his willingness to do so. They arrived the day after dad's funeral. Mom had initially believed he was present for only moral support, but when she learned that he also intended to assist with family affairs, she became upset. She failed to comprehend the necessity of handling notifications and other business matters. Although dad had stored important documents in a file cabinet, whenever Mom saw any of us near it, she grew agitated and demanded that we leave it alone. Father Philip had brought his laptop computer with him; so whenever Mom would lie down or was in the garden, I would smuggle a few folders to Father Philip from dad's desk or file cabinet. He would then hide the folders behind his laptop in order to covertly review their contents. Occasionally Mom would appear, look around and inquire about our activities. Eventually she would take her sleeping medication and retire for the evening, a point at which we could freely review dad's documents.

Dad had a very easy to navigate filing system, and we soon came upon a file labeled "Upon My Death." Its contents included a letter with instructions on who to contact and other pertinent directions. I also reviewed dad's check ledger and noticed that over the last month there had been several donations to various animal rescue shelters, which we found ironic since dad had always complained about a lack of capital. Also, it saddened me to observe his increased dementia; he often had written duplicate checks.

We located information on selling the family home and found several life insurance policies; the first one had been taken out around the time dad had graduated West Point in 1942. We contacted all of the insurance companies, but one significant obstacle was that I did not possess a power of attorney. I asked Mom to complete a limited power of attorney document, but she repeatedly declined to do so, despite the fact that often a contact would not let me conduct the necessary action because I did not have power of attorney. Many of the contacts I made would ask to speak to Mom, which was not possible with her hearing impairment. My frustration was growing because I was trying to tie up loose ends in L.A. and close out accounts. Father Philip, who had to leave on Saturday to serve Divine Liturgy on Sunday morning, had flown back to Tucson, but his brother remained in L.A. with some friends and offered to assist in packing up some larger items for me. He also assisted me in cataloging the property items. Those we decided to discard were piled in the driveway, since the new owner was to dispose of them. The attic and garage were full and Father Philip's brother took care of getting all that organized for me. Mom took to him since he was helping and played with Maddy, her boxer. Anyone that showed Maddy attention was a friend of Mom's.

One difficult task was to sell the church organ that dad had been constructing since Frank had been sent to death row. It had been his outlet and passion, and he had spent many long hours working on it. The instrument could be played, but it was not complete. Dad was a lifelong organ aficionado; he had often traveled as a child to see famous theater organs. After he retired from the presidency of Theta Cable, he established an organ repair business, and worked on several well-known church organs in Los Angeles. His handmade organ was indeed a mighty accomplishment, but its having remained unfinished precluded his hope of donating it to West Nottingham Academy and also greatly diminished its value. At least I was able to locate someone who had a genuine appreciation for dad's finely detailed work to

Frankie's dad with the organ he built.

purchase the organ. His mastery at wood working had required shop tools that were unique in nature; so the organ's purchaser, a gentleman from San Diego who owned an organ business, also acquired dad's many tools. It was nice to have received a letter from the organ business owner who upon returning to San Diego had set up dad's organ. He expressed amazement at dad's ability and appreciation for dad's great work.

The week after dad's death, the realtor, who was also a family friend and offered much help, came over to discuss the family home's sale. He put the estate on the market and it sold in two days, for the full asking price. It was yet another blessing from God, given the state of the economy and housing market. I was happy that the area of Brentwood, California evidently didn't know the country was in a recession! The purchaser was a home builder who lived in the neighborhood; the day that he had looked at our home, he purchased it. His plan was to tear down the existing structure and to then construct a mansion on the property. Meanwhile, there was a home across the street from our residence in Tucson that had been on the market for several months. The seller was a Christian man who, after inheriting the home from his uncle, had done quite a bit of remodeling. My father (Pa) spoke to him and was able to arrange for Mom to take up residence prior to the closing on her California home. Thus, Pa worked on Tucson details, while I labored at packing up the Los Angeles home. I had less than a month to pack up and get out of the Saltair residence. As I looked around at all there was to do, and I being the one that would have the task, I prayed that the Lord have mercy on me!

A family friend, who worked as a registered nurse and had attended Christ Community Church with me, offered to journey to Los Angeles and assist me in packing and caring for Mom. We had spoken frequently by telephone while I was in L.A. and she knew that I was struggling. In fact, she also offered to transport Mom to Tucson. Her two weeks at the family home in Los Angeles, helping care for Mom, was truly appreciated.

Mom had become very nervous and extremely agitated. She was not thinking clearly in regards to all that needed to be done, and at one point I had to contact her doctor, who prescribed some medication to help calm her down. With the driveway piled with items we were discarding, I had, on several occasions, observed Mom on top of the pile digging through the property, and I became very concerned for her safety. When I tried to encourage her to return indoors, she stubbornly refused and became agitated. It seemed that her irrational behavior was a desperate attempt to assert some semblance of control in a life that had so suddenly spun out of kilter. She had lost her husband of nearly sixty years and was about to leave the home in which she had resided for fifty-five years. There were moments when she would yell at me for the decisions I made, which I found so very frustrating, since I had to make all of the decisions that she was unable to address. And there were times when Mom and I would be looking through family photo albums and reminiscing about good times, and she would suddenly grow quite upset. Of course, the loss of her husband and home had to inflict tremendous grief; still, her erratic behavior added to our already very stressful predicament.

Initially, the plan was to depart Los Angeles in early July; however, we altered it to the end of June. Mom had anticipated remaining until the sale of the estate closed, so leaving before then was upsetting for her. I explained that the owner of the home in Tucson had agreed to permit her residency there for a month prior to receiving funds from our purchase. I also let Mom know of my need to return to work. Furthermore, I believed that to not leave for Tucson immediately could lead to Mom attempting to remain in Los Angeles, on her own. She had already queried the realtor on the availability of a small house in another area of L.A.; thankfully, he had said that it was financially unfeasible and that she must be with me. Still, the closer we were to leaving, the more agitated Mom became. I had to continually explain the arrangements I had set up for the transport of her property to Tucson. Her doctor desperately attempted to convince her to fly to Tucson, but she remained adamant in her refusal, which gave us grounds for concern. Driving across the Mojave Desert in 110° temperatures was certainly very dangerous. Her main concern was to have Maddy with her, which would not have been possible on a plane. She continued to be irrational and to do things that were not safe.

Ruth's husband, DJ, and his father-in-law traveled to Los Angeles and I rented a moving truck for them. We planned to begin packing on a Friday and to complete the job on Saturday. Saturday morning came, and Mom took forever to get ready. A favorite pastime of hers had been to pick dead leaves from the ivy by the pool, and she went to do it one last time; it broke my heart. I just watched her out the window and began to cry, thinking of all the good memories we all had of the Saltair home. Finally, at about 11:00 a.m., she entered the car with her dog, Maddy and the nurse. Clutched tightly in her hand was the letter of encouragement my husband had sent. It was all extremely emotional, and as I watched the car leave the home that she had loved so much, I cannot even imagine the pain she must have felt as the car turned out of Saltair for the last time.

Once Mom and the nurse were underway, DJ, his father-in-law and I finished loading the moving truck. We all stayed in a hotel that night, and in the morning DJ and his father-in-law left for Tucson in the truck, while I headed to the airport. Flying home would enable me to begin preparing Mom's new home for her afternoon arrival. Mom and the nurse spent Saturday night in a hotel, after having traveled half of the way to Tucson. The trip was very rough for her. On Sunday evening Mom and the moving truck arrived at her new residence at around the same time. I was very nervous over how Mom would react to her new home, as she had only seen photographs of it. Thanks be to God that she appeared to be pleased, She was disappointed at the absence of grass and wished for a few changes, but I was able to get her bed and a few other items set up so that she could spend her first night in relative comfort. I was able to unpack and arrange

Mom's property over the next few days.

After a few days Father Philip brought over his daughter, Ashley, to meet Mom. Ashley needed a job and Mom required a care giver. After they visited for about twenty minutes, Mom asked when Ashley could start. Ashley said she could begin at once, so they arranged a four-hour schedule from 4:00 p.m. to 8:00 p.m., a period that enabled Ashley's presence for jause.

Jause. In Austrian households supper is frequently a late evening meal, so a mid-afternoon (usually at 4:00 p.m. or so) gathering occurs at which coffee or tea and some form of pastry is served, which is known as jause. We have been honored to have established this tradition in honor of Mom and her beloved homeland in some segments of Tucson. At first, when Ashley was off for one day a week, Pa and I would be with Mom in the afternoon/evening to celebrate jause with her. In fact, over the next year and a half everyone who came into contact with Mom loved jause.

It was a chore of several weeks' time to unpack all of Mom's things and arrange them as she wished. We had planned to store some of the extra items in a shed in the backyard and/or in a storage shed that was on the street in front of the house. Mom pronounced both sheds as unsightly and wanted the one in front removed at once. I had to explain that it could not be razed until after the closing. At the end of July the Los Angeles estate closed the day before the Tucson residence; yet on that day Mom refused to sign any papers until both sheds were gone. Consequently, I had to quickly unload the backyard shed and squeeze its contents into the already full house, as well as hire people to tear down and remove that shed and arrange for the shed out front to be hauled away. Mom then signed the papers. Once again, she was trying to control what little she could.

Another task was getting Mom's yard landscaped. My dad and I labored in the scalding sun of southern Arizona to lay some sod and plant some flowers, and we had a local nursery put in a tree. It was a real pleasure to see the home develop and to notice that Mom was calming down; she was not as contrary and began to view the house as her home. I had also adopted the tradition of bringing her fresh flowers from the store every week to have on the kitchen table. She would beam when I walked in and handed them to her. Ashley and others would bring her flowers occasionally, too.

Around the end of September 2008, I went over to Mom's on a Saturday morning and found that she was already dressed and wanted to go to the hospital. She held up her hand and it was obvious that she had broken her wrist. I rushed her to the emergency room, where the doctor intended to give her anesthetic and set the bone, but after some discussion it was decided that such a course of care would be too much for Mom. Her wrist was splinted and after the swelling went down in a few days, a cast was put on her arm. The cast was left on for six weeks and Mom suffered extensive pain. From that point on, I remained anxious that Mom would have another fall. I had known that it had been an all too often occurrence when dad was still alive. He didn't tell me every time she fell, but he told me enough that I was able to get the picture.

As winter approached, Mom was amazed at how cold it was in Tucson. She said that she liked the snow on Mt. Lemmon and joked about having forgotten her skis! She enjoyed our Thanksgiving dinner and the special tablecloth I had purchased for her. Shortly after Thanksgiving I began to put up Mom's Christmas decorations. We got her a small tree, put out various trinkets, and Pa put up Christmas lights on the house. When we took her outside to surprise her, she was overjoyed. Mom was quite funny when she was surprised; she became exceedingly excited and sort of squealed, like a kid.

Pa and I loved to bring flowers from the nursery to plant in Mom's garden as a surprise for her, and when Mom wanted some geraniums as Christmas neared, we got her a nice red one to plant. I also did a lot of baking and brought much of it to Mom; she absolutely loved it. For Christmas Mom came over to our house and we enjoyed a fine feast along with some family friends. I did notice that Christmas of 2008 was hard for Mom, it being the first one after dad's death; for as she opened her presents, she was happy and sad at the same time. We just hugged and cried; we missed dad and Frank, too.

After Christmas Mom wanted another tree, an orange tree; so we took her to the nursery to select her own tree. Since the trees were quite a distance from the entrance, the nursery kindly provided a golf cart for her to ride on. She found the perfect orange tree for her home. We also found a beautiful bird bath and quail blocks, as Mom absolutely loved to watch birds.

Mom turned ninety-three years old on her birthday, March 12th. In early March I decided to get her a patio table with matching chairs. Pa, Ashley and I formulated a plan for surprising Mom. We brought over balloons, flowers and apple strudel, and while Ashley occupied Mom in her bedroom, Pa and I set up the patio furniture. We tied balloons on the table and chairs before then guiding Mom onto the porch to surprise her... and was she ever pleasantly surprised! On the evening of her birthday, we served her Wiener schnitzel, a Viennese specialty that I was most happy to cook for her. We also gave her dad's favorite dessert, angel food cake. The excitement of the day really exhausted her, but she had a beautiful, special occasion.

About two months after Pa and I had given Mom her special day, Pa had a big scare. He had fallen in his bedroom and his ribs hurt a lot; then, a day or two later, he began to have a cold. Pa developed a bad cough, one that kept him up at night. After a week of coughing, he finally agreed to let me take him to the emergency room. After an examination, the doctor said that he had pneumonia and further related that his liver and kidneys were not functioning well; they admitted him at once. I was very scared that I was going to lose my dad; I had never seen him so sick.

Pa was hospitalized for three weeks. For a while he thought his life was ending, but by God's grace, he pulled through. He had to undergo myriad tests, was unable to eat solid food and ended up losing twenty-five pounds. It was a very frightening experience for all of us, especially that first week when Pa was in serious condition. During the whole of Pa's hospitalization, Mom was very afraid and nervous. Thankfully he returned home, but it still took him several months to regain his strength and stamina. When he came home and went over to see Mom, she was over-joyed. She and Pa had developed a very strong friendship. He has the patience of Job, which, many times, was necessary when dealing with Mom.

Frank's mom in Tucson, 91 years old.   Rachel's dad (Bob or Pa).

Toward the end of the summer of 2009, Ashley had decid-ed to move to Portland, Oregon, and intended to leave in early October. Near the end of September Mom had a bad fall. At about midnight my phone rang; it was Mom saying that she needed help. I quickly ran across the street to Mom's home and found her on the floor in the kitchen area, with her right leg twisted almost out to the side. She was in great pain, and I knew at once that the hip that had been replaced about a dozen years ago was dislocat-ed. I called my dad to come over after calling 911. That particular fall was the beginning of the end for Mom.

Mom was rushed to the hospital and after she was sedated,

doctors were able to put the hip back in. Afterward, she went to a rehabilitation facility and seemed to recover quickly. In hindsight, it probably would have been better to have brought her directly home from the hospital to have begun physical therapy. The rehab center was quite an unpleasant experience for her, as she remained highly agitated throughout and refused to follow instructions. Ashley had opted to delay her move until the end of October so she could aid in Mom's rehabilitation. Unsure of how much assistance Mom would require, Ashley remained with her for the first three nights before then returning to the usual four hours in the evening routine. Mom was insistent that she did not need someone with her at night, even though all of her falls had occurred at night. Over the next few weeks Mom endured a twice weekly in-home physical therapy schedule. She handled the sessions fairly well, but failed to follow home safety recommendations. For instance, upon the physical therapist's recommendation, I rolled up and put away all decorative Persian rugs prior to her returning home. However, after returning to Mom's a few hours later, I found Mom, clad in only undergarments, dragging the rugs back into the living room. When we inquired as to her action, she stated that she was "working" and that her rugs would remain in the living room... I had to relent and allow the rugs to remain.

Locating Ashley's replacement was a harrowing experience and required about three weeks to complete. We all loved Ashley so much. Mom and Ashley had a very special relationship that could be very volatile at times, but always ended with the two hugging. Ashley spent an extraordinary amount of time communicating with Mom. All communication with her had to be done on paper and Ashley would tell her stories and make her laugh by writing everything to her. It was crucial that the next care giver be willing to converse with Mom on paper. I never wanted her to feel left out because she didn't know what was being discussed. Mom could be quite finicky and the first four interviewees were, for one unknown reason or another, simply not right for her, but finally we found Lorrie and Mom was very pleased. Of course, all of us were very sad when Ashley left at the end of October, but Mom quickly adjusted to Lorrie and also liked Lorrie's boyfriend. He was able to converse with Mom in her native language of German, a real treat for her. Lorrie and her boyfriend began to call Mom "Oma" a German term of endearment for grandma or an elderly woman. Mom truly enjoyed their help.

For Thanksgiving of 2009 we provided a special dinner for Mom and she thoroughly enjoyed herself. It remains as one of my poignant memories, since day by day I had noticed how much more she was sleeping and how much less she was communicating. As with the previous year, after Thanksgiving we put up lights and Christmas decorations for her. It was also around this time that I began to notice wounds on her arms and legs. When I asked her about them, she insisted that a fall had caused them "weeks ago". We became very concerned and began to keep a closer watch over her, particularly as confusion and a significant increase in incontinence had set in.

Chapter Fourteen

Enduring to the End

A S 2007 dawned upon us, Rachel began the official process of her catechism and to also attend Sunday services regularly at the Holy Resurrection Antiochian Orthodox Church in Tucson, Arizona. She participated in catechist classes and met with Father Philip rather frequently. Moreover, our continued study of Church history served as a sort of auxiliary catechism, as we examined all seven Ecumenical Councils, some regional councils and a few individual Church Father canons. Our sources of reference included The Rudder, an exhaustive work wherein Church councils are rigorously analyzed, as well as works by early Church Fathers, such as Justin Martyr. Our undertaking definitely afforded a beautiful panorama of the rich, centuries-old, unbroken history of the Apostolic Church. In Protestantism there is a claim that after Christ Jesus and His Apostles in the first century, any type of Christianity that existed was not authentic. What they term as "authentic Christianity" was resurrected in the sixteenth century by Martin Luther's Reformation; of course this begs the question of what occurred in the intervening millennium and a half.

Included also in our studies of Church history, from The Rudder as well as some of the works by early Church Fathers (e.g., Justin Martyr, a latter second century Church Father, et al.), were many of the heresies defeated by the Church[8] and Church Father canons on morality. These were especially enlightening and I could see in Rachel a growing eagerness to embrace and be guided by the Holy Orthodox Church's doctrines. The schedule for Rachel's baptism was that she maintain the regimen of a catechumen until Pascha of 2007 (In the Orthodox Church Easter is called Pascha.), when she would be baptized into Christ and enter the Holy Apostolic Church. Rachel had completed her catechism and was baptized on that glorious day. The next time I would see her, on Monday of Bright Week (April 9th, the day after Pascha), my beautiful wife would be an Orthodox Christian. It was a momentous occasion. Although we had been pursuing Christ together for over nineteen years (with sixteen of those years as man and wife), it really felt that we could at that point truly embark upon a joint voyage, enduring to the end for salvation.

It so happened that an entirely distinct event that seemed to cement the onset of our labor in perseverance took place. Abbot Epiphanios (Abbot of Machairas Monastery in Cyprus), Father Theoklitos (a monk at Machairas Monastery) and Abbot Nicholas (Abbot of another monastery in Cyprus) received the blessing of Metropolitan Athanasios (the bishop who had gently ushered me toward Orthodoxy in 1998-99) to visit St. Anthony's Greek Orthodox Monastery here in Florence, Arizona, in April of 2007, mere weeks after Rachel's baptism. Having never met any Orthodox Christians besides Father Paisios, I was so nervous that I was almost in tears. For me, this was a huge event, but the grace of God that accompanied these humble men of God into the visitation room immediately put me at ease. As a means by which to facilitate our communication, as Abbot Nicholas and Abbot Epiphanios spoke very little English, I began to show them the

---

8   Frank's previously referenced work (cf. footnote 6) covers much of this
     topic.

photographs of Rachel's baptism that I had received the previous day. It was with great pride that I presented my Orthodox Christian wife to them. I fondly remember how they eagerly leaned forward toward the visitation window in anticipation as I displayed each photograph for their inspection. Then, with Father Paisios and Father Theoklitos, both of whom speak fluent Greek and English, serving as interpreters, I was able to obtain instruction from the Cypriot abbots. It was a heavenly experience out of which I received two special admonitions which have remained with me. One occurred during discussions about the execution of a man from California that was to occur in the near future. Since "Gypsy" was a Californian Aryan Brother, I had referred to him as my "brother" during our conversation, and Father Theoklitos asked me what I meant by that reference. I explained to him that Gypsy and I were "California brothers." After a moment of surprise, Father Theoklitos patiently instructed me on the importance of extinguishing prior habits once we have become members of the body of Christ. I had lapsed into a pattern of past identification without thinking, a habit which could lead to other temptations, so I was exceedingly grateful for Father Theoklitos' correction.

The other admonition actually served as the impetus for this book, because Abbot Epiphanios, who was quite taken with the story of Rachel and me, suggested that we write our autobiography. Quite frankly, I was caught off guard and emitted a nervous laugh, which Father Theoklitos immediately rebuked saying, "You can't laugh at the Abbot's instruction." May God bless this precious monk whose correction humbled me and led to the preparation of this autobiography. I am vastly thankful for the grace I received, and my sole regret is that it took so long to obey the Abbot.

The day after I had been blessed with that visit, my precious Rachel, who had received the name of Sarah at her baptism, had the chance to visit with Father Theoklitos, Abbot Nicholas and Abbot Epiphanios at St. Anthony's Monastery, an occasion that she tremendously enjoyed. On our next visit Rachel and I experienced a sweet time of thanksgiving to God as we shared our encounters with the faithful from Cyprus. The Good Lord had provided a magnificent start to our journey for salvation as an Orthodox Christian couple. He also bestowed upon us the grace that would be required as we confronted several concurrent obstacles to our endeavor of enduring until the end.

Perseverance in the working out of our salvation has not always been at all easy. I have previously detailed some of the impediments that I confront in SMU II, which reveal just how a long road it has been for me to even begin looking upon difficulties as the medicine of purification. A potentially devastating encumbrance, which some cooperation with God's grace has turned into a significant blessing, were a few developments in court. My conviction and sentencing, a direct appeal to the state supreme court and state court post-conviction relief proceedings had been held before my case was admitted into federal court. We used what is called a writ of habeas corpus (a pleading which asserts some federal constitutional infirmity and which seeks a release from custody). Even though I had been assigned a great attorney, the frustration involved demanded the application of patience. Then, late in 2003 I became aware of evidence that proved law enforcement had surreptitiously placed the sole purported physical evidence on my car.

The government alleged that after having struck the little girl on her bicycle with my automobile, I had placed her in it, and then drove twenty to twenty-five miles to the desert, where I murdered her. In support of their specious contentions the only shred of physical evidence was a purported streak of pinkish paint (the girl's bicycle was pink) on the bumper of my car. In 2003, facts began to emerge that no such smudge was on the bumper at the time of my arrest and that the bumper had been removed from the car, transported to the Pima County Sheriff's evidence area in Tucson, and then returned to Texas where it was sloppily reattached... all while my vehicle was in the sole custody of law enforcement. Clearly, my evolving patience had begun to produce fruit.

Almost eight years earlier, in 1996, I had been denied an evidentiary hearing, which should have been granted me because of the post-trial discovery of burial. Had I been granted that hearing, the fact that the time required to have driven from where the girl had disappeared to where her partial remains were eventually located, dig a grave and bury the child, then drive back to a downtown park would have precluded me as the perpetrator. Although the evidentiary hearing was mandated by law, Rachel and I had accepted that it had not been granted because it simply was not God's will for me to have been released at that time.

Thus in 2003-2004, seven or eight years later, another opening for my cooperation with God's grace had emerged, along with the opportunity for freedom from incarceration. After a few more years (Yes, the exercise of additional patience was necessary.) in the spring of 2007, the federal judge ruled that there was sufficient new evidence regarding law enforcement misconduct with the paint to warrant an evidentiary hearing, which he indicated would be held within three or four months. Then the government complained that the issue should be returned to state court. (In a case brought by a state government, the state court possesses the right to hear all evidence first. Since many facts supporting the police manipulation of paint evidence were new and had never been presented in a state court, the state insisted that the issue be remanded to state court.) The federal judge had no choice but to send the planted paint claim back to state court for the required evidentiary hearing, and the attorneys began preparing for a post-conviction relief proceeding in state court. Our hope for success increased because the investigation by our expert proved that some marks on the underside of my automobile, which government had alleged could have come from the girl's bicycle, were not present on the vehicle's gravel pan at the time of my arrest. In fact, proof was uncovered that the state's accident reconstruction expert had caused the indentations back in 1985.

So, it was with confidence that we presented the post-conviction relief petition as a precursor to the required evidentiary hearing. Further patience was required when, in January of 2009, contrary to state and federal law, the state court judge refused to hold the hearing. We would not be able to call witnesses and present evidence because that particular judge dismissed the paint claim. Not only did he ignore the overwhelming proof that police had tampered with the paint, he also disregarded the fact that the state expert had fabricated the gravel pan evidence.

While impossible to quantify, there has been an almost constant correlation between cooperation with God's grace and opportunities in court. Consequently, I am deathly afraid that as my obedience to the commandments of Christ and to my spiritual father falters, what will follow is a commensurate closing of the door to my release from prison. Certainly, this is what is demonstrated by the sudden and outrageous denial of the evidentiary hearing in January of 2009. Furthermore, what has impacted me more than the delay in any potential for my freedom is the despair that my sloth in my struggle for salvation inflicts on my blessed and faithful wife; I pray her forgiveness.

In addition to the tribulations regarding the paint tampering claims, several challenges in regards to my health have arisen in recent years. These have also encouraged the need for constancy in enduring to the end. The refusal by the Arizona Department of Corrections (ADOC) to provide any treatment for the Hepatitis C virus that had been diagnosed in 1997 turned out to have dire consequences. However, with Father Paisios' guidance in the virtue of patience, categorical evidence of God's grace emerged. During many of my visits with Geronda (Father Paisios), I expressed despair over my inability to access care for a potentially terminal illness. Hepatitis C kills tens of thousands annually; when left untreated, the probability of a fatal outcome skyrockets. With this in mind, my beloved spiritual father has prescribed a regimen of reading about the lives of some saints, patience, writing to St. John Maximovitch and fervent prayer. Then, in December of

2005, when I was at a doctor's appointment on a completely unrelated matter, the doctor inquired about the status of my Hepatitis C, completely out of the blue. I eagerly grasped the opportunity to explain my twenty-year history of Hepatitis C absent any treatment. The protocol for Hepatitis C therapy is complex and fiscal concerns heavily favor the withholding of care. However, this doctor took it upon herself to bypass the required lengthy approval process by ordering a FibroSure analysis (a blood test that mimics a liver biopsy). Since Hepatitis C attacks the liver and can cause cirrhosis (which can culminate in liver cancer), a biopsy or FibroSure determines the degree of harm that the virus has done to the liver. I underwent FibroSure testing in January of 2006, even though I did not meet all of the ADOC central office requirements for the procedure. In March the devastating results were delivered: I had cirrhosis of the liver and was in stage four (the final phase) of Hepatitis C virus. Ever since, it has been a real struggle to not be consumed by "what ifs"... what if I had received the necessary medicine earlier... what if the biopsy had been ordered in 2000-2001? Perhaps the disease would not have progressed to stage four cirrhosis.

The doctor had submitted the request for treatment, a combination of interferon injections and ribivarin capsules over nearly a six-month period, but complications emerged once that physician was rotated to another unit. The new health care provider took issue with the deviation from established protocol and delayed treatment by going through the formulary for a FibroSure approval. The re-test occurred in May of 2006 and once the result of cirrhosis had been confirmed, the recommendation for interferon therapy was re-submitted. I sent another letter to St. John Maximovitch for divine intervention as Rachel and I maintained our prayer vigil. The delays inherent in governmental procedure certainly taxed our patience, as our pleas for the necessary medication had fallen on deaf ears for so long. Then, through the grace of God, St. John Maximovitch of Shanghai and San Francisco performed a miracle when the course of treatment began in

August. Interferon therapy is no fun at all; it is like a mild form of chemo. Nausea and emotional instability are common elements. Upon its completion, there was no detectable Hepatitis C virus in my blood. Thanks to a continuous miracle by St. John, I have enjoyed both the absence of virus and a remission of liver cirrhosis.

Around the same time that the prison system was denying my Hepatitis C therapy, I was facing frustrating decisions regarding eye surgery. I had experienced an alarming loss of vision in 2004 that had resulted in corrective surgery and required a similar procedure on the other eye. However, the ADOC central office denied permission to proceed, and actually asserted that one good eye was adequate. Hence, a nearly two-and-a-half-year battle with the state (as well as with patience) ensued. It was not until May of 2007 that the medically necessary surgery on the other eye occurred. While both surgeries had met with success, I still had some difficulty with vision. Although laser surgery was simultaneously performed on both eyes in January 2009, even with corrective glasses, my eyesight has remained quite problematic.

The need for nurturing the virtue of patience in the face of serious health concerns did not cease with Hepatitis C and liver cirrhosis or my eyes. Some of my other more anxious moments include:

- A battle with skin cancer began just prior to December of 2005. Thankfully, all of the cancer had been excised during surgery, although another scare arose in early 2009 when a second surgery was performed. By God's grace there was no cancer.
- In addition to having suffered from a degenerative back since 1990, x-rays revealed that four cervical disks in my neck had significant narrowing. Both the concomitant pain and ADOC failure to refer me to an outside specialist have required much patience.
- Around September of 2002 I underwent a procedure for the removal of kidney stones. In 2007, when it was thought

that more stones had developed, ultrasound revealed the presence of gallstones, and I underwent surgery to have my gallbladder removed.

- A follow-up CAT scan in March of 2008 showed a tumor-like mass on my liver. Given the Hepatitis C and cirrhosis history, that revelation gave rise to abject fear. Again, prayer, a letter to St. John Maximovitch and patience were assigned by Father Paisios. A liver biopsy was performed in June. I will never cease to marvel at God's grace, for the biopsy evidenced no cancer. However, my liver would not stop bleeding after the invasive procedure and I landed in the intensive care unit for several days.

- Pain in my mid-section led to several diagnostic procedures, including an endoscopy (a tube placed down the throat and into the stomach), during which it was discovered that all of the medication I had been taking for back pain had caused an ulcer and severe stomach inflammation.

- An eventual MRI on my neck revealed that my entire cervical spine has endured significant damage.

- I have required the use of a wheelchair since 2015 and was referred to a neurosurgeon for probable surgery.

The list is not meant to infer that I was always persistent in the exercise of patience; in fact, on several occasions I seriously considered filing a lawsuit. My precious wife, who always more consistently cooperates with God's grace, forbade that course of action. Nevertheless, the cultivation of patience had been greatly enhanced by my many health problems over the span of only a few years. Also, frustrations throughout recent court processes have facilitated the fostering of this virtue, and our desire of enduring to the end has been amplified. Nonetheless, my health concerns and my legal issues are nothing in comparison to one of the most difficult challenges in my life. In May of 2008, my dad, whom I adored, died.

In the year after Rachel's entry into the One Holy Apostolic Church, we zealously struggled in working out our salvation. Although it has not always been easy, it can be seen as the absolute necessity for what was to come. Truly, there is no way that either of us could have navigated the sorrows and stresses of my father's death without a year of preparation together in the Orthodox Church. God's grace is miraculous.

As an only child and spoiled brat, a son who had depended on mommy and daddy throughout his entire life, there really is no way to explain the devastation inflicted by the loss of one of the two bedrocks that I had known since birth. As I recall the developments leading up to Memorial Day of 2008, the day on which my precious dad died, I can only marvel at God's provision. My father had desired to relocate the family home, both as a pre-emptive measure prior to my parents becoming too elderly to move and as a means by which to free up some capital to ensure adequate funding in a worsening economy for their remaining years. Nonetheless, to leave their residence after over fifty years in the Brentwood area was a daunting proposition. To determine the fiscal feasibility and benefits versus drawbacks, Rachel and I labored tirelessly to crunch the numbers, solicit the advice of experts and construct factual charts for my parents to consider. Our efforts had not been intended to impress my dad; yet he had been pleased with our undertaking. In fact, a mere two weeks prior to his death, he wrote in a card to my mom, "This indeed is a joyous Mother's Day; our son has finally grown up."

At the end of May 2008, my dad had to be hospitalized. I was informed via a phone call with my wife that evening. We decided that she should visit me the following day in order to discuss plans before she departed for Los Angeles. Afterwards, I wrote a note of encouragement to my dad, which expressed my profound appreciation for his perennial example of honor; related my undying love for him; proclaimed that he had always been and would always be my coach; and I promised that Mom would be taken care of. My hope was to recruit someone in the visitation area to pass the letter to Rachel, and I was successful in that endeavor.

On Sunday, May 25th, my wife visited my father in the hospital. Thus, in his heart, my father knew that his beloved wife would be well cared for and safe. The next day was Memorial Day and I received a surprise visit from Father Paisios. The session began ordinarily enough; he inquired about my dad and I related the details from the previous night's conversation. Then it happened – the difficult and dire words of, "Anthony, he's gone." Initially I was unable to comprehend the meaning of his words; I could only stammer some unintelligible babble. Then it dawned on me that by "gone" Father Paisios meant "dead." Again, a feeling of bewilderment and disbelief permeated me. I was devastated. I thank God that Father Paisios was with me.

As tremendously unbearable as I had found that news, I cannot even begin to imagine my mother's absolute despair. For her to merely contemplate a few weeks away from her husband had been anguishing; but to have to face the permanence of the fact that her husband of fifty-eight years was gone... Graciously, God provided for Rachel's comforting presence. I prayed that my mother's deeply wounded heart would continue to be graced. The subsequent weeks were intense, but God saw all of us through every trial and tribulation. The merciful Lord shepherded my precious mother to Tucson, and within a month of my dad's passing, dear Mom began the painful ordeal of settling into a new home in a strange land.

Rachel and her father, whom everyone knows as Bob but I affectionately call "Pa", after the patriarch in the 1960's western television program Bonanza, truly loved caring for my mother, God bless their kind hearts. Rachel arranged for her dad's doctor (an expert in geriatric care) to be my mom's primary health care provider. God's grace has been pervasive; I am sure that my father is well pleased.

Speaking of God's grace, from a secular point of view, the potential for disaster as a result of my dad's death was extremely high. We escaped, solely due to God's divine providence:

- God granted Rachel and me a year as an Orthodox Christian couple to prepare.
- Dad had the comfort of knowing that his wife would be well cared for and safe.
- Dad joyfully realized that his son had become an adult.
- Dad read my letter the day before he died.
- Having visited with Rachel twice on the day prior to his death, dad knew of and was confident in her absolute competence.
- Mom had her daughter-in-law by her side for consolation.
- I was blessed by the presence of my spiritual father when I learned of my dad's death.
- There was a sudden "mysterious" phone system glitch that permitted me to make two daily calls.
- The family home sold immediately, for the full asking price.
- My mother's new residence was right next to my wife.
- Mom had loving help to pack and re-locate.
- A nurse transported my mom to Tucson safely.
- My mother received excellent care from a caregiver, family and her doctor.
- Mom had a lot of company around her, most of it Orthodox Christian.

Clearly, God's grace reigned supreme through an intensely difficult time for my mother, Rachel and me. Toward the end of 2008, it seemed as if we had begun to adjust a little to life without dad. My mom and I took comfort in knowing that he is alive and without pain in heaven and lives on in our hearts.

As an interesting aside, in the year before my dad's death, Father Paisios had visited my parents at our family home in Brentwood. I have a photograph of that glorious occasion, one of Father Paisios with my dad, on the wall of my cell. My beloved father used to call me "Trooper," and when my thoughts begin to dwell on the challenges that one must inherently endure on death row, I often glance at that photograph and, just like when I was a boy, I can hear him lovingly guide me with a "Clean it up, Trooper."

I am beginning to realize that with God's grace, even the darkest moments can become fuel for the voyage of enduring to the end. The adversities I have faced – the judicial abuses of discretion in death case appeals; my own health difficulties (along with the continued refusals of the ADOC to provide medically necessary health care); my father's death; a scare with the well-being of Rachel's dad; etc. – all have led Rachel and me to a more firm belief that sufferings are in fact blessings. They are intended by God as provisions for the cultivation of patience and the development of other virtues, like humility, faith, wisdom, prayer, on the pilgrimage of working out our salvation and enduring to the end. Assuredly, "... we know that all things work together for the good of those who love God" (Ro. 8:28).

Chapter Fifteen

And The Two Have Become One

Rachel:

TWO days before celebrating the Nativity of the Lord Jesus Christ in 2009, I arose early and began my day by going across the street to see about Mom. As usual I entered through the front door, but immediately sensed that something was very wrong. Accompanying the aura of foreboding was an awful smell. Nervously, I clicked on the lights in order to peer down the hallway that led to the bedrooms. The chilling vision that confronted me will remain forever etched in my memory. Mom lay sprawled across the floor by her bed. Initially I thought, "Oh my God, Mom is dead!" Mom's dog, Maddy, a sweet boxer everyone affectionately called Maderl (the Austrian term of endearment for Maddy) lay right beside Mom on the floor.

With trembling hands, I quickly dialed 911 to request emergency medical aid and then, with a great deal of fear and anxiety, continued down the hallway. Upon nearing the room

I could hear Mom moaning and see that she was alive, but just barely. Obviously, she had suffered a terrible fall and had also soiled herself, which made everything much worse. The paramedics soon arrived and after some initial assessment, she was gently lifted onto her bed. Mom was quite agitated that I had summoned the paramedics and repeatedly declared that she was not going to the hospital! The paramedics examined Mom closely and then, since the law states that they could not transport her without her consent, they left the premises.

Extremely upset and fearing that there was something seriously wrong with Mom, I called my dad and a friend to come help and get Mom cleaned up and determine what to do next. It became rapidly apparent that the same hip that had dislocated a few months prior had once again dislocated. Mom also seemed very confused and agitated with all that was happening. I decided to call 911, again; this time Mom was going to the hospital!

As Mom was completely deaf, the situation was made even more complicated by the necessity of having to communicate everything in writing to her. As patiently as I could, I explained why at least a brief journey to the emergency room was necessary. When a new team of paramedics arrived, I was thankful that I knew one of them. He happened to have a sympathetic ear and I knew he would listen, while I explained, about Mom's obstinacy and her medical history. Moreover, Mom's blood pressure was dangerously high (well over 200). Given the totality of circumstances, the paramedics agreed to rush Mom to the hospital and placed her on a gurney. Even so, while they were exiting her bedroom, Mom desperately grabbed the door frame while yelling at me, "You're a pest!"

Eventually, the paramedics were able to safely get Mom loaded into the ambulance and en route to the hospital, with me following closely behind in my car. The emergency room personnel summoned the same doctor that had treated Mom for a dislocated hip a few months prior. I was thankful that he was available to treat her since Mom really trusted him. Taken into surgery that afternoon, Mom's hip was put back into place successfully, but there was still concern over her very high blood pressure. It was the next day, the day before Christmas, when I realized that Mom wasn't going to bounce back the way she had a few months before. As Christmas 2009 dawned, Mom had begun to sleep more, was eating less and exhibited an overall sense of disinterest; she was beginning the dying process.

Knowing that Christmas with Mom would be celebrated at the hospital, my dad and I brought her gifts, a poinsettia and a Christmas balloon to her room in order to make the atmosphere more festive. She had such little strength and her blood pressure was still very high, but she seemed to appreciate the efforts. However, she had increased periods of confusion, such as asking about me, even though I was right next to her.

Every night, just before bed, I would call the night nurse to check on Mom's condition, and then again in the morning before going to work. As 2009 drew to a close, I was not working as much, because I was making arrangements for Mom's care. Mom's release from the hospital became the predominant concern. There were many decisions that needed to made, and it was I who had to make them. One decision concerned Lorrie, Mom's caregiver, who had been working about four hours a day, but was not sure of being available on a twenty-four hour a day basis. I knew that Mom would require around the clock care for the rest of her life, even if it fell on me to provide it.

The nursing staff at Saint Joseph's, the Catholic hospital where Mom was, was very kind and helpful in directing me to a number of in-home care services. The day after Christmas Mom's doctor related, in no uncertain terms, that some grave decisions about Mom's care had to be made. There were several serious conditions impacting her, not the least of which was preventing a stroke, for despite the medication she was being given, Mom's blood pressure had remained over 200. The doctor highly recommended hospice care. Up to that point, everything had transpired without Frank's knowledge.

Frank:

After a letter I received from my mother in late August of 2009, in which she stated that it was "extremely important" for her to come to visit, I understood the situation. Both Mom and I sensed the end was upon her. Arrangements were made for Mom to visit me with Rachel and her dad. The visit occurred on September 14th, one of the twelve great feasts of the Orthodox Church, the Elevation of the Holy and Life-Saving Cross. As it turned out, it was the last time I ever saw my mother.

A few weeks after their visit, I was informed of Mom's serious fall. I was acutely aware of the horrific experience that the in-patient rehab hospital had inflicted on Mom. In late November 2009, my knee gave out; I collapsed and was brought to the building's health unit by wheelchair. In mid-December I was troubled by significant conflict with other inmates. Neither episode however, could come close to the devastating news delivered merely days before Christmas of 2009. On the afternoon of December 23rd I was granted an emergency phone call and learned of my beloved mother's hospitalization, as well as plans for her return to a rehab hospital.

As Rachel was to visit me on December 27th, she met beforehand with a case manager for the hospital, in order to get hospice care in place for Mom. Initially, Rachel felt it best for Mom to be in an in-patient hospice facility, but after we discussed things during our visit, she changed her mind. It had been a very difficult discussion because I knew how hard it had been on Rachel to care for Mom when she had previously returned from the rehab hospital. I was also aware of what an awful experience the "in-patient" experience had been for Mom. I found it nearly impossible to ask Rachel to take on Mom's home care. Not only would the physical effort be monumental, but the emotional toll had to be considered as well. Additionally, although Rachel had previously looked after Mom when she had returned from the hospital in October, it was not anywhere near the same as caring for someone who was under hospice and preparing to die. I wondered if Rachel was at all ready for the journey she would have to endure over the following weeks.

Rachel:

It had been exceedingly difficult on me to inform my husband about his mother's decline, a task made even more troublesome by the news I received upon arriving at the prison. Just as I had pulled into the visitor's parking lot, my cell phone rang; it was the hospital informing me that Mom's blood pressure had plummeted... they were losing her. I was seventy-five miles away, and about to tell my husband of Mom's status. Quickly, I called my dad to have him rush to hospital to see about Mom, and then, I went in for the visit. At least if Mom passed while I was at the prison, I would be the one to deliver the news to Frank. As Frank listened to the facts about his mother being at death's door, his shoulders drooped and the blood drained from his face. To say that he was devastated would be a gross understatement.

I had planned to stay with Frank for both two hour visits, so that while I was in my car for the hour between the visits, I would be able to call the hospital. I was informed that Mom had recovered from the sudden drop in blood pressure and was doing better. At least, I had some good news for Frank.

Mom was to be released from the hospital on Tuesday, December 29, 2009, for entry into hospice. The day before, Mom's bed was removed to make room for the hospital bed that was to be delivered. All of the supplies that would be needed for her care would be provided by hospice. I had also hired a care giving agency recommended by the hospital. Mom's regular caregiver would be available for eight hours a day, leaving two shifts for the agency to fill. I was very pleased with the caregivers that were provided.

The Comfort Keepers, Inc. picked Mom up from the hospital and brought her home. She was delighted to be back in her home, with Maddy and her family. She was not too upset with the changes that had been made to her room, as she understood it was for her care and safety. We did not tell Mom that she was under hospice care or what her prognosis was. Both Frank and I felt it wasn't necessary to deliver that kind of news to her; all that was needed was to make her as comfortable as possible. She sat up in a wheelchair for a while and visited, while having jause, before declaring that she was very tired and wanted to rest. I never dreamed it would be her last jause and her last day out of bed.

Frank:

God's grace continued to embrace us through the difficult journey of those days. I had enjoyed the benefit of two visits with my adorable wife on Sunday, the 27th, the second of which brought the news that my mother had slightly receded from the jaws of death and that she would return home in two days. I was also permitted my weekly phone call on Monday and then gained an extra call on Tuesday. Knowing that Mom had arrived home and was receiving great care gave me at least some comfort. Nevertheless, satan and his minions by no means ceased their provocations. The stress I endured during that time was monumental and, unfortunately, had become known to the other inmates. I had used the phone while in my cell, which permitted others to hear my comments about hospice and become aware of my mother's imminent death. There were several miscreants, with whom I was enduring difficulties, who began a barrage of vile comments, such as, "I'm glad your mom is dying," "I hope the rotten bitch croaks soon," and other derogatory remarks. Having more than enough to deal with, I retreated into the loving arms of Christ Jesus. Unfortunately, my failure to respond to their comments enraged them even more. The aspersions became even more wicked, with statements along the lines of desiring to engage in sexual intercourse, sodomy and oral copulation with my dying mother, along with several threats on my life. My mother being near death and attacks by inmates were not all I had to endure. Amidst the stress, I received the sudden directive to pack and be moved (I worried it would be to an area wherein physical assault would become part of the agenda). I had an anxiety attack and came very close to passing out.

The day after having been moved, I was able to receive God's grace via a visit with Father Paisios, the first meeting I had had with my spiritual father since my mother's decline. Father Paisios instructed me to recite the Jesus Prayer for my mother and my wife. Meanwhile, Rachel also was reciting the Jesus Prayer with greater frequency and ardor. Thus, as 2009 came to a close, Rachel and I increased our focus and reliance on the Son of God.

I have often wondered why it had fallen to my wife to usher my mother into eternal life with God. I am resolute in the knowledge that it is because Rachel is more firm in the Lord. That knowledge, however, did not make it any easier for Rachel to stomach the anguish she had to endure as she experienced Mom's rapid decline.

Rachel:

Frank's mom began to fail quickly. The day after her return home, a man from hospice came to the residence to explain the protocols and procedures of hospice. For instance, Atavan would be provided for anxiety and morphine for pain, but the caregivers were not able to administer it since they were only aides. That task would have to fall on either me or my dad. Hospice made sure that I knew to call at any time, as there would be many questions that would arise in the coming days. I did call hospice a few times, but nothing prepared me for what I would experience over the next two weeks.

Mom did eat some in the first few days after returning home, but not nearly as much as she had in the past. We had placed Maddy's bed next to the hospital bed, so Mom had her sweet dog with her, which gave her immense joy. Of course, Mom kept trying to get out of bed on her own; plus, the continuing change of faces around her caused much frustration. The care giving agency was very good about trying to ease Mom's apprehensions, as they attempted to provide the same three or four nurses for her care. One nurse was 80 years old, and worked the night shift (11 p.m.-7 a.m.); despite her age, she was an excellent caregiver. Unfortunately, Mom declared that she was "too old" and gave her a very difficult time. I had to go over a few times, in the middle of the night, to ease Mom's worries. All too soon, she became too weak to fight over it. On top of it all, Maddy became very nervous and started to cry incessantly; she knew Mom was dying.

As hard as it was on me to see Mom in such a condition, it was unbearable for my dad to see Mom's helplessness as she approached death. Toward the end, he simply could not bear to observe Mom sleeping all the time and not eating. Mom really had a close relationship with my dad. When she had first moved to Tucson in the summer of 2008, he would go across the street many times a day to check on her and have lunch with her. Upon entering her home, he always gave her a kiss on the cheek. Mom had told Ashley, when she had first moved here, that she and he were courting. Everyone laughed a lot over that, except my dad who didn't find it as funny as everyone else did.

As difficult as I found it to see Mom's condition, not all of it was unexpected. Hospice had provided me with a very helpful booklet that explained the dying process. The booklet, Gone From My Sight, by Barbara Karnes, R.N., is given to the family in order for them to understand the stages of death. For example, it explains that one to three months prior to death a withdrawal takes place. As I looked back, I realized that Mom had not been herself after "recovering" from her fall in 2009. I also recalled that there had been more and more times when Mom would sit and stare off into the distance, and that she had spent more time sleeping. I had always felt that losing Ashley had played a big role in Mom's depression. Mom loved Ashley and had a very special relationship with her. Hospice had informed me that Mom could pass away quickly or linger for a month or two. I prayed for Mom to pass quickly, as watching her in her condition for a month was unthinkable. As 2010 began, Mom deteriorated quickly.

The pamphlet on the stages of death explained that as the body prepares to die, the person stops eating. Mom was hardly eating, a huge change for her as she had always had a good appetite and would eat anything she was served. About a week before her death Mom began to not eat at all. Just providing her with water was frightening, because great care had to be exercised to ensure she did not choke or get water into her lungs. We gave her water from a small sponge that was attached to a stick, which Mom would try to jam into her mouth because she was so thirsty. It was heartbreaking for me to watch Mom basically starve to death and for Pa... well, it tore him up.

I also read that disorientation occurs a week or two before death. In Mom's case some of that took the form of her repeatedly asking for Frank; it seemed as if all that kept Mom alive was waiting for her son. I put a photograph of Frank in Mom's hand to hold; sometimes the picture rested by her cheek on her pillow. I also hung an icon of the Theotokos (the Mother of God) so Mom could see it and pray. There was a large picture of dad on the wall that I would point to and tell Mom to go be with dad. It was all so very hard.

Visiting Frank several times in the week before Mom's death, I tried to describe how his mother was dying, but Frank did not really get the full picture. That was very frustrating because I knew Mom would be gone within a week or two.

Frank:

I know Rachel endeavored to prepare me for the inevitable, but I was less than receptive. Three days prior to Mom's death, I was able to speak with her on the telephone. The call left no doubt in my mind that my precious mother was very close to death. After stating a crystal clear "Frank J," Mom could only labor for every breath and softly moan "Frankie J." The moaning of my name along with the hissing sound of the oxygen machine confirmed the gravity of my mother's state.

I believe that there was also a more subliminal, sort of telepathic, correspondence between my mother and me. The one utterance of "Frank J," as clear and strong as if Mom were thirty years younger, conveyed my mother's loving declaration that it was time to leave and rejoin her beloved husband in heaven. Furthermore, it expressed a mother's eternal love for her only child. That one utterance made it clear that she knew Father Paisios and Rachel would take good care of me. Quite simply, it said goodbye. With that, Mom began her final descent.

Shortly afterward, Mom's blood pressure rose again to dangerously high levels, requiring the administration of medication, which was difficult since Mom could no longer swallow. Mom's blood pressure medicine had to be administered rectally, and it fell upon Rachel to accomplish that task. Rachel has bravely opined that when faced with difficult situations, one simply must do things that a person never previously envisioned oneself doing. She also insists that Mom was a great patient during those efforts. God bless Rachel, an angel from heaven.

What a predicament, to see a person you love dying, and to fervently try to keep that person comfortable without prolonging the inevitable. One could reasonably ask, "Why give Mom blood pressure medication?" Rachel has rightly stated that she simply felt it was what she needed to do. She was the one making all of the decisions and she had to be able to live with them. Again, God bless her.

Rachel:

Mom began picking at her clothes and reaching out, further highlighting her impending death. She also became very agitated and, in spite of her debilitated condition, frequently attempted to get out of bed; it is truly amazing how the body has sudden bursts of strength. There were also some physical changes. Mom had always been a small woman, about 5' 3" tall and 105 lbs., but she grew very gaunt in the days preceding her death and slept almost constantly. Also, although she had always felt cold (Her home had always been a furnace with the heat up very high.), she suddenly often felt warm and did not want the covers on her or the space heater on. As her death drew closer, her skin color became yellow like someone with jaundice. A day or two before her death, some major changes took place: she began to breathe much slower and there was a noticeable alteration in the color of her hands and feet. On Saturday, January 9th, a hospice nurse came to Mom's house twice; that was the day before Mom died. The nurse declared that Mom would pass within twenty-four hours or less. She pointed out that the earlobes turn back when death is near, and that both the palms of the hands and the soles of the feet turn purple as circulation begins to stop. I was awake all night waiting for the night nurse to call; Mom's death was extremely close.

On Sunday, January 10, 2010 – the day of St. Gregory of Nyssa and of Theosebia the Deaconess (sister of St. Basil the Great and St. Gregory of Nyssa) – I arose from bed at about 6:15 and went over to Mom's house, where I was met by a very concerned night nurse. Mom had been very still and her respiration was very slow. I phoned my dad to come over quickly, and also phoned the hospice nurse, who had been waiting for the call. I also summoned Father Philip.

At about 7:00 a.m. Mom began to make gurgling and gasping sounds. Her skin had atrophied overnight from the dehydration; her body felt a bit cold to the touch and her blood pressure was very low. I began to say "Lord Jesus Christ have mercy on Mom, a sinner," knowing that Mom was departing this earth. A few minutes later, a mucous-like substance came from Mom's mouth. She seemed to cease breathing before taking three or four huge gasps... and then, she was gone.

Just as Mom was departing, Father Philip arrived and immediately began performing the Trisagion Prayer. Afterwards, Father Philip then recited the prayers for the departed before leaving to prepare for Sunday Divine Liturgy services at our church.

The Trisagion Prayer originated in the fifth century. After an earthquake in Constantinople, the people had gathered on a plain, pleading for mercy. They were joined by Emperor Theodosius II and Patriarch of Constantinople Proclus, and God instructed them to pray what became known as the Trisagion:

"Holy God, Holy Mighty, Holy Immortal, have mercy on us."

Nearly always, there are set prayers that are recited before and after the Trisagion:

"O heavenly King, The Comforter, the Spirit of Truth, Who is in all places and fills all things, Treasure of blessings and Giver of life, come dwell in us and cleanse us of every blemish, and of Thy goodness save our souls O Blessed One."

Then the Trisagion, followed by:

"O Most Holy Trinity have mercy on us. O Lord cleanse us from our sins. O Master forgive our transgressions. O Holy One come visit us and heal our infirmities for Thy name's sake. Lord have mercy. Lord have mercy. Lord have mercy."

After this, the Lord's Prayer is recited:

"Our Father, Who art in heaven, hallowed be Thy name, Thy kingdom come, Thy will be done, on earth as it is in heaven. Give us this day our daily bread, and forgive us our trespasses, as we forgive those who trespass against us. And lead us not into temptation but deliver us from the evil one. For thine is the kingdom, the power, the glory, both now and ever and unto ages of ages. Amen."

Somewhere around 7:30 a.m. hospice arrived to pronounce Mom dead. With that dreaded task done, my dad made coffee while I signed necessary papers. The hospice nurse, who was very kind, arranged for a mortuary to come for Mom. She explained the procedures and informed me of a one year follow-up during which I could call at any time and hospice would occasionally check on me. The nurse stayed until approximately 9:00 a.m., when two nicely dressed men arrived from the mortuary. Prior to entering Mom's bedroom they gave my dad and me a few minutes alone with Mom. I didn't think I could endure being present while they prepared Mom's body for transport, and so I did not stay in Mom's room. Not long after, the mortuary attendants came out of Mom's room. Mom's body had been placed in a black body bag on a gurney that was wheeled out of the house, down the sidewalk, and placed into the back of the van. Maddy, who was beside herself, had been put on a leash. As the van drove off into the distance, I just stood outside for a while... alone. Eventually, I returned indoors where I finalized papers for the hospice nurse. Once hospice had departed, I began making notifications of Mom's death and contacted the same funeral director in Santa Monica, California who had directed the funeral for Frank's dad.

My dad and I were concerned over what to do with Maddy. The beloved boxer had initially remained in Mom's house, with my dad staying over with her, until we decided to bring her to our home. Maddy had been very upset and agitated, to the point of having to be prescribed medication from the vet, so it was best to have her at home with my dad and me. She stayed in my dad's room and was slowly introduced to the other pets, two King Charles Cavalier Spaniels and five Persian cats.

Frank:

Rachel was scheduled to visit me the day after Mom's death. She must have found the prospect of delivering the news to me quite daunting. As she entered the visiting room and sat down, I asked her how my mother was doing. From the look on Rachel's face I knew that my precious mother had died. Although Mom's death had been expected, I still reacted with shock and disbelief.

"Mom is dead."

I just sat there, feeling numb. Memories of Little League baseball, ski trips, days on southern California beaches, cub scouts and so many others flooded my mind. They were such special times, times that had always permitted me to have felt loved and to have maintained a relative sense of stability throughout what I had turned into a decidedly tragic adult life. The news of Mom's death seemed to rip the memories away and I felt a pervasive sense of desperation. However, in the distant recesses of my mind God's grace beckoned. Mom had worked out her salvation and God had delivered her from further struggle.

A battle began between the temptation to submit to abject sorrow and the reliance on the lifeline that was God's grace. I was desperately trying to hold back tears, lest a total breakdown ensue. As my gaze fell upon my terribly anxious wife, I uttered, "I'm an orphan" just before God's grace smashed the temptation of Machiavellian thoughts. I was confronted with the reality that God had truly granted Mom rest and that He had graced me with such a devoted wife, who had so bravely comforted and taken care of Mom in her final weeks. Unfortunately, I failed to completely run into the sanctuary of the Lord Jesus Christ. I had many conflicting feelings, ranging from relief over an end to Mom's suffering to despair from a sense of utter loss. Nevertheless, hope in God provided a road to sanity and salvation.

Rachel:

The days after Mom's death were extremely difficult for me. I found myself going over to Mom's house several times a day or simply wandering around, overwhelmed by feelings of vacancy. My grief was made more difficult when I realized there would be no more 4 p.m. afternoon gatherings around Mom's table for jause. It was heartbreaking to clean out Mom's room and to face the emptiness there after the medical equipment company had retrieved the hospital bed and other equipment.

A few days after Mom's death, the funeral director informed me that the funeral would be delayed until January 20th. With the date for the funeral set, I began making travel plans and ensuring several friends were aware of them. I would travel from Tucson to Los Angeles with my dad, Father John and Lorrie; Ashley would join us from Portland. Everyone was scheduled to arrive on Tuesday for the Wednesday funeral.

Other arrangements included selecting Mom's burial clothes. I decided on a very pretty, light blue suit that Mom had really liked to wear, and the pink slippers that Nancy and Andy (DJ & Ruth's children) had given her for Christmas, but had never been able to wear. Mom's feet were always cold, so it seemed only right to have slippers on her feet. There were other items that the mortuary in Tucson would send to Los Angeles with Mom's body. Amongst these were the cross that Frank had worn for nearly 20 years. It had been a wedding gift that I had given him in 1991, and Frank had virtually never taken it off. When his mother fell ill, he had sent it to her. All of the letters Frank had written to his mom the last ten days of her life, a photograph of Frank, an icon of the Mother of God (the Theotokos) and an icon of St. John Maximovitch also accompanied her body. Father Paisios had had Frank pray to St. John for healing from Hepatitis C, and the icon that had been blessed at St. John's grave (one of Frank's prized possessions) would now "accompany" his mother's journey to heaven. Of course, all of these details simply broke my heart.

The care of the pets also had to be arranged for while we were in Los Angeles, especially for Maddy since she had been so upset. In fact, whenever my dad and I left her sight, she would howl mournfully and continuously. Eventually it was decided to keep Maddy at the vet's office where there were lots of people that loved her and would care for her, while the longtime neighbors and Ruth would take care of the other pets.

Everyone arrived in Los Angeles on Tuesday, January 19th, as planned; our plane landed about half an hour after Ashley's, and then together, we all took the airport shuttle van to the hotel. Unfortunately, it was one of the rainiest seasons that Los Angeles had experienced in years. I was worried about complications during the funeral and knew that the following day would be extremely dreary... in more ways than one.

On the morning of January 20th, 2010, everyone arose early to prepare for the mid-morning funeral that would take place in the pouring rain. There was a tight schedule because the burial would be in the early afternoon in Riverside, California, a two and a half hour drive from Los Angeles. At the funeral home I was able to say goodbye to Mom in the viewing room, and everyone had some time to pray and be alone until the service. It all seemed so surreal, especially as I had just gone through the same things for Frank's dad only a year and a half prior. When it was time to congregate in the chapel, I said my last goodbye and the casket was closed. It was brought into the chapel which had been adorned with pink and white roses. The service was very small; in addition to us, the only other ones present were Chad (Frank's childhood friend) and my cousin Beth along with her husband, Jake.

Prior to the beginning of the service, Chad had said that he wished to say a few words. He spoke, very movingly, for 15-20 minutes about his cherished memories of Mom and the Atwood family. He had spent quite a lot of time with them as a child. Then Father John began the funeral, during which Ashley and I read

aloud some Sacred Scripture and Father John spoke affectionately about Mom. He related his memories of her over the past
20 years and expressed his fondness for having experienced the
tradition of jause with Mom. After the service several beautiful
photographs were taken and then the caravan, with the funeral
director and I traveling in the hearse and the others in the rent-
al car, began the two-and-a-half-hour trek to Riverside National
Cemetery. It was raining very hard, the weather truly making the
day even sadder.

At the cemetery, a governing official greeted everyone
and hustled us to the burial site, while Mom's casket, the same
kind as her husband's, was brought over from the hearse. I was
pleased to see that the location, where Frank's dad had been buried nearly two years previously, had turned from bare dirt to lush
thick grass. The grave for Frank's dad had been opened and covered with a board in an effort to keep some rain out; the board
was removed to place Mom's casket on top of her husband's.
As preparations for the burial were underway, everyone huddled
under an umbrella in the cold and the rain. It was especially upsetting for my dad to see so much rain pounding on both caskets.
I later learned that sixty-five interments had been scheduled that
day, in the driving rain. Although the workers tried to treat the
caskets with respect, the ground was such a mess. After placing
a few roses on Mom's casket, I stood back and then watched, as
Mom's body was lowered into the ground. It was a horrifying and
surreal experience.

Cemetery workers were to fill in the grave and then place
the spray of roses that had been on Mom's casket on top of
the grave. After getting into the car, everyone sat a minute and
watched before they began the long drive back to Los Angeles.
As we left the large cemetery Father John drove past the beautiful
lake that was near its entrance. It had a large fountain in its center
and was surrounded by lots of trees. I knew Mom would have
liked the scenery.

Thankfully, Father John was driving, as the treacherous

weather remained a great concern. As we reached downtown Los Angeles, there was the rush hour traffic to contend with, and it was still raining. There was just enough time to retrieve Father John's luggage from the hotel, and to quickly get to the airport for Father John to make his plane. My cousin, Beth had invited everyone over to her home for a while. There, Frank called and I related all of the details of his dear mother's funeral.

The next day, Pa, Lorrie, Ashley and I made our way to LAX airport to make our departure. Ashley was able to obtain her boarding pass for her flight to Portland; however due to very high winds, all travel to Arizona had been cancelled. We saw Ashley off, and then I struggled to obtain a hotel for Pa, Lorrie and myself, as nearby hotels were booked. Finding one at last, the shuttle bus picked us up and delivered us to the front of the hotel... and it was still raining.

By the next day, the winds in Arizona had calmed and we were able to catch a flight back to Tucson on the afternoon of January 22nd. Home at last, my dad and I were physically and emotionally exhausted. We also experienced an overwhelming sense of emptiness... there was no Mom.

Toward the end of January, I decided to take a much needed vacation to San Antonio to visit Aunt Mary and family. Aunt Mary was such a great source of support to me and helped me through some initial emotional feelings. Returning home in early February 2010, I immediately had to face making notifications of Mom's death. Frank, my dad and I took up the routine of life again, without Mom.

Rachel and her Aunt Mary.

Chapter Sixteen

Life as One

Rachel:

In the weeks following my return from Los Angeles, I had to make a big decision: whether to continue working or retire. There were, of course, financial considerations. Plus, twenty-five years of cleaning houses had taken a toll on my back. I am an energetic person and enjoy a life of routine, so I found it discomfiting to change that routine. I have had feelings of guilt for not "working". The decision was quite a struggle, but in February of 2010, with the blessing of Father Paisios, I opted for retirement. The transition was, as I had expected, a difficult one.

Loyalty to my clients found me ensuring that Ruth (who had worked with me for four years) was fully prepared to take over the business. I had to say goodbye to some clients I had had for over twenty years, which was very emotional for me. For the next month or so the absence of routine caused me to feel out of sorts; it was the first time in thirty years that I was not going to work in the morning. It took the better part of a year for me to become comfortable with retirement and my new life.

At the time, a mound of notifications, arrangements (finances, accounts, taxes, etc.), and other affairs served as both a frustration and a welcome distraction. There was simply so much to do, much of it unanticipated, and had to do with issues with which I had little experience. Still, having a full slate of activities made me feel less awkward about no longer working.

One especially enjoyable distraction was that I arranged my dad's eightieth birthday party. I thought it would be nice to have it at our old guest ranch, El Corona. The ranch had become a catering hall, but retained a lot of the old touches it had had when my family had owned it. My dad had made contact earlier in the year with the current manager and owner, Kerry. They immediately became friends with Kerry asking numerous questions about the ranch. When I called Kerry to ask whether they could accommodate for my dad's party, he quickly responded that he would be delighted. I busied myself with sending invitations and making all the arrangements to have family flown in from Texas and Los Angeles for the party. Trying to keep one step ahead, I let my dad know about the party, but not about all the relatives flying in. He truly was touched and very surprised by all the faces he had not seen in a very long time. He conducted tours (on a whim) for all who wanted to see and hear the history of the ranch and was, truly, in his glory! The smile on my dad's face was there the entire evening.

Frank:

By 2010, developments with my case continued as had become the common rule: slowly and unsuccessfully. My attorney interviewed four government witnesses (two detectives and two experts), culling some seeds of hope from those sessions. To begin with, the scenarios they proclaimed contradicted each other and advanced preposterous representations of government involvement with my car back in 1984. Moreover, several hundred previously "misplaced" photographs, for which there were no negatives, had suddenly been "found" and which, upon inspection by my experts, revealed a number of infirmities. Given the developments, we hoped that the judge would provide the required evidentiary hearing. Unfortunately, hope in everything other than the Lord Jesus Christ returned void.

In early 2010 the judge summarily dismissed the request for relief, without, as the law mandates, construing the assertions as true and, once again, absent the evidentiary hearing prescribed by Arizona statutes. Subsequent to this judicially abusive denial, there were interminable delays in seeking review by the Arizona Supreme Court. Eventually the matter was ripe for review by the state's highest court in 2011. As expected, the Arizona Supreme Court rubber-stamped the trial court's corruption.

When it rains, it pours. Other challenges suffered as 2010 unfolded make this adage clear. I have always endured difficulties with other prisoners, with only the degree of severity wavering. The summer of 2010 really tested my patience. In August I was "darted", twice. The first occurred when I was on the way to visit my wife and her priest and an inmate "darted" me with a piece of metal; the second occurred when I was returning from a visit and a prisoner "speared" me with a pencil. While the injuries were inconsequential, I suffered significant emotional trauma – especially since staff knew of both incidents. Staff also knew that liquids had been thrown on me, yet refused to move me to a safer environment. It was only when my attorneys intervened that prison officials transferred me to another area.

Apparently, the Arizona Department of Corrections did not appreciate what they viewed as interference by outsiders. A series of calculated retaliatory actions were undertaken by the Department, including: seizure of religious items (books, icons, holy oil, etc.); attempts to issue vengeful disciplinary reports; cessation of an eleven-year religious diet; the temporary removal of all property from my cell; threats of transfer to isolation rooms; the withholding of all books. Although these impositions were temporary inconveniences that have been remedied, they did make the Nativity Fast of 2010 especially challenging for both Rachel and me.

In retrospect, the failing must be placed squarely on both of our shoulders. Although we both struggle for purification faithfully and pray daily for humility, all too often I react with pride to the very events God lovingly provides. Thus, I pollute not only my own inner self with passion, but also infect my precious wife's internal well-being. Thanks to the grace of God, I have begun to recognize the Good Lord's constant provisions, at least in hindsight.

Rachel:

Thanks to God's visible grace, I am, at long last, "home." It was on the celebration of the Presentation of Our Lord (2 February 2011) that the new church was completed and enjoyed its very first service, presided over by Bishop Joseph. Previously, the Antiochian Orthodox Christian Church had held weekly services in an annex building of St. Demetrios. To have its own church is a most wonderful blessing.

In fact, God's grace has been continuously present, as both my dad and brother became familiar with the One Holy Apostolic Church. My dad began to occasionally attend church with me, and in 2010 attended catechumen classes. He was baptized into the Orthodox Christian Church on Holy Saturday, 2011.

Frank:

Apparently the enemy of mankind was outraged over Pa's entry to Orthodoxy, as well as by Rachel's and my own efforts toward humility and cooperating with God's grace. Events from the spring of 2011 and onward have been rife with tribulation, beginning with a serious attempt to undermine my safety.

In May of 2011 an inmate, having been sent to death row for murdering a correctional officer while in prison, put out a contract on me. This included the inmate trying to arrange the sending of monies to another prisoner, who lived near me, in exchange for assaulting me. An emergency relocation quickly ensued once the plot had been uncovered.

However, events in the new housing area remained unstable. I had resided with some of the inmates previously and sought to avoid confrontation by remaining silent. The prisoners still engaged in continual verbal attacks until December of 2011, when boiling water was thrown on me as I was returning to my cell. In response, the unit administration via the Associate Deputy Warden, rather than move the offending inmate, placed me in the gang member violent control area. That was on 6 January 2012, on the Theophany. Within hours I ended up in the mental health pod, on suicide watch.

In 2012 my case also re-entered federal court. Previously, all forty plus claims had been denied in 2007, other than the one that centered on law enforcement having placed paint on the bumper of my car. At that time, the judge had intended to conduct an evidentiary hearing so that incontrovertible proof of police misconduct could be presented. The State, however, had forced a return of those proceedings to State court, where, as has been mentioned, the court refused to hold the required hearing. The entire episode spanned five years, so when the opportunity to return to federal court emerged, further pleadings were lodged in support of an anticipated evidentiary hearing.

Evidence was extraordinarily convincing. Technological advances in photography permitted the uncovering of facts that proved the paint had not been on the bumper at the time of my arrest and that post-arrest law enforcement had taken the bumper to Arizona and back. (I had been taken into custody in Texas.) The same federal judge, who in 2007 was eager to conduct an evidentiary hearing, categorized the claim as "unbridled speculation" in

2012, and denied all relief[9].

It was also at the same time, in September of 2012, that the Arizona Department of Corrections (ADOC) decided to severely limit my religious services with Father Paisios. Since 1999, the practice had been the allowance of at least one two hour visit weekly, although Father usually came every other week. The new allowance restricted services to one hour each month. Every effort to resolve the new policy fell on deaf ears, and in January of 2013, I filed a lawsuit.

There was one positive development in criminal court: My extensive history of psychiatric problems had not been presented at the 1987 death sentencing and the new laws determined that those problems required remedy. In the fall of 2012 I was examined by a renowned psychologist who directs the South Carolina prison system's violent sexual predator program and works at the national training center for government prosecutors. Her evaluation determined that my having been sexually assaulted at the age of fourteen in 1970 accounts for the night and day difference between my behavior and activities prior to the assault: sports, church, military school, family involvement, etc. and my behavior and activities subsequent to the assault: drugs, sexual promiscuity, crimes. My behavior had transpired as a result of post-traumatic stress disorder (PTSD). The facts of my life supported this conclusion unequivocally and the federal judge agreed to hold an evidentiary hearing.

In the summer of 2013 the government "expert" evaluated me. That so-called evaluator had treated only one person who had been sexually assaulted and one who had committed a sexual offense (as it turned out, it was the same person) in contrast to the doctor who had evaluated me in 2012 and who had treated hundreds, if not thousands, of victims and predators. The renowned doctor had also determined that I was not a risk to re-offend and

---

9   A book, with the working title: *Injustice for All: The Frank Jarvis Atwood Story*, is currently being prepared for publication; it details the myriad infirmities having infected Frank's case.

posed no danger to society. Seeking to reach out to my fellow citizens, I also engaged in a book-length interview, "Victimly Insane" which encompasses my entire history.[10]

The evidentiary hearing took place in the fall of 2013, with experts and other witnesses testifying. It really seemed like a reversal of the death sentence would occur, but once again all relief was denied. At the time of this writing, my last appeal to the federal appellate court (the Ninth Circuit, in San Francisco) has been denied, and execution could occur as soon as 2018. Nevertheless, having previously received a master's degree, I subsequently earned a degree in theology from St. Stephen's M.A. Program (Antiochian House of Studies, School of Orthodox Theology), and am currently working towards attaining a doctorate in theology. God willing, I will attain this degree.

Danger to my safety has been a continuous issue. Another troubling experience occurred with the prisoner who in 2011 had tried to have me attacked. After being escorted to my housing area in July of 2013 to use the recreation room, he broke away from staff escort to run up to my cell and spit in my face. In June of 2014, on Pentecost, the same inmate from 2011 and 2013 was yet again allowed entrance into my pod, and again, ran away from the officer to charge my cell. Also, in May of 2014, an inmate tried to dart me.

At my mother's January 2010 passing into Paradise, I had decided to put my welfare in the hands of ADOC. While a proper course of action, it has been frustrating to experience the neglect of their duty to protect. I have been assaulted six times, and not once has the attacking prisoner been disciplined. May God have mercy on the inmates and on the staff members responsible.

In August of 2014 I successfully settled the religious lawsuit and Father Paisios can come for two hours every other week to serve the Sacraments. As a result, all hell broke loose. For years the prison had declined to allow a cap (known as a skoufos

---

10   Interview to be published in 2018 or later; please see: www.freebirdpublishers.com/victimlyinsane.

or skufiya). Then, in 2014, the item received approval. The monastery sent the cap and I made several requests for its delivery to my cell, all to no avail. The religious lawsuit settlement had really angered ADOC. Finally, while I was in the property room area at the end of August I was able to secure possession of the skoufos. Shortly afterwards, a book and icon, which had been authorized by the religion department and which the monastery had sent, were delayed by several months in being delivered to my cell. One must wonder about the reasons the ADOC were so intent on retaliating... Why? Was it because of the lawsuit? Was it because I had fought the government for the right to follow the precepts of Orthodoxy, to grow in my faith and love for Jesus Christ? On the day of the lawsuit settlement, the associate deputy warden refused to allow for me to be served Holy Communion. He knowingly and maliciously defied a court order.

Amidst this madness in August and September of 2014, prison guards began to harass me. There was one in particular, who often worked my housing area. In late September, after a visit with my wife and Father Philip, this particular officer showed up to take me back to my cell. The guard knew that I had a medical order to not be handcuffed behind the back, but did so anyway. As I began to ascend the stairs, the guard knocked me, face first, into the metal stairs. After returning me to my cell, he told me to keep my mouth shut and not complain to the nurse. Terrified, I remained silent for several days, but on the fourth day my severe injuries forced disclosure of the attack.

That, too, was a mistake. Nursing refused to examine me or refer me to the doctor. After two days I went on a six-day hunger strike, and still did not receive any attention by medical staff. Finally, a lieutenant arranged for a doctor's appointment. The doctor said my toe was probably broken, ribs bruised or cracked, and my cheek had a possible fracture (facial nerve damage was identified).

At the same time, Rachel suffered a major medical emergency. Some of her colon had to be removed (a colectomy) and her recovery remains a slow, arduous and frustrating process. It would have helped for Rachel to have enjoyed visits with me, her husband, but the same officer who had refused to allow me to receive Holy Communion, imposed a thirty day visit suspension. Additionally, my complaints about the assault and medical care treatment, as well as prevailing anger over the lawsuit success, had reached the highest levels in Browning Unit. The deputy warden, Staci Fay, whether relying on an altered disciplinary report or not, indefinitely suspended all of my visits, even though ADOC policy does not allow for such action as a consequence of the misconduct I had allegedly committed.

The retaliatory conduct did not end there. During a discussion on the improper visitation loss, I pled with the sergeant to seek a reversal of the action, but to no avail. In fact, the sergeant wrote up a disciplinary report on what he viewed as my threatening comments to him. The obvious intent of ADOC is to create a separation between Rachel and me through the continuation of visitation loss. It is too late, the two have already become one! We humbly request your prayers for the prison officials, and ask that you please pray the following for us:

O Lord and Master of my life!
Take from me the spirit of sloth, faintheartedness, lust of power, idle talk.
But give rather the spirit of chastity, humility, patience and love to Thy servant.
Yea, O Lord and King! Grant me to see my own errors and not to judge my brother.
For thou art blessed unto ages of ages.
Amen!

Afterword by Frank

A Candid Look at the Orthodox Church
as the Spiritual Hospital

Many people have questioned my potential to truly change. Due to my criminal conduct in California, people have expressed concern over the possibility that I could once again engage in felonious conduct. I understand their concerns. In no way do I assert an "I'm all better" claim; I still entertain passions all too frequently. What I do state, however, is that my obedience to God and to my spiritual father (which is a means of participating in God's grace) has healed my inner self to the degree that I in no way desire to inflict harm on anyone. What follows is a small treatise on how I came to an understanding of the Orthodox Church as a spiritual hospital.

Having been created in the image and likeness of God, meant that Adam and Eve had only the single thought of union with God; they were not concerned about bodily needs or external matters. Adam and Eve were created with the potential for perfection and to love unselfishly. However, once they accepted satan's suggestion to become like God through self-will, humanity's entire being experienced a radical deformation via separation from God. Mankind was infected with evil thoughts, including passions such as pride, self-love and sexual indulgence, which tore apart and disabled the image of God within. This condition – our senses turned outward to the world rather than inward and focused on God – permits the evil one and his demons to assault us with provocations. When these provocations are not cut off immediately, carnal life ensues. Our existence becomes unrealized and impoverished, far from the Creator. What I have referenced here has been far more clearly stated by Fathers of the Church.

One contemporary faithful servant of God puts it this way: "The sickness of human nature is the fallen condition of mankind," which is to say that the "notorious 'ancestral sin' is precisely man's failure, at the very outset of his presence in history, to preserve the remembrance of God (and all) descendants of the first-fashioned human beings share in this morbid condition... a sickness of man's nature is transmitted from person to person." Continuing, Protopresbyter Metallinos states, "Inactivity (of the) remembrance of God... enslaves man to angst and to the environment, and also to the quest for happiness through individualism and (an) anti-social outlook. In the sickness of his fallen state, man manipulates God and his fellow-man in order to reinforce his individual security and happiness... This, therefore, is the sickness man seeks to cure by becoming fully incorporated into the 'spiritual hospital' of the Church." The good Father concludes, "The unique and absolute goal of the life in Christ is theosis (movement toward perfection), namely union with God, so that man, through participation in the uncreated energy of God, becomes by Grace that which God is by nature... This is, in Christian terms, the meaning of salvation. It is not a matter of man's moral improvement, but of the re-creation and re-formation in Christ of man (via) a real and existential relationship with Christ." Salvation through a re-formation in Christ is precisely what I have been seeking, and it is why I hope to endure to the end.

In 2012-2013 I was evaluated by psychologists for the

government and the defense, who carefully reviewed documents about the contrast in my life prior to having been raped at age fourteen, as well as documents about the traumatic outcome of my post-sexual assault life. The doctors took especial note of my resultant sexualization, extreme substance abuse and risk-taking conduct, and of the facts that I had obtained drugs by prostituting myself, ending up in several mental hospitals by age fifteen. Both experts agreed that my sexualization at such a young age was the product of post-traumatic stress disorder. Orthodoxy further determines that my manner of thinking and behavior were the result of my weakened state having become susceptible to demonic attack, which further infected me with sexual indulgence to the extent that I became an abuser of children. As this autobiography makes evident, until my entry into the Greek Orthodox Church – our Spiritual Hospital – I was tossed to and fro by demonic provocation, particularly by carnal passions.

It must also be pointed out that my journey to Orthodoxy differs dramatically from the jailhouse conversions of myriad prisoners. When inmates are locked in a cell, there is a great deal of time for reflection, and momentary traces of conscience often trigger self-serving claims of religious affiliation. However, without being involved in the One Holy Apostolic Church, even sincere self-professed Christian inmates drown in Protestantism, which is spiritually devoid. For example, the Evangelical precept of "once saved, always saved," by which a person makes an emotionally charged confession of belief in the Lord Jesus Christ for "salvation", leaves that individual without the grace of the Orthodox Church. This is precisely what I had experienced when I was involved with Fundamentalist "Christianity" from 1988-98. It was only when I was thrown a lifeline by a Greek Orthodox bishop that I began to have any hope of a cure.

I have learned that the Eastern Orthodox Christian Church serves as the "hospital" wherein spiritual fathers ("doctors") diagnose and then help to administer and foster the cure for our souls. The cure is nothing less than the grace of God. Consequently, rather than continue with my previous intellectual and ultimately vacant approach to Christ, I had stumbled across – and made my own – a specific method by which to seek the Kingdom of God. The method requires that I actively practice repentance, obedience, humility, prayer, fasting, etc. When this method is neglected, Christianity loses its very essence. Such an experience in God's energies centers on the criterion of Orthodoxy, that is, a correct diagnosis (followed by an application of the necessary treatments) made by my spiritual father. Thus, Eastern Orthodox Christian theology functions as the therapeutic provision of the Church (as medicine for our cure). While the West understands theology as something extraneous to one's self, the Orthodox Church reveals theology to be the fruit of one's experience of his/her ontological union with God.

Returning to the inspired words of Protopresbyter Metallinos: "(Orthodox Christianity) offers man the possibility of deification (theosis), just as medical science provides him with the possibility of maintaining or restoring his health, in both cases through a definite therapeutic process and a specific way of life," and, "This salvific work of the Church is accomplished through a specific therapeutic method, whereby the Church, in essence, operates in history as a universal infirmary. St. John Chrysostom thus calls the Church a spiritual hospital." Also, "salvific therapy depends directly upon the interior functioning of each person... (the) purpose of the Church's presence in the world, as a communion in Christ, is to cure man through the restoration of the communion of his heart with God," meaning, "man's need to be cured (extends to) his self-interest, which ultimately functions as self-love, (and) must be transformed into selflessness."

Although it has been excruciatingly painful to undergo the diagnosing of my spiritual illnesses, Father Paisios has exposed the void in my inner self and the accumulation of spiritual diseases from carnal living. As any failure to voluntarily flee worldly concerns could only result in involuntary sin, I have submitted to spiritual surgery and continue to struggle toward purification. As a Protestant, I had pronounced my belief in Christ, but was then left to my own devices and self-will. Upon entry into the spiritual hospital of the Eastern Orthodox Church, I began laboring to cleanse the obscured, yet indestructible image of God within myself. Every single person has the potential to scrub the filth from that image by rejecting the self. In rejecting the self, one works to renounce worldly concerns, his own will, and conceit.[11]

I continue to work on crushing my own self, because I have recognized that simply by having been created I am compelled to cooperate with uncreated God in order to inwardly transform my own self and be healed. To do so requires the revelation of all illness, no matter how ugly, and then to give myself over to the treatment provided by my spiritual father. In addition to total obedience to my spiritual father, another aspect of cutting off self-will requires repentance. Repentance, "a change of mind" (metanoia), allows me to grieve over former sin, but not with a sorrow born of human origin; instead the energy of God is at work.

Saint Theophan the Recluse (1815-1894) highlighted a treatment for human illness in The Path to Salvation. To paraphrase: When first coming to know inner sinfulness, one must construct an exact history of being, in much the same way as accounting requires numerical precision; a complete examination of sinful acts (when, where, who, how, why, etc.) has to be undertaken. Then, eventually, one must travel beyond this thorough investigation and enter the sinful heart, since here dwells the heart's condition that comprises our inner being. The performance of this will uncover a person's chief governing passion. (Everybody has a main passion to and by which all other passions, or habits and tendencies, submit and are inspired.) This will provide an accurate portrait of sinfulness and one can now use the medicine of self-reproach, a treatment whereby one acknowledges that one should not have participated in a sin, yet still did so, even when

---

11 St. John Climacus, *The Ladder of Divine Ascent*, Faber & Faber, London, 1959, p. 59.

able to have not done so. (So, all obstacles, such as conscience and external deterrents, are to be carefully noted.) Self-reproach is a window to understanding one's inner self and will facilitate the realization of "I am wretched." Repentance and shame, which are the foundations of correction, then develop. It is precisely this therapeutic method that provides the possibility of changing the unchangeable. One is ready, at such a point, to turn from sin and instead, work for God by being obedient to His commandments, since one now will be aided by God's grace.

The continued exodus of self, that is repentance, has assisted me onto the path from what is unnatural (satan) to what is natural (God), as this grace continues to work from within and uncover sickness. In this manner, I have been working to unite my senses toward God and have come to more fully appreciate St. Isaac the Syrian's proclamation of, "This fetid sea, which lies between us and the noetic paradise (perfection), we can cross with the boat of repentance... (thusly do) we cross over the sea of this world to God... Repentance is the ship"[12].

Together with repentance, I attempt to cooperate with God's grace in an effort to transform my passions by cutting off demonic provocation at the very moment of inception. I rely on Church Father teachings on "remembrance of God" to expel all thoughts (logismoi), even "good" ones, via a continued invocation of the Jesus Prayer. By repeatedly reciting, "Lord Jesus Christ, have mercy on me," no other thought is allowed. Other techniques that my spiritual father has suggested include contemplating hell, in order to banish carnal desire; death, in order to focus attention; and the horrible evil of past sins. The hope is that such contemplations will place my senses in submission while I seek to irrigate my inner self with godly thoughts, rather than worldly poison. When my senses were unrestrained, I could only be guided by passionate, worldly ideas and flooded with demonic temptations, which, in turn, led to the formation of

---

12   St. John Climacus, *The Ladder of Divine Ascent*, Faber & Faber, London, 1959, p. 59.

new passions in which, of course, the demons delighted. Casting out old thoughts promotes an opportunity to plant new thoughts, thoughts involving Christ Jesus.

Another tactic centers on the examination of the approach of passions. That is, I attempt to examine the conditions under which various passions increase and decrease, along with realizing which thoughts arise, in order to expose and guard against demonic assault. I combine these practices with reading about the lives of saints in order to further scrub my mind of evil thoughts. The reading is then wielded as weapons against any wandering of my mind, and serves to fix my thoughts on holy servants of God. St. John Chrysostom stated that "there can be no salvation without reading the saint's lives."

I begin each day by remembering God – before my thoughts can become defiled by my daily life – and follow that with some reading. I conclude each day with a little more reading, before going to sleep while reciting the Jesus Prayer. When lustful thoughts seek to invade, I recite St. Isaac the Syrian's method of rebuke, saying, "This is defilement which leads to destruction. Lo, the tombs are filled with the bones of the dead" (The Ascetical Homilies).

As it is essential that I not "become wise in (my) own conceits" (Ro. 11:25), my approach to God is not pursued via intellect (through rational investigation and analysis of the Divine), but is instead sought out via synergy, which is cooperation with the will of God by submitting our will to His; in a word – grace. I actively seek to rely on simple faith, rather than intellectual knowledge, as an obedience to the teaching of Christ: "Assuredly, I say to you, unless you are converted and become as little children, you will by no means enter the Kingdom of Heaven" (Mt. 18:3).

Another key to excising passions rests in adapting asceticism as a way of life. Asceticism includes such practices as vigil, fasting, obedience, prayer; it is best described as the collaboration between man (the created) and God (the uncreated). As St.

Isaac the Syrian said, "Asceticism is our chariot from impurity to purification." Through the use of "praxis," (practice) which is the cooperation with God's grace through the practical application of Church Father teachings, I attempt to ascetically uproot internal passions and restore my soul to its natural function. Ascetical praxis points to a huge difference between Western and Eastern Christianity, as the West halts at mere belief, whereas the Orthodox Church prescribes participation in God's grace (energies). I endeavor to observe Christ's commandments (such as the Beatitudes in Mt. 5:3-12) in my daily life, which includes seeking to follow the Gospel from moment to moment.

Returning briefly to Protopresbyter Metallinos, he teaches that the "therapeutic method provided by the Church is the spiritual life (which) is experienced as ascesis and as participation in the Uncreated Grace... The aim of ascesis is victory over the passions, for the purpose of overcoming internal enslavement to the breeding grounds of (spiritual) sickness... (a) Christian who practices self-restraint under the guidance of his spiritual father (therapist) becomes receptive to grace."

One crucial ascetic ingredient that I have been assigned by my spiritual father includes nightly vigils, which are a process wherein one goes to bed at 9:00-10:00 pm and arises at 1:30 am to engage in a couple of hours of prayer. The prayers are medicines and include both liturgical and personal prayers, prostrations, and up to an hour of the Jesus Prayer, prior to reading lives of the saints. Such a practice, however, cannot exist alone, because nightly labor must not be spoiled by daytime sloth. In fact, day labor has to conform to night vigil, so that no separation between the two exists. One way to accomplish this is by adhering to the Church's fasting regimen, which is generally, every Wednesday and Friday, forty days before Easter and Christmas, and a few brief annual periods. The combination of vigil and fasting must accompany every struggle undertaken against carnal thoughts and other evil. Sacred Scripture speaks of fasting, both as having been commanded from the very beginning, when the requirement in Paradise was to refrain from the tree of the knowledge of good and evil (cf. Gen. 2:16-17), and through the Lord's example of fasting following His Transfiguration (Mt. 4:1-2).

The point of fasting is to weaken the body, so that the soul will be strengthened in combat against the evil one and his demons. Fasting from both food (body) and senses (soul) is required, as both body and soul must labor in order to avoid eternal death. Just as Adam broke the command to fast in Paradise, so too will we be condemned if we do not fast. It is essential to combine fasting and the practice of hesychia (stillness) of both the body and thought (soul) in order to shut the doors through which demons enter. My engagement in these endeavors under the guidance of my spiritual father shows that I am actively seeking to renounce my own will. It also sets the stage for obedience, a critical component, since mixing in self-will constitutes spiritual adultery. At any rate, the Orthodox Christian tradition of asceticism and Sacraments explains the biblical transformation of prostitutes and tax collectors... and it explains how I am working toward attaining transformation.

I find it necessary to also refer to my quest to arrive at an understanding of authentic, unselfish love. Condemned to death for a notorious child murder I did not commit, I have suffered more than three decades of horrendous abuse that has made my quest for the original destiny of humans to love God and others unselfishly a fairly bloody struggle. The Bible points to our having been created not to seek our own self-centered desires, but to instead seek the fulfillment of others' interests (cf., 1 Cor. 10:24; Php. 2:4); "love seeketh not its own" (1 Cor. 13:5). We are to give to and suffer for others (cf., Ro. 12:10), and we are to love others as Jesus Christ loves us (cf., Jn. 15:13) and "others" includes our enemies (Mt. 5:44). Initially, Adam's transgression led to the corruption of unselfish love, which is an illness comprised of self-centered love. It has so evolved that each person now tends to his own life's needs (self-interests) and is ignorant of humanity's original destiny. Consequently, we are unable to experience a relationship of unselfish love with others and have fallen into an individualism wherein communion with Jesus Christ does not and cannot exist. It is precisely such a condition in which I found myself, an arena of selfishness that had kept my soul separated from grace. The true struggle for purification is a desperate attempt to avoid eternal death. Through asceticism, I hope to attain the humility of unselfish love.

My struggle towards purification does not differ from the struggle of any other Orthodox Christian, which means that I also face tribulation. Through developing an understanding of affliction as a necessary attribute for purification, I have come to look upon my life as a death-row inmate as the seeds which I now water with ascetic endeavors for union with God. The Lord Jesus Christ tells us that we will experience tribulation in the world (cf., Jn. 16:33), so I had to learn to endure adversity on the condemned row as the means by which to extricate myself from the claws of demons. Sacred Scripture also offers much needed encouragement, for example: "should you suffer for (salvation), you are blessed" (1 Pet. 3:14); "For to you it has been granted on behalf of Christ, not only to believe in Him, but also to suffer for His sake" (Php. 1:29); "rejoice to the extent that you partake in Christ's sufferings, that when His glory is revealed, you may also be glad with exceeding joy" (1 Pet. 4:13). For me, the ascetic exercise of enduring tribulation has become a labor of sacrifice to God:

> "Still others had trial of mockings and scourgings, yes, and of chains and imprisonment. They were stoned, they were sawn in two, were tempted, were slain with the sword. They wandered about in sheepskins and goatskins, being destitute, afflicted, tormented − of whom the world was not worthy. They wandered in deserts and mountains, in dens and caves of the earth" (Heb. 11:36-38).

Thusly armed against evil, I have sought to confront temptation with patience in order to crucify my flesh.

Church Fathers have taught that without tribulation we cannot know the truth, that it is only through affliction that we gain spiritual knowledge. I certainly face significant adversity, yet I am beginning to perceive it as instruction. The Physician of souls permits the medicine of daily trials for the healing of the soul. The Lord commands one who yearns after Him to "deny himself, and take up his cross" (Mt. 16:24). This "denial of self" is the denial of flesh. Thus, seeking to endure the continued scorn with patience becomes a means by which to capture a sense of unworthiness. Part of this requires seeing myself as inferior to those who abuse me and, rather than to judge them (and bring disease to my soul), I must consider myself as the cause of their fall. This is especially valid in a prison setting, where felons strut around like proud peacocks; self-esteem can easily creep in. When the temptation to act in a prideful manner arises, God's grace has allowed provocations, such as profane verbal insults, to fall thickly on my ears as a means by which to encourage humility... if I can manage to embrace those offenses patiently. Unfortunately, there are too many times when I still react with anger. God be praised for the sacrament of confession, to further my progress.

I have understood that "taking up the cross" is the means to abolish sin and transform passions.[13] "The cross" also references a will that has been prepared for affliction: whereas my previous actions were the result of rage over having been sexually assaulted and from anger at perceived offenses, I have finally begun to accept tribulation as deserving. Just as raw metal is extracted from the earth in an unrefined and ugly state, purified in fire, and then pounded into a beautiful sword, so do the fires and pounding of tribulation cleanse and beautify the soul.

It is not my intention to infer that I am adept at enduring

---

13 Additional information may be found in: *Spiritual Alchemy* (by Anthony of the Desert; Xlibris, 2010) and *Noetic Jerusalem* (by Anthony Atwood and Sarah Atwood; Amazon 2015).

contempt and humiliation (especially those I could avoid) with good will. Rather, I have become aware of the need to suffer temptation in order to realize both my human weakness and my need for God. I beseech your prayer that I humbly embrace every trial, which is initially so very sour yet later sweetens. Only with tribulation can any one of us enter the Kingdom of God (cf. Acts 14:22).

In conclusion, what I have recognized – and what I hope some, if not all readers will recognize – is that every individual's desire – no, need – for purification requires their entry into the Orthodox Church and cannot be based on an intellectual and/or emotional acceptance of Christ. I have entered the spiritual hospital that is the Orthodox Church, where, under the guidance of my spiritual father, I remain under treatment. I continue to learn to humbly pick up my cross in order to eternally follow Christ: "Rejoice, and be exceedingly glad (when suffering afflictions), for great is your reward in heaven" (Mt. 5:12)!

EPILOGUE

The idea behind publishing a book with the Orthodox Christian reader in mind (as well as others, especially those who are seekers into Orthodoxy) is to make the reading something that draws the readers and enables them to engender a sense of empathy – and especially in our case, something that will cause the readers to desire to lift their hearts and voices in prayer. Looked at in this light, the readers' prayers can then become a "treasure box" of prayers that will come to our aid when we most need them... this, of course, is a mystery.

Like many converts to Orthodoxy, having become disillusioned with Evangelical Protestantism, we were searching for the one, ancient, catholic (universal) and apostolic Church. In the course of my constant and prodigious reading, it is no accident that I, Anthony, stumbled upon the Eastern Orthodox Church. Every person, at different points in their lives, experiences what they at first perceive to be a coincidence. It is, however, when and how we act on the coincidence with which we have been presented that determines our way forward. The choice I made, to write to Metropolitan Athanasios, who was then Abbot of Machairas Monastery in Cyprus, was borne of my desire for (Christ) Truth. The tremendously helpful advice he sent me, to "Be brave and trust God." is advice which I have shared with Sarah. It has been the single, most precious piece of profound advice we have ever received, and it is in fact the chief motivating factor in everything we do, including writing this book.

Although I did not know then, my choice also became the door to salvation. It was only natural that I would share that doorway with my beloved wife, who then shared it with Pa. Clearly, love grows when it is shared, and so, it is our fondest wish to share that doorway to salvation with every reader, "... that they may all be one even as thou, Father, art in me, and I in thee, that they also may be in us, so that the world may believe that thou hast sent me." (John 17:21)

Frank Jarvis Atwood (Anthony), 2018, still on death row.

DRAWINGS

MADE BY FRANK IN PRISON

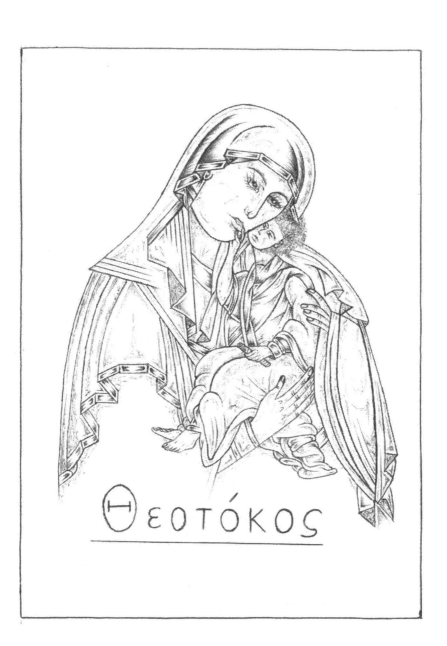

Θεοτόκος

Elder Gabriel

Ἀποκεφαλίζω

ὁ Ἅγιος Ἰωάννης
ὁ Πρόδρομος

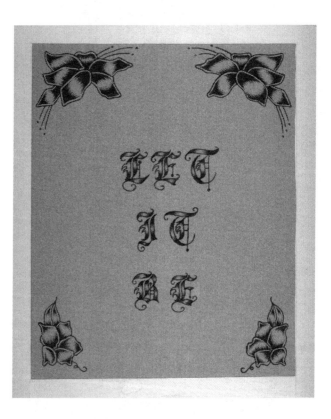

Κύριε
Ἰησοῦ Χριστὲ
Ἐλέησόν με Ἐ

Made in the USA
Columbia, SC
15 December 2021

51549155R00188